2343866-1

10/9/07

Child Language: The Parametric Approach

In memory of Roger Brown

Child Language

The Parametric Approach

WILLIAM SNYDER

OXFORD
UNIVERSITY PRESS

Great Clarendon Street, Oxford OX2 6DP

Oxford University Press is a department of the University of Oxford.
It furthers the University's objective of excellence in research, scholarship,
and education by publishing worldwide in

Oxford New York

Auckland Cape Town Dar es Salaam Hong Kong Karachi
Kuala Lumpur Madrid Melbourne Mexico City Nairobi
New Delhi Shanghai Taipei Toronto

With offices in

Argentina Austria Brazil Chile Czech Republic France Greece
Guatemala Hungary Italy Japan Poland Portugal Singapore
South Korea Switzerland Thailand Turkey Ukraine Vietnam

Oxford is a registered trade mark of Oxford University Press
in the UK and in certain other countries

Published in the United States
by Oxford University Press Inc., New York

British Library Cataloguing in Publication Data

Data available

Library of Congress Cataloging in Publication Data

Data available

Typeset by SPI Publisher Services, Pondicherry, India
Printed in Great Britain
on acid-free paper by
Biddles Ltd., King's Lynn, Norfolk

ISBN 978–0–19–929669–9 (Hbk.)
      978–0–19–929670–5 (Pbk.)

1 3 5 7 9 10 8 6 4 2

Contents

Acknowledgements   vii

Abbreviations   x

1 **A Brief Introduction**   1

2 **The View from Syntactic Theory**   4
 2.1 The Principles-and-Parameters framework   4
 2.2 The Minimalist Program   9
 Appendix: A typical derivation in Minimalism   27

3 **The View from Phonological Theory**   32
 3.1 Optimality Theory   32
 3.2 Government Phonology   41
 3.3 Acquisitional predictions of GP versus OT   47

4 **The View from Children's Spontaneous Speech**   51
 4.1 Diary studies   51
 4.2 Longitudinal recordings   52
 4.3 CHILDES corpora   52
 4.4 Example: the English verb–particle construction   55
 4.5 Conclusion: grammatical conservatism   72

5 **Statistical Methods for Longitudinal Studies**   74
 5.1 Checking for concurrent acquisition   74
 5.2 Checking for ordered acquisition   80
 5.3 Example: particles and compounds in English   81

6 **Experimental and Statistical Methods for
 Cross-Sectional Studies**   96
 6.1 Experimental methods   96
 6.2 Statistical hypothesis testing   109
 6.3 Example: scrambling and case-marking in Korean   115

7 **Case Studies in the Parametric Approach**   119
 7.1 Syllable structure in Dutch   119
 7.2 Noun-drop in Spanish   129
 7.3 Preposition-stranding in English   146
 Appendix: FRUs from Section 7.3   157

8 Conclusions: Grammatical Conservatism and
Cross-Linguistic Variation   159
  8.1 What must the child acquire?   160
  8.2 Is the child grammatically conservative?   164
  8.3 How can we translate hypotheses about grammatical
      variation into testable, acquisitional predictions?   173
  8.4 What are the relative merits of child language acquisition
      versus other domains in which to test parametric
      hypotheses?   176
  8.5 What are the implications of grammatical conservatism for
      linguistic theory?   180
  8.6 Concluding remarks   190

References   193
Language Index   205
General Index   206

Acknowledgements

I am pleased to acknowledge the many people who have helped me, directly or indirectly, in the writing of this book.

Prominent among them are the students I have had the privilege to teach, advise, and in a number of cases collaborate with. Koji Sugisaki is a co-author on much of the work discussed in this book. It was a distinct pleasure to serve as his doctoral advisor, and I am delighted that we are continuing to work together now that he is a professor. Ning Pan, likewise, began as a student but quickly became a research collaborator. This book includes a considerable body of research conducted with Koji and Ning, as well as smaller projects conducted with Deborah Chen Pichler, Kelly Inman, and Maki Yamane, all of whom were at one time students with me at the University of Connecticut.

The reader will also find numerous references in this book to the work of Bosook Kang and Miwa Isobe. Bosook was my student at the University of Connecticut, while Miwa was a student at Keio University, where I had the privilege of serving as an outside member of her dissertation committee. Both students had a great deal to teach me.

A number of other students, past and present, have helped make the University of Connecticut a stimulating environment for language acquisition research. These include my advisees Jean Crawford, Kazuko Hiramatsu, Koichi Ohtaki, and Natasha Rakhlin, as well as other students who have taken a strong interest in acquisition: Klaus Abels, Jeffrey Bernath, Carlos Buesa-García, Laura Conway (Palumbo), Sarah Felber, Keiko Ishii, Pei-Jung Kuo, Laurel Laporte-Grimes, Nobu Miyoshi, Masashi Nomura, Lara Reglero, Miguel Rodríguez-Mondoñedo, Nilufer Şener, Serkan Şener, Arthur Stepanov, Oksana Tarasenkova, Emma Ticio, and Sandra Wood, among many others. Special thanks are due to Helen Koulidobrova for her work on the index.

The faculty at the University of Connecticut have been a major source of intellectual stimulation. I am especially indebted to Jonathan Bobaljik, Len Katz, Diane Lillo-Martin, and Mamoru Saito for extensive discussions of the material in this book. I am also grateful more generally to my other colleagues in the Department of Linguistics:

Arthur Abramson, Mona Anderson, Eva Bar-Shalom, Željko Bošković, Andrea Calabrese, Jon Gajewski, Harry van der Hulst, Howard Lasnik, David Michaels, Nancy Ritter, Yael Sharvit, Doreen Simons-Marques, and Susi Wurmbrand; as well as Inge-Marie Eigsti, Carol Fowler, Letty Naigles, Jay Rueckl, and Whit Tabor in Psychology; and Bernard Grela in Communication Disorders.

Colleagues at other universities have likewise played important roles in making this book possible. The sections of the book on syntax, and especially syntactic variation, have benefited enormously from conversations over the years with Noam Chomsky at MIT, Richard Kayne at New York University, and Luigi Rizzi at the University of Siena. When writing the sections on phonology I had the considerable benefit of conversations with Heather Goad at McGill University and Joe Pater at the University of Massachusetts–Amherst, as well as e-mail correspondence with Tania Zamuner at the University of British Columbia. I am also grateful to Silvina Montrul at the University of Illinois, Bonnie D. Schwartz at the University of Hawai'i, Roumyana Slabakova at the University of Iowa, and Lydia White at McGill University for discussions of second-language acquisition and a variety of related topics. Finally, in a position of special prominence, let me mention Karin Stromswold of Rutgers University, who has been a mentor, colleague, and friend for many years now. Indeed, it was Karin who first trained me in spontaneous-speech methods for child language research.

Other scholars who have given me the benefit of their wisdom, at one point or another, on material discussed in this book include (but are by no means limited to) Sigrid Beck, Rajesh Bhatt, Tonia Bleam, Stephen Crain, Kamil Ud Deen, Marcel Den Dikken, Jill DeVilliers, Nigel Duffield, Janet Fodor, Diamandis Gafos, Anastasia Giannakidou, Irene Heim, Nina Hyams, Kyle Johnson, John J. Kim, Tony Kroch, Jeff Lidz, Gary Marcus, Alec Marantz, Theo Marinis, Jason Merchant, Edson Miyamoto, Keiko Murasugi, Yukio Otsu, David Pesetsky, Colin Phillips, Steve Pinker, David Poeppel, Sandeep Prasada, Tom Roeper, Joey Sabbagh, Jerry Saddock, Tetsuya Sano, Ann Senghas, Dan Slobin, Rozz Thornton, Lisa Travis, Virginia Valian, Josh Viau, and Ken Wexler.

I am quite grateful to have had the opportunity to present some of the material in this book in talks at CUNY Graduate Center, Keio University, the Max-Planck Institute in Nijmegen, McGill University, Meiji Gakuin University, MIT, Nanzan University, Northwestern University, SUNY Stony Brook, the University of Chicago, the

University of Maryland, the University of Massachusetts–Amherst, and the University of Pennsylvania, among others.

The National Institutes of Health (Grant DCD-00183) and the University of Connecticut Research Foundation both supported some of the work reported in this book. I am likewise grateful for the good will of the teachers, the parents, and (most of all) the children at the University of Connecticut Child Labs.

Throughout the process of writing this book I have had the good fortune to work with John Davey at Oxford University Press. His support has meant a great deal to me. I would also like to thank Jenny Breaker, Karen Morgan, and Chloe Plummer for their efforts on behalf of the book.

Finally, I owe a tremendous debt to my parents, Bill and Annie Redd Snyder, and to my partner, Raymond Lamm.

Abbreviations

A	adjective
ACC	accusative (in glosses)
acc	accusative (as syntactic feature)
AGRo	object agreement
AGRoP	object agreement phrase
AGRs	subject agreement
AGRsP	subject agreement phrase
A-P	articulatory-perceptual
AP	adjective phrase
BR	branching rhyme
C	complementizer, or consonant
CD	Constraint Demotion
CHILDES	Child Language Data Exchange System
C_{HL}	computational component of the human language faculty
C-I	conceptual-intentional
CLAN	Child Language Analysis
COMBO	combination search (CLAN program)
COMP	complementizer (in glosses)
CON	universal set of constraints
CP	complementizer phrase
CV	consonant-vowel
D	determiner
DP	determiner phrase
EDCD	Error-Driven Constraint Demotion
Eval-H	evaluation procedure (from "Evaluate Harmony")
Freq	frequency analysis (CLAN program)
FRU	first of repeated uses
GEN	generation function, or genitive (in glosses)
GP	Government Phonology
HIRC	head internal relative clause
imit	imitation (in coding children's speech)
IP	inflection phrase

IPFV	imperfective (in glosses)
LGB	*Lectures on Government and Binding*
LI	lexical item
MEN	Magic Empty Nucleus
MLU	mean length of utterance
MLU$_m$	mean length of utterance in morphemes
MP	Minimalist Program
N	noun, or nucleus (in Government Phonology)
N-drop	noun drop
NOM	nominative (in glosses)
nom	nominative (as syntactic feature)
NP	noun phrase
Nuc	nucleus (in Optimality Theory)
O	onset (in Government Phonology)
Ons	onset (in Optimality Theory)
OT	Optimality Theory
P	preposition, or postposition
p	probability
P&P	Principles-and-Parameters framework
PL	plural (in glosses)
PP	preposition phrase, or postposition phrase
pro	phonetically silent pronoun
PST	past (in glosses)
P-stranding	stranding of a preposition or postposition
R	Rhyme
+Ref	referential
rep	repetition (in coding children's speech)
+s	string (in CLAN programs)
SIP	Split IP Parameter
Spec	specifier
UG	universal grammar
T	tense
+t	tier (in CLAN programs)
TCP	The Compounding Parameter
TEC	transitive expletive construction
TOP	topic (in glosses)

TP   tense phrase
V   verb, or vowel
v   voice
VP   verb phrase
vP   voice phrase

1

A Brief Introduction

This book is dedicated to a single, foundational issue in the study of child language acquisition: What exactly is the child acquiring?

Even the most ardent of nativists will acknowledge that languages differ from one another, and that the child uses her input to choose among the various grammars permitted by human biology. What exactly are the decisions that the child has to make?

At the other end of the spectrum, those with an empiricist inclination expect the process of language acquisition to depend much more heavily on the input. Yet, these researchers too acknowledge that the final state of language acquisition includes grammatical knowledge of a general nature, more abstract than the specific examples encountered in the input. Again, what form does this grammatical knowledge take?

The parametric approach to child language is a broad research program dedicated to this issue. Here the word *parametric* is a convenient cover term for any kind of abstract grammatical knowledge, regardless of how it is implemented: Possible instantiations include actual parameter settings, constraint rankings, or abstract features of functional heads, to name but a few.

My central empirical claim will be that the time course of child language acquisition is itself a rich source of evidence about the nature of what the child is acquiring. First, theories of grammatical variation across languages make strong, testable predictions about the process of language acquisition in children. This book will show, in considerable detail, how to derive these predictions and then test them with various types of evidence from children. Second, certain broad observations about the process of language acquisition, in and of themselves, have direct implications for the nature of what the child is acquiring. I will elaborate on this point in the final chapter of the book.

My objective in writing the book is to create a resource for fellow child-language researchers who are interested in parametric questions.

One of the major challenges of this type of research is that it requires a command of technical information from both theoretical linguistics and experimental psychology. Here I will do my best to make the essential information accessible to readers from a range of academic backgrounds. In so doing I run the risk of boring certain readers, or perhaps even offending them, by including material that they will find overly basic. To minimize this problem I have organized the book into relatively self-contained chapters, so that readers can comfortably skip ahead to whatever interests them.

Throughout the book I will illustrate methodological points with concrete examples drawn from my own research or from the research of close colleagues. This approach has the advantage that I am well-qualified to discuss the examples, but the disadvantage that I will necessarily give short shrift to work conducted by many other fine researchers. I apologize in advance to those whose work I am neglecting.

This book also presents some material that I expect to be controversial. Within the child language community there exist strongly held and often sharply conflicting views on research methodology. My personal stance can be summarized as follows: each available technique has its own particular strengths and weaknesses, none is perfect, and the most compelling arguments are based on converging evidence from multiple approaches. An important objective is therefore to elucidate the particular strengths and weaknesses of a number of the most widely used research methods.

The plan of the book is as follows. Chapters 2 and 3 provide a sketch of the leading approaches to cross-linguistic variation in contemporary syntax and phonology. There I discuss how acquisitional predictions can be derived from grammatical hypotheses in each of the major frameworks. Chapter 4 is a hands-on exploration of children's spontaneous speech, both as an instructive exercise for those who have not worked with it before, and as a source of evidence for my claim of grammatical conservatism.

Chapter 5 presents some of the quantitative methods that are available for statistical hypothesis testing with longitudinal, spontaneous speech data. The methods are demonstrated with data from my work on children's acquisition of compounding and prepositional particles in English (Snyder 2001). Chapter 6 provides corresponding methods for work with cross-sectional data (from data-collection methods such as elicited production and truth-value judgement). As an example I discuss Kang's (2005) findings for scrambling and case-marking in the acquisition of Korean.

Chapter 7 provides three further case studies, drawn from research that I have conducted with students and other collaborators: investigations of children's acquisition of syllable structure in Dutch, noun-drop in Spanish, and preposition-stranding in English.

Chapter 8 gathers together the main conclusions on the following questions: What sort of information exactly must the child acquire, in order to know the grammar of her native language? How can we translate theories of grammatical variation into testable acquisitional predictions? What are the strengths and weaknesses of first-language acquisition as a testing ground, when compared with evidence from historical change and second-language acquisition in adults? What is the empirical evidence for the claim that children are grammatically conservative? Finally, and perhaps most importantly, what are the implications of grammatical conservatism for the nature of grammatical knowledge?

My broad agenda in this book is to demonstrate that the study of grammatical variation, like the study of grammatical universals, is a "deep" domain of scientific inquiry, one where we can expect to discover richly explanatory principles. Child language provides a unique window into this aspect of human language. To those who are new to the parametric approach, welcome!

2

The View from Syntactic Theory

This chapter surveys the ideas on cross-linguistic variation that are prominent in contemporary syntactic theory. Two major frameworks are considered: the Principles-and-Parameters framework and the Minimalist Program. For each framework I provide a brief overview and at least one example of how cross-linguistic variation is treated, together with ways of using acquisitional data to test specific proposals. In the first section, on the Principles-and-Parameters framework, I also introduce the idea that the child is grammatically conservative, at least in spontaneous production, and discuss the relevance of this characteristic when generating acquisitional predictions.

2.1 The Principles-and-Parameters framework

2.1.1 An overview

The term *parameter* gained prominence in linguistics around 1981, the year Noam Chomsky published *Lectures on Government and Binding* (LGB). There he wrote that "in a tightly integrated theory with fairly rich internal structure, change in a single parameter may have complex effects, with proliferating consequences in various parts of the grammar" (Chomsky 1981: 6). The Principles-and-Parameters framework (P&P), which began with LGB, remains one of the major influences on present-day syntactic research.

James Higginbotham has suggested the metaphor of a switchbox: it is as though the human language faculty came equipped with a box of switches, each of which must be set to one of just a few possible positions (Chomsky 1986b: 146). The grammar of a particular language is effectively a list of the settings in the switchbox. The

X,Y,Z ∈ {V, N, A, P}

XP dominates X′ and an optional specifier ZP.
X′ dominates X and an optional complement YP.

Specifier Parameter: ZP {precedes, follows} X′.
Headedness Parameter: X {precedes, follows} YP.

English: "precedes", "precedes"

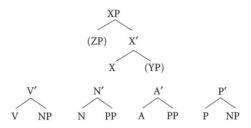

FIGURE 2.1 Principles and Parameters of phrase structure, circa 1981

child's task in acquiring a grammar reduces to setting the switches appropriately.

The P&P model represents a departure from grammars with numerous, idiosyncratic rules. In earlier work, for example, a syntactic rule of English specified that a transitive verb is followed by a direct-object noun phrase. The claim was that any native speaker of English had this particular rule as part of his tacit knowledge of English syntax. In the switchbox model, however, this knowledge takes the form of a parameter setting.

In one formulation (see Figure 2.1), a principle of phrase structure indicates that every syntactic phrase (XP) contains a head (X), an optional complement (YP), and an optional specifier (ZP). A parameter (the "Head Parameter"; cf. Chomsky 1981: 95) stipulates that the head {precedes, follows} its complement. Each language uses one of the two options in the set, and English takes "precedes". Given that a verb (V) is the head of a verb phrase (VP), and the direct-object noun phrase (NP) is a complement of this V, the English setting of the Head Parameter requires the V to precede the NP.

The advent of syntactic parameter theory, in the form of the switchbox model, was a major advance towards explanatory adequacy (Chomsky 1964). A linguistic theory is explanatorily adequate only if it provides an answer to the logical problem of language acquisition: How can a child possibly arrive at a suitable grammar for the language of her adult caretakers, given the types of experience that are in fact sufficient for this purpose? Syntactic parameters can, in principle, be set appropriately with far less information than would be needed to construct a grammar from the ground up. Hence the burden of explanatory adequacy, while still present, becomes much lighter.

It would be possible to have a parameter corresponding to each and every surface phenomenon found in any language, but the express hope in P&P is that this will not be necessary. For example in the case of the Head Parameter, as formulated above, the separate word order rules for complement of a transitive V, complement of a preposition or postposition (P), complement of a noun (N) and complement of an adjective (A) are subsumed under a single parameter, which abstracts away from the syntactic category of the head.

In general, a small number of highly abstract parameters can account for a much larger number of superficial differences between languages. Hence, from the perspective of explanatory adequacy, highly abstract parameters have at least two major advantages over narrower, more specific parameters. First, the fewer the choices that the child must make, the less room there is for error. Second, the broader the consequences of each parametric choice, the greater the range of evidence that a child can use to set the parameter correctly.

2.1.2 Limited success of the P&P framework

In the years since LGB, syntacticians have worked hard to identify parameters, but their efforts have met with only limited empirical success. Why is this so? One possibility, of course, is that the entire project is misguided, and that there are no real parameters there to discover. Another possibility is that researchers have made unfortunate methodological choices.

The latter possibility merits consideration. For example, linguists in the 1980s were often looking for lists of superficial properties that clustered together across languages. An immediate problem is that the points of parametric variation they were trying to discover are (by hypothesis) considerably more abstract than the surface characteristics one can determine through casual inspection of a language: Simple, superficial diagnostics can often be satisfied by any of several, similar-looking constructions, each with a distinct grammatical basis.

Hence, a "comparative" approach to finding parameters calls for in-depth analysis of each language in the sample. Moreover, as discussed by Baker (1996), the sample must include truly diverse, typologically distinct languages (rather than simply a collection of Romance dialects, for example), if one is to detect the operation of "macro-parameters", or major points of syntactic variation. Baker proposes that we have so far identified very few candidates for macro-parameters precisely because few researchers have attempted the in-depth comparison of typologically diverse languages. Hence, methodological difficulties are plausibly responsible for the limited success, to date, of the search for syntactic parameters.

2.1.3 Acquisitional testing of P&P and grammatical conservatism

Child language provides an extremely valuable source of data in the search for P&P-style parameters. Recall that a theory of syntactic para-meters is simultaneously a theory of the child's hypothesis space during language acquisition. The child's task is to identify the correct grammar for the community's language from among the possibilities permitted by the parameters of universal grammar (UG). In principle, then, we can gain insight into the nature of UG parameters by studying how the child's grammar changes during the course of acquisition.

Concretely, for any proposed parameter we can derive acquisitional predictions as indicated in (1) and (2):

(1)   If the grammatical knowledge (including parameter settings and lexical information) required for construction A, in a given lan-guage, is identical to the knowledge required for construction B, then any child learning the language is predicted to acquire A and B at the same time.

(2)   If the grammatical knowledge (including parameter settings and lexical information) required for construction A, in a given lan-guage, is a proper subset of the knowledge required for construc-tion B, then the age of acquisition for A should always be less than or equal to the age of acquisition for B. (No child should acquire B significantly earlier than A.)

Deriving and testing acquisitional predictions of the types in (1) and (2) has several major advantages over the comparative approach. First, we can focus on a single, well-studied language. In-depth analysis of diverse languages is not required. Furthermore, in testing the acqui-sitional predictions, each child provides evidence comparable to a new language in the comparative approach. Just as each new language presents an opportunity for two (putatively associated) grammatical characteristics to diverge, each new child presents an opportunity for the two grammatical characteristics to be acquired at different times.

A possible disadvantage of the acquisitional approach is that our information about a particular child's grammar at a particular point in development is normally quite limited. For example, younger children are notoriously bad at providing grammaticality judgements, which are the mainstay of research on adult languages.

Yet, the disadvantage is not as severe as it might seem. In Chapters 4 and 7 I will present evidence that children's spontaneous speech exhibits the remarkable property of grammatical conservatism: children do not begin making productive use of a new grammatical construction in their spontaneous speech until they have both determined that the construction is permitted in the adult language, and identified the adults' grammatical basis for it.

Specifically, in Chapter 4 we will examine the onset of verb–particle combinations in the speech of young children acquiring English. Initially the construction is absent from the child's speech, but fairly abruptly it comes into frequent, and overwhelmingly correct, use. The scarcity of substantive errors tells us that the child's use of the construction has a grammatical basis (indeed, almost certainly the correct grammatical basis), because extra-grammatical strategies (or incorrect grammatical analyses) that merely approximate the adult grammar are inevitably error-prone.

Further evidence for children's grammatical conservatism in spontaneous speech will be seen in Chapter 7, when I discuss children's acquisition of preposition-stranding in English *wh*-movement: while pied-piping of the preposition is cross-linguistically much more common than preposition-stranding, and would make a natural "unmarked option", English-learning children do not pass through any pied-piping stage along the way to acquiring preposition-stranding. Pied-piping is not the correct option for adult English, and children acquiring English actually refrain from *wh*-movement of prepositional objects until they know how it is accomplished in the adult language.

Quite generally, the evidence from spontaneous speech shows the child making steady progress towards the adult grammar, with astonishingly few substantive errors (i.e. errors of comission). Hence if a grammatical construction is present in the child's spontaneous speech, if the construction occurs with a variety of different lexical items, and if the child's use of the construction appears to be fully adult-like, then we may reasonably conclude that the construction indeed has the same grammatical basis as it has for the adult speaker. Moreover, if the child exhibits a rapid transition from never using the construction to using it frequently and correctly, then we can surmise that the child has acquired the final pre-requisite for the construction at the point of the transition.

If this view is correct, then even fairly superficial diagnostics will be adequate to determine when the child acquires a given point of grammatical knowledge. Parametric proposals within the P&P framework will lead to predictions of concurrent or ordered acquisition (as in (1) and (2)) that we can test using longitudinal records of children's spontaneous speech, provided we can find constructions that are expected to depend on the proposed parameters and that are used with high frequency once they have been acquired. (These points will be discussed in greater detail in Chapter 5.)

2.2 The Minimalist Program

2.2.1 An overview

One of the principal developments in syntactic theory since LGB has been Chomsky's (1995, 2001*b*) Minimalist Program. Minimalism is still more of a research program than a theory, but many of its proposals have gained widespread acceptance. Here I will attempt a relatively brief sketch, and then discuss some examples of recent Minimalist accounts of cross-linguistic variation. This section will be considerably more detailed than the previous one, because the Minimalist literature tends to be difficult for acquisitionists to break into, and I hope that I may be able to provide some help. Throughout this section I will stay as close as possible to the technical implementation found in (Adger 2003), which I recommend as a highly accessible (but book-length) introduction to the framework.

Perhaps the most important point is that Minimalist syntax is purely derivational, rather than representational. The goal is to eliminate any syntactic requirements that would be tied to a level of representation, such as the D-Structure or S-Structure of LGB. Instead, syntactic requirements are tied to individual lexical items (LIs; roughly speaking, words), and get satisfied through operations that occur during the derivation. LIs are added to the derivation one by one, and each can have immediate effects: a new LI can satisfy requirements of the LIs that were already present, and it can impose additional requirements of its own.

These requirements take the form of uninterpretable features that are present on a given LI and need to be checked off (i.e. marked for eventual deletion) during the course of the derivation. The guiding intuition is that a feature is uninterpretable if it will have no meaning to the conceptual-intentional (C-I) systems that assign a semantic interpretation to the derivation's output. For the derivation to succeed (or "converge"), all of its uninterpretable features need to have been checked and deleted by the time the output is sent to the C-I systems. A feature is checked off when it enters into a checking relation with a matching feature on another LI.

At some point during the derivation, the structure that has been constructed is sent to the articulatory-perceptual (A-P) systems for pronunciation. This point is called spell-out, and occurs as soon as the LIs that were originally chosen for use in the sentence have all both been incorporated into a single tree structure, and had any uninterpretable features checked off. The derivation can continue beyond spell-out (as will be discussed in the context of Bošković's DP Parameter, in Section 2.2.5), but no more LIs can be added.[1]

Features play an absolutely central role in Minimalism. The information expressed by a feature can be phonological, semantic, morphological, or syntactic. A feature that has only syntactic consequences is called "purely formal". For purposes of the syntactic derivation, features are divided into several important subtypes. First there is the distinction between interpretable and uninterpretable features just mentioned, which in turn is related to the syntactic category of the LI that contains the feature. For example, the feature [Plural] is considered to be interpretable when it occurs on a noun, but uninterpretable if it occurs on T, the syntactic head that carries tense information.

Second, the uninterpretable features are divided into selectional and non-selectional features. A selectional feature is one that is tied to a theta role (e.g. Agent, Theme, Goal) that the LI assigns. The selectional

---

[1] My statement that after spell-out "no more LI's can be added" is accurate for much of the Minimalist literature (e.g. Bošković 2004), but does not hold for the literature that assumes Phase Theory (first introduced in Chomsky 2001b). In Phase Theory the derivation proceeds in chunks, and each individual chunk (or "phase") is spelled out as soon as it is completed. The reader who ventures into the most recent Minimalist literature will probably encounter phases, but I have elected not to cover them in this overview because they play no role in the discussion of Minimalist approaches to cross-linguistic variation, below.

feature ensures that a constituent of the right syntactic category appears in a position where it can receive the theta role.

For example, the English verb *meet* assigns a theta role (Theme/Patient) to its direct object. In Minimalism the direct object is taken to be a Determiner Phrase (DP), which bears the syntactic feature D on its topmost node. The verb *meet* will therefore contain the selectional feature [*u*D], which will be checked off if (and only if) the verb is combined with a DP. (The prefix *u*- indicates that the feature is uninterpretable.)

Selectional features are always satisfied by means of the operation Merge, which takes two constituents (such as *meet* and a DP) and combines them as sisters within a single phrase. In Adger's (2003) implementation of Minimalism, Merge can be used only to check off a selectional feature or to satisfy a requirement of the Hierarchy of Projections. The latter is what requires, for example that a VP should be dominated by a vP (the shell where agentive subjects are introduced), which in turn must be dominated by a TP. The idea that Merge can only occur when strictly necessary (i.e. to satisfy a selectional feature or the Hierarchy of Projections) is sometimes called Last Resort, and will play an important role in the discussion of Bošković's DP Parameter below.[2]

Finally, features that are both uninterpretable and non-selectional are further divided into the categories of strong and weak. If a feature is strong, then checking requires a strictly local relationship, namely syntactic sisterhood, between the checker and the check-ee. This relationship can be created by the operation Move (i.e. by moving a constituent with a matching feature up from a position lower in the tree) or by the operation Adjoin (i.e. by adjoining a constituent that was not yet part of the tree).

Weak features, in contrast, are checked off by the operation of Agree, which permits checking at a distance. This operation applies whenever two LI's α and β have a given feature in common, provided that both of the following conditions hold: (i) Either α c-commands β or β c-commands α, and (ii) there is no element γ that has the relevant feature and intervenes between α and β (in terms of c-command).

---

[2] I should mention that the Hierarchy of Projections is part of Adger's implementation of Minimalism, and other authors more typically employ the mechanism of "selection" to achieve similar effects. The main difference is that selection operates top-down, whereas the Hierarchy of Projection operates bottom-up. Also, selectional requirements are permitted to vary as a function of the particular LI that does the selecting.

For the reader who would like to see a concrete example of a Minimalist derivation, I provide one in an appendix to this chapter. For present purposes, however, the information above should be sufficient. Let's now turn to the Minimalist view of cross-linguistic variation.[3]

2.2.2 Cross-linguistic variation in Minimalism

The express goal in Minimalism is to keep cross-linguistic variation entirely outside the computational system where the syntactic derivation occurs (termed C_{HL}, for "computational component of the human language faculty"). C_{HL} has the same repertoire of operations (Merge, Move, Agree, and a few others) in every language, and satisfies any given featural requirement in exactly the same way. The locus of syntactic variation is supposed to be the choice of features that are included in LIs. The LIs of a given language, in turn, are stored in the lexicon, outside C_{HL}. Thus, in (Chomsky 1995: 7) we find the following statement: "If these ideas prove to be on the right track, there is a single computational system C_{HL} for human language and only limited lexical variety."

We will see that in practice this ideal is not too strictly adhered to. Two of the three examples to be discussed in the following subsections, of Minimalist approaches to actual cross-linguistic variation, violate it to some degree, or at least require rather special interpretations of the word *lexical*. Additionally, Minimalist discussions of word order (linearization) are revealing. One approach, which I take to be the official view, says that linearization occurs after spell-out. In other words, determination of word order is stipulated to be "not part of syntax proper". This move will be justified if it turns out that linearization is well explained in terms of independently needed principles of (morpho-)phonology. A less interesting prospect is that the syntactic machinery concerned with word order will be retained, and simply relabeled as "morphology" or "phonology".

---

[3] One closing word of advice for the reader who is preparing to venture into the Minimalist literature for the first time: the vocabulary of Minimalism is constantly changing. For example in some recent work, "Merge" and "Move" are replaced by "External Merge" and "Internal Merge" (or "re-merge"). Similarly, a feature that drives movement may be called a "generalized EPP feature" or "OCC" (short for "occurrence feature"). My hope is that this overview of the leading ideas will help one break the code, even when the present terminology is obsolete.

Still another possibility, however, is to accept word order as part of syntax, and to argue that the parameters of word order are "lexical" in a way that makes them compatible with Minimalism. For example, Lasnik and Uriagereka (2005: 36) suggest that head–complement order might be regarded as lexical, on the grounds that idiom chunks (e.g. *break + bread, the ice, ground, the news*) commonly involve a head–complement combination, and need to be stored in the lexicon (given that their meanings are non-compositional).

This move leads one to ask whether a highly general property of word-level elements, such as head–complement order, is "lexical" in the sense demanded by Minimalism. Suppose we interpret *lexical variation* in the context of Minimalism to refer to the listed idiosyncrasies of particular, individual words. Recasting the Head Parameter as a point of lexical variation in this sense will be difficult, at best. Lasnik and Uriagereka do not attempt it.

Indeed, the conceptual appeal of reducing syntactic variation to lexical variation lies precisely in the fact that the lexicon is independently required as a repository of listed, idiosyncratic properties of individual LIs. If we allow the lexicon to include global syntactic properties of the language, that is, properties such as head–complement order that are not connected to any particular LI, then the meaning of the term *lexical* becomes nebulous. Thus, it is not entirely clear why the setting of the Head Parameter would have a greater right to be stored in the lexicon than the settings of other types of parameters.

In any case, the tendency in the Minimalist literature on comparative syntax seems to be to propose P&P-style parameters where needed, albeit with a certain degree of discomfort. Thus, in (Bošković 2004), the source of the parametric proposal discussed in Subsection 2.2.5 below, the word *parameter* never occurs. On the other hand, some researchers do succeed in reducing interesting cases of syntactic variation to differences in the uninterpretable features of individual LIs, exactly as demanded by Minimalism. Longobardi's proposal in the next subsection is a case in point.

2.2.3 Example I: the Referentiality Parameter

Longobardi (2001) uses the idea of strong and weak features to unify two characteristics of Italian syntax. First, in the Italian equivalent of (3a), the proper name *Maria* "Mary" can be preceded by the feminine-singular definite article *La*, as in (4b).

(3a)   Mary telephoned me.

(3b)   *The Mary telephoned me.

(4a)   Maria mi ha telefonato.
       Maria me has telephoned
       "Maria telephoned me."

(4b)   L-a   Maria mi ha telefonato.
       the-FEM.SG Maria me has telephoned
       "Maria telephoned me."

According to Longobardi, the choice between (4a) and (4b) is essentially free, although it is sometimes influenced by stylistic preferences.

   A second difference between Italian and English concerns the
position of certain adjectives when they modify a proper name. In
English (5), the word *only* must precede *Mary* to express the meaning
"No one except Mary telephoned me".

(5a)   Only Mary telephoned me.

(5b)   (*)Mary only telephoned me. [*on reading of "no one except
       Mary"]

In Italian, however, if no definite article is present then the adjective
sola "only" follows the name *Maria*, as in (6b). (The examples in (6)
are adapted from Longobardi 1994: 625–6.)

(6a)   *Sola Maria mi ha telefonato.
       only Maria me has telephoned
       "Only Maria telephoned me."

(6b)   Maria sola mi ha telefonato.
       Maria only me has telephoned

(6c)   L-a   sola Maria mi ha telefonato.
       the-FEM.SG only Maria me has telephoned

(6d)   (*)L-a   Maria sola mi ha telefonato.
       the-FEM.SG Maria only me has telephoned
       [*on the relevant reading]

Yet, if the definite article is used, as in (6c–6d), the adjective *sola* must
now precede *Maria*. If *sola* follows *Maria*, as in (6d), the relevant meaning is lost; (6d) can only mean something like "Lonely Mary telephoned
me", where *sola* is construed as the (homophonous) adjective meaning
"lonely", and is taken as part of an epithet.

Longobardi proposes that these differences from English can be reduced to a single point of syntactic variation: in Italian, but not English, "referential D" has a strong N feature. The idea is that, in all languages, a proper name must be accompanied by a determiner (often phonetically null) that bears the feature [+Referential]. This referential D in turn has an uninterpretable N feature that can be either weak or strong. Longobardi terms this the Referentiality Parameter, although it is not a syntactic parameter in the usual sense of the P&P framework. Rather, it is a listed idiosyncrasy of a single item in the lexicon.

The fact that the feature is strong in Italian means that any referential D must, by the point of spell-out, be a sister to a constituent with an N feature. As noted in Section 2.2.1, in the discussion of Last Resort, this type of non-selectional feature cannot be satisfied simply by merging the D with an NP. Only selectional features can be satisfied in that way. Instead Minimalism provides two other methods for satisfying the feature, as illustrated in Figure 2.2.

Within Minimalism, the more typical way for a strong N feature to be checked off and rendered invisible is through movement and adjunction of N to D. This is illustrated in the upper half of Figure 2.2, and yields the form in (6b). Longobardi notes that a second way to render the strong N feature invisible is through the use of an expletive D, as illustrated in the lower half of Figure 2.2. The expletive D in Italian takes the form of a definite article, and can bear an N feature. (Here I am modifying Longobardi's 2001 discussion slightly, for consistency

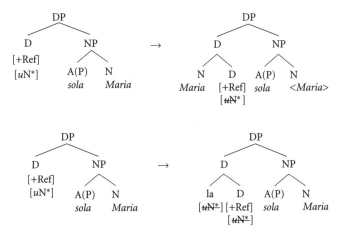

FIGURE 2.2 Two ways of checking the strong N feature on [+Referential] D

with the implementation of Minimalism found in Adger 2003.) The result is the form in (6c).[4]

Hence, Longobardi's account unifies two distinctive characteristics of Italian syntax, namely the possibility of a definite article with proper names, and the fact that (in the absence of this article) the proper name must precede any adjective that modifies it. The basis of the unification is the idea that the [+Referential] D in Italian has a strong N feature. Some testable acquisitional predictions of this account will now be discussed.

Longobardi's Referentiality Parameter conforms strictly to the Minimalist ideal: it is implemented as an abstract feature, stored in the lexical entry for a single LI. Nonetheless, the logic used in Section 2.1.3 to derive acquisitional predictions for a P&P parameter applies in exactly the same way here.

Consider the grammatical pre-requisites for an expression such as (7).

(7)   L-a   sola Maria
      the-FEM.SG only Mary
      "only Mary"

According to Longobardi's account, the construction of an expression like (7) requires two main bits of information about Italian: (i) Italian has a strong N feature ($[uN^*]$) on its (phonetically null) referential determiner; and (ii) Italian makes available an expletive determiner that bears an N feature.

From this situation we can derive a prediction of ordered acquisition: as soon as a child can construct utterances of the type in (7), she will necessarily be able to construct expressions of the types in (8) and (9). In other words, utterances of the type in (8) or (9) will become grammatically available to the child prior to, or concurrently with, but never significantly later than, utterances of the type in (7).

(8)   Maria sola
      Mary only
      "only Mary"

---

[4] Longobardi is less explicit than I would like about the details of his proposed expletive determiner. In Figure 2.2 I have simply represented the insertion of the expletive determiner as if expletive-insertion were some type of special syntactic operation, outside the usual mechanisms of MP. This simplification should be adequate for present purposes.

(9)   L-a   Maria
      the-FEM.SG Mary
      "Mary"

This prediction follows from the fact that, according to Longobardi's analysis, the grammatical pre-requisites for either (8) or (9) are a proper subset of the grammatical pre-requisites for utterances such as (7). Utterances like (8) require the knowledge that Italian has a strong N feature on its referential determiner, as well as knowledge about the structural location of adjectives in the semantic class to which *sola* belongs. Utterances like (7) require all this, plus the additional knowledge that Italian provides an expletive determiner with an N feature.

Similarly, utterances like (9) require the knowledge that Italian has a strong N feature on its referential determiner, as well as knowledge that Italian provides an expletive determiner with an N feature. Utterances like (7) require all this, plus additional knowledge about the structural location of adjectives in the semantic class to which *sola* belongs.

Hence, to test Longobardi's account acquisitionally, we might examine longitudinal corpora of spontaneous speech from each of a number of children acquiring Italian. With luck, the same utterance types in (7–9) will occur in the children's speech sufficiently often for us to test the predicted pattern of ordered acquisition with the methods that are detailed in Chapter 5. If luck is not with us, we might find alternative, more frequently occurring diagnostics, or we might conduct a cross-sectional study using a method such as Elicited Production, as discussed in Chapter 6.

I should hasten to add that I have not myself conducted these studies. I have no idea what the outcome will be when someone does. (See Slabakova 2006 for related research on adults acquiring Italian as a second language.) But I submit that logically, child language acquisition provides an excellent way to test Longobardi's Minimalist proposal.

2.2.4 Example II: the Split IP Parameter

Bobaljik and Thráinsson (1998) propose the Split IP Parameter (SIP; cf. also Thráinsson 1996, 2003) as a way to connect a total of five points of grammatical variation that are observed within the Germanic language family:

(10a)   Does the finite verb remain within the vP, or does it raise into the inflectional system?

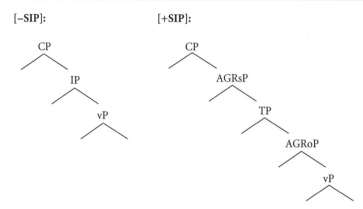

FIGURE 2.3 The Split IP Parameter

(10b)   Does the verb stem bear distinct inflectional affixes for both tense and agreement?

(10c)   Is there more than one syntactic position available to subjects?

(10d)   Is there more than one syntactic position available to objects?

(10e)   Are transitive expletive constructions (TECs) permitted?

The SIP has two values, as illustrated in Figure 2.3. Languages that are [−SIP], such as English, Norwegian, Danish, and Swedish, have only a single inflectional head, I, between CP and vP. Languages that are [+SIP], such as Icelandic, German, and Dutch, have a system of three inflectional heads, AGRs, T and AGRo, between CP and vP. (For simplicity the illustration in Figure 2.3 assumes head-initial order throughout, although in fact the Germanic languages vary in that respect too.) In the terms of Adger (2003), the SIP amounts to a parameterization of the Hierarchy of Projections.

To handle (10a), the key proposal is that both I (in [−SIP] languages) and T (in [+SIP] languages) require a special relationship with a verbal constituent. In the case of I, the requirement is satisfied simply by Merging with a vP complement. In the case of T, however, the requirement triggers Movement of the V+v complex up to T. In the system of Adger (2003) we might say that I is required to dominate vP by the Hierarchy of Projections, and hence must Merge with vP. In contrast, T simply bears a strong non-selectional feature [uV] that is satisfied by Move. Thus in [−SIP] languages, the verb will normally remain inside vP at spell-out, while in [+SIP] languages the verb will always have raised into the inflectional system.

This difference in verb-raising is illustrated for Danish ([–SIP]) in (11), and Icelandic [+SIP] in (12). (Both examples are drawn from Platzack 1986: 209.)

(11)   …at han *ikke* **købte**   bogen.   *Danish*
        that he   not bought book-the
        "…that he did not buy the book."

(12)   …að hann **keypti**   *ekki* bókina.   *Icelandic*
        that he   bought not book-the
        "…that he did not buy the book."

The negation word *ikke/ekki* "not" marks the left edge of vP. Hence, the crucial point is that the finite verb *købte* "bought" in Danish appears to the right of negation, inside vP, while its counterpart *keypti* in Icelandic appears to the left of negation, outside vP.

The remaining properties (10b–10e) can all be related to whether the inflectional system contains only a single head, or a set of three heads. In the case of (10b), Bobaljik and Thráinsson propose (1998: 57) that inflectional morphemes correspond directly to inflectional heads in the syntax. Hence, in a [–SIP] language there can be at most one inflectional affix on the verb stem, while in a [+SIP] language it will be possible to have fully distinct inflectional affixes for tense and agreement.

This pattern is well exemplified by English ([–SIP]) and Icelandic ([+SIP]). For example, in English we find verb forms like *walk-s* and *walk-ed*, where -*s* is (arguably) a marker of 3sg subject agreement, and -*ed* is a marker of past tense, but we never find verbs with two separate markers for tense and agreement, as in **walk-ed-s*. In Icelandic, however, such combinations of markers are common, as in *köstu-ðu-m* "throw-past-1pl".

Properties (10c–10d) refer to the following: in [+SIP] languages it is common to find that subjects appear in one of two structural positions, depending on whether they refer to an entity that is "old" or "new" to the discourse. The same is true of direct objects. This type of alternation is absent from [–SIP] languages. According to Bobaljik and Thráinsson, the difference relates to whether the inflectional system provides only a single specifier position (Spec,IP), or three specifier positions (Spec,AGRsP; Spec,TP; Spec,AGRoP). In the latter case, subjects can occupy either Spec,AGRsP (when they refer to old information), or Spec,TP (when they refer to new information). Likewise, objects can occupy either Spec,AGRoP (old information) or the complement position of V (new information).

Finally, Bobaljik and Thráinsson consider Transitive Expletive Constructions (TEC). The TEC has an expletive in the usual subject position, and has the logical subject in another position somewhere lower than the expletive but higher than the vP. According to Bobaljik and Thráinsson, this situation is possible only in a [+SIP] language, which has more than one specifier position available in the inflectional system. The predicted pattern is borne out:

(13)   *Det har **en katt** ete   mysene.   *Norwegian*
         EXPL has a   cat eaten mice-the
         "There has a cat eaten the mice."

(14)   það   hefur **einhver köttur** étið   mýsnar.   *Icelandic*
         EXPL has   some   cat   eaten mice-the
         "There has a cat eaten the mice."

A [–SIP] language such as Norwegian disallows the TEC, as shown in (13) (cf. Bobaljik & Thráinsson 1998: 56, ex. 24a). In contrast, a [+SIP] language such as Icelandic allows it, as shown in (14) (cf. Bobaljik & Thráinsson 1998: 56, ex. 25a).

At this point a few comments are in order. First, according to Bobaljik and Thráinsson, most of the characteristics of [+SIP] languages are options, rather than necessities. For example, the presence of multiple inflectional heads in a given language makes it *possible* to have multiple inflectional affixes on the finite verb, but nothing requires it. Similarly, [+SIP] languages have the *potential* for multiple subject positions, multiple object positions, and/or TECs, but none of these are obligatory. The one necessary characteristic of [+SIP] languages is that any finite verb has to be outside the vP by the point of spell-out. This situation will have important implications for acquisitional predictions, to be discussed below.

Second, while the bulk of Bobaljik and Thráinsson's syntactic assumptions are well within the boundaries of Minimalism, their recourse to a P&P-style parameter, the SIP, is (arguably) a rejection of Chomsky's (1995) call to derive cross-linguistic variation in syntax entirely from information that is stored in the lexicon.[5] As noted earlier,

---

[5] Jonathan Bobaljik (p.c., 28 July 2006) has brought it to my attention that the SIP can in fact be regarded as a point of lexical variation, albeit in a rather special sense, and that this was at least implicit in Bobaljik (1995). The reasoning goes as follows. In the framework of Distributed Morphology (Halle and Marantz 1993), abstract features must be "bundled" together to create the lexical items that are included in a syntactic numeration. We might therefore say that SIP is not a parameter of syntax proper, but rather a parameter

the proposal of P&P-style parameters is actually rather common in current Minimalist work on cross-linguistic variation. Thus, acquisitionists should be wary of the Minimalist rhetoric: the demise of parameters has been greatly exaggerated. We will see another, comparable example below (Section 2.2.5), in the proposals of Bošković. In Chapter 8, Section 8.1, however, I will return to the question of exactly what it means for a point of variation to be "lexical", and whether the SIP might in fact qualify.

The acquisitional predictions of SIP are derived in the same way as for any other P&P-style parameter. In particular, for a [+SIP] language like Icelandic, the fact that the V+v complex raises into the inflectional system will follow directly from the [+SIP] setting, while a number of additional properties will follow from the combination of the [+SIP] setting with other points of grammatical knowledge: the fact that Icelandic verbs can simultaneously bear a tense marker and an agreement marker; the fact that subjects and objects each have two syntactic positions (old information/new information) available to them; and the fact that Icelandic permits the Transitive Expletive Construction (TEC).

The subset/superset relation in the grammatical pre-requisites for V+v raising versus the other properties leads directly to a prediction of ordered acquisition: any given child learning Icelandic should acquire V+v raising into the inflectional system prior to, or at the same time as, but never significantly later than, any of the remaining properties.

The practical difficulty, however, will lie in finding diagnostics for these grammatical properties that are appropriate for use with young children. Most importantly, we need a diagnostic for the first part of the predicted ordering, the raising of V+v into the inflectional system. Unfortunately all the [+SIP] Germanic languages that Bobaljik and Thráinsson discuss are verb-second (V2) languages: Dutch and German have V2 in matrix clauses but not embedded clauses, while Icelandic has V2 both in matrix clauses and in most embedded clauses.

---

of how features are bundled together, prior to their insertion in the numeration. In a [−SIP] language such as English or Danish, the features of tense and subject agreement are bundled together into a single lexical item (Infl), while in a [+SIP] language such as Icelandic, the features are introduced into the numeration as separate lexical items (T, AGRs). This approach has the effect of moving the parameter outside of syntax proper, and into a domain that we might call "lexical". Yet, it still does not reduce the parameter to information that is stored in the lexical entry of any single lexical item.

The trouble is that once V2 has applied, we can no longer discern whether the verbal complex was previously in vP or in the inflectional system.

In principle we might devise elicitation tasks for the special, rather complex sentence-types that would be informative in a language like Icelandic or Dutch, but a more practical approach is probably to look for a [+SIP] language that does not have V2, and test the predictions of the SIP there. Bobaljik and Thráinsson have relatively little to say about such languages, but the Romance family provides some candidates.

For example, Spanish has cases where a tense-marker and a (distinct) agreement-marker co-occur on a single verb stem: where Icelandic has *köstu-ðu-m* "throw-past-1pl", Spanish likewise has *lanz-ába-mos* "throw-past-1pl". Furthermore, the v+V complex in Spanish appears to be outside the vP at spell-out, as illustrated in (15).

(15)   Juan no **come nunca** las fresas.
        John not eats   (n)ever the strawberries
        "John doesn't ever eat strawberries."

The main verb *come* "eats" appears to have moved out of the vP, as it precedes the word *nunca* "(n)ever" which (arguably) marks the left edge of the vP. (In contrast, in the English gloss, the main verb *eats* remains to the right of *ever*).

If consultation with experts on the morphology and syntax of Spanish supports these initial impressions, and Spanish is appropriately analyzed as [+SIP], then we might reasonably test the following acquisitional prediction: Children acquiring Spanish will begin to move V+v out of vP (as in (15)) at least as early as they begin making productive use of morphological complexes such as *-ába-mos*. For example, it will be problematic for Bobaljik and Thráinsson if we ever find a child who has acquired *both* the use of forms like *ába-mos* and the other prerequisites for an example like (15), such as knowledge of the lexical item *nunca*, yet the child systematically refrains from producing utterances in which the finite verb precedes *nunca*.

A possible concern about this prediction is that the child might initially misanalyze a morphological complex such as *-ába-mos* as a single morpheme, rather than a sequence of two morphemes. Yet, if a child uses the complex to express both tense and agreement, as the adult does, then Bobaljik and Thráinsson's account requires that the child, like the adult, has a bimorphemic analysis: according to their proposal, universal grammar allows no other possibility.

Once again, I emphasize that I have not myself tested the acquisitional prediction discussed here, and I have no idea what the outcome will be when someone does. I should mention that Conradie (2006) has studied the SIP in the context of adult second-language acquisition (English speakers acquiring Afrikaans), although unfortunately her materials are unsuitable for use with young children. Also, Conradie's work does not address the time course of language acquisition, but rather focuses on the degree to which the stable-state grammar of an advanced second-language learner corresponds to the grammar of a native speaker. Her work thus focuses on the second-language learner's possible knowledge in the absence of directly relevant experience. This important class of parametric predictions (which are valid for first-language as well as second-language acquisition) will be discussed in Chapter 8, Section 8.3.

2.2.5 Example III: the DP Parameter

Bošković's (2004) is concerned with explaining why some languages allow scrambling, or more precisely "Japanese-style scrambling", while others do not. An example of this type of scrambling from Japanese is provided in (16a–16b) (based on Bošković 2004: 614, exs. 2a–2b).

(16a)   [$_{IP}$ John-ga [$_{CP}$[$_{IP}$ Mary-ga [$_{VP}$ sono hon-o   katta]] to]
      John-NOM   Mary-NOM that book-ACC bought that
      omotteiru]
      thinks
      "John thinks that Mary bought that book."

(16b)   [$_{IP}$ Sono hon-o[$_{IP}$ John-ga[$_{CP}$[$_{IP}$ Mary-ga[$_{VP}$ katta]] to]
      that book-ACC John-NOM   Mary-NOM bought that
      omotteiru]]
      thinks
      "John thinks that Mary bought that book."

The unscrambled version of the sentence is (16a). In (16b) the direct object of the embedded clause, *sono hon-o* "that book (acc.)", has been scrambled to the front of the matrix clause. Despite the difference in word order, the two sentences in (16a) and (16b) mean the same thing.[6]

The example in (16b) illustrates two major properties of Japanese-style scrambling: an argument can be scrambled "long-distance", across a clause boundary; and the scrambling is semantically vacuous. Additional characteristics include the fact that multiple arguments can be scrambled to the front of the same clause; and the fact that the scrambling of adjuncts, while not impossible, is far more restricted than the scrambling of arguments.

An important generalization concerning Japanese-style scrambling is that it is found *only* in languages that lack articles. Bošković (2004: 629–33) proposes that a crucial requirement for this type of scrambling is the negative setting of what we might call the "DP Parameter" (although Bošković himself never gives it a name):

(17)   THE DP PARAMETER: The Hierarchy of Projections {does, does not} include a DP layer above NP.

The effect of the negative setting of (17) is that "noun phrases", in the traditional sense, will be bare NPs, rather than DPs. Bošković argues that in these [–DP] languages, the counterparts to demonstrative and possessive determiners are actually adjectives, located inside the NP. Moreover, in the absence of a DP, true articles are simply absent.

Following (Bošković and Takahashi 1998), Bošković adopts a distinctly Minimalist approach to Japanese-style scrambling: The scrambled constituent is merged in its surface position, and later *lowers* into its unscrambled position by covert movement (i.e. an application of Move after spell-out). This idea is specifically Minimalist in the sense that it rejects two important assumptions of pre-Minimalist work in the P&P framework: the prohibition on movement into a theta-position, and the requirement that a moved constituent must c-command its trace (the Proper Binding Condition).

For his account to work, Bošković needs to modify the standard Minimalist approach to features that I reviewed in Section 2.2.1. First, he proposes that theta roles are themselves a type of feature. The theta features on an NP/DP must be checked against the corresponding

---

[6] The claim that Japanese scrambling is always semantically vacuous is an oversimplification, however, as discussed for example by Dejima (1999) and Saito (2006).

feature of the theta-role assigner, and the checker and check-ee must be sisters when this checking occurs, but (in a [–DP] language, at least) the checking can be deferred until after spell-out. Further, Boškovic's proposes that the case feature on an NP can likewise be checked covertly. (In the system of Adger 2003, the unchecked, uninterpretable case feature on a scrambled NP would block spell-out.)

What then prohibits Japanese-style scrambling in a [+DP] language? Boškovic proposes an explanation in terms of Last Resort. In my overview of Minimalism in Section 2.2.1, I mentioned "Last Resort" as the idea that the operation Merge can apply only when its use is forced by a selectional feature or the Hierarchy of Projections. Boškovic proposes that Last Resort is specific to functional projections: a DP is a functional projection, and therefore can be merged into a tree only if the operation satisfies a selectional requirement (i.e. a theta-feature) of the constituent with which it is merged. In contrast, an NP is a non-functional projection, and can be merged either in a theta-position or in a "scrambled" position at the beginning of the clause (where it does not satisfy any selectional feature).

To conclude, Boškovic's account falls squarely within Minimalism, but is similar to the Bobaljik–Thráinsson proposal of Section 2.2.4 in violating Chomsky's (1995) injunction against parameterization of C_{HL}. From the perspective of child language acquisition, then, Minimalism appears to be a modest adjustment to the earlier P&P framework, rather than a fundamental change in direction. The issue of what exactly it means to move syntactic variation "into the lexicon", however, and the question of whether the DP Parameter and/or the Bobaljik–Thráinsson SIP might qualify as lexical, will be considered in some detail in Chapter 8, Section 8.1. Let us turn now to some acquisitional predictions of Boškovic's analysis.

The main cross-linguistic prediction of the DP Parameter is that if a language has Japanese-style scrambling, then it will necessarily be an NP language and lack true articles. Correspondingly, the strongest acquisitional prediction is that if a child is acquiring a language with Japanese-style scrambling, then as soon as her grammar in fact allows this type of scrambling it will also lack true articles.

Unfortunately, this prediction is rather uninteresting. If the adult language permits Japanese-style scrambling (according to Boškovic's account), it will lack articles. Grammatical conservatism then makes it extremely unlikely that the child will invent a system of articles for which there is no evidence in the input. Hence, no matter how early or late the child starts using Japanese-style scrambling, it will necessarily be true at that point that her grammar lacks articles.

Likewise, if a child is acquiring a DP language, Bošković's account predicts that as soon as her grammar includes determiners, she will refrain from Japanese-style scrambling. Yet, grammatical conservatism makes it quite unlikely that the child will ever use Japanese-style scrambling when there is no evidence for it in the input. Hence, while the prediction is likely true, it does not provide a useful test of the theory.

Kang (2005) has found and tested a much more interesting acquisitional prediction of Bošković's work. Instead of focusing on the negative setting of the DP Parameter, she examines another pre-requisite for Japanese-style scrambling: the existence of overt case-marking. Bošković (2004: 633) notes that an account of Japanese-style scrambling should ideally account for two generalizations: first, languages with this type of scrambling lack true articles, and second, these languages always have a system of overt case-marking.[7]

Bošković (2004) accounts for the first generalization with the DP Parameter, but the second generalization requires him to add what he terms the Argument Identification Requirement: an argument noun phrase must be "identified" in overt syntax (i.e. at some point in the derivation prior to spell-out). The two mechanisms available for identification are marking the noun phrase overtly for case, and placing the noun phrase in a theta-position. In a [+DP] language the second mechanism is always sufficient, given that DPs are necessarily merged in their theta-positions. In a [−DP] language, an NP can also be merged in a "scrambled", non-theta position, but only if it bears overt case-marking, because it will not occupy a theta-position until after spell-out.

Kang observes that the addition of the Argument Identification Requirement leads to a new acquisitional prediction: if a child is acquiring a language with Japanese-style scrambling, then overt case-marking will be acquired prior to, or concurrently with, but never significantly

---

[7] According to Bošković (2004: 633, fn.27), the latter generalization has roots going back at least to (Sapir 1921). Yet, it is important to note that Bošković's version is specific to languages with JSS. Sapir's proposal extended to all languages with free word order, and is falsified (for example) by polysynthetic languages, many of which have free word order but no case-marking on their noun phrases. Thanks to Jonathan Bobaljik for bringing this to my attention.

later than, this type of scrambling. Kang evaluates this prediction with a cross-sectional comprehension study on two- and three-year-old children acquiring Korean, a language with Japanese-style scrambling, and the results are as predicted: children understand scrambling of an object across a subject only if they understand both nominative and accusative case-marking. The details of this study, including the precise logic of the prediction, will be presented in Chapter 6.

Appendix: A typical derivation in Minimalism

Armed with the information about Minimalism in this chapter, let us work through an example: the derivation of the English sentence *John met Mary*. First recall that Minimalism makes no use of the level of D-structure. Instead, the derivation begins with a "numeration" N that lists the LIs that will be used in the derivation, and (if the same LI will be used more than once) the number of times that it will occur. Hence, we begin with (A1).

(A1) N = {*John*[D, *u*case:], *Mary*[D, *u*case:], *meet*[V, *u*D],
     v [*u*D, *u*case:acc, *u*V*, *u*infl:],
     T[*u*D*, tense:past, *u*case:nom]}

Here I am closely following the notational practices of (Adger 2003). Each LI in N is a "bundle" of features, and if it has a phonological realization then (for convenience) I use the English spelling of that realization to stand for the bundle. If the bundle has no phonological realization, I use the syntactic category (e.g. v, T). This is followed by a list of other relevant features in square brackets.

   The names *John* and *Mary* are followed by [D], their syntactic category, indicating that they will function as the head of a DP; and by [*u*case:], which indicates that they have an uninterpretable "case" feature. The latter feature is followed simply by a colon, which indicates that a value, such as nom(inative) or acc(usative), is required but has not yet been assigned. The next LI, *meet*, is associated with the features [V, *u*D]. The first feature indicates that the LI's syntactic category is V; and the second is a selectional feature indicating that the LI requires a sister of category D, to which a theta role will be assigned. (Note that the selectional/non-selectional distinction is not explicit in this notation. The fact that *meet* is a V, with theta roles to assign, is what tells us that its [*u*D] feature is selectional.)

The LI v (or "little v") is used in Minimalism to introduce an agentive subject. Hence, v assigns the theta role of Agent, and has a selectional feature [*u*D]. Additionally, v is taken as the source of accusative case for the direct object. Hence, v contains the feature [*u*case:acc]. (Note that case is a purely formal feature, and is uninterpretable on both the provider and the recipient.)

The two remaining features on v are [*u*infl:] and [*u*V*]. The first is a weak, uninterpretable feature that requires an "inflectional" value such as "past tense" to be assigned to it. The latter is a strong feature (as indicated by the asterisk), and will force V to raise and adjoin to v. The details will be given below.

Finally, the LI T has the feature [tense:past], in other words an interpretable tense feature with the value "past"; and the feature [*u*case:nom], indicating that it needs to serve as the source for nominative case on a DP. The remaining feature, [*u*D*], requires the establishment of a sisterhood relationship with a DP. This feature is sometimes termed an "EPP" feature, in reference to the Extended Projection Principle of LGB: Every clause must contain a subject. The [*u*D*] feature on T likewise serves to ensure that the clause will have a DP subject within the TP. Note that this is not a selectional feature, because T assigns no theta role to the DP.

The next step in the derivation is to select two LIs from the numeration and merge them, as shown in (A2).

(A2)   V
                    ⎛‾‾‾‾‾‾‾‾‾‾⎞
            meet [V,u̶D̶]   *Mary* [D, *u*case:]

This choice of LIs is guided by the "Hierarchy of Projections", which requires the following architecture in the verbal domain: T > v > V. In other words, LIs will be added to a given structure in such a way that VP is dominated by vP, and vP is dominated by TP. The choice of the LI *Mary* at this point will have an effect on the interpretation (i.e. the person named *Mary* is the Theme, the one who was met), but the choice of *John* would also have led to a convergent derivation (with a different interpretation).

The operation of Merge serves to create a checking relation (sisterhood) between the two LIs, which allows the uninterpretable feature [*u*D] of *meet* to be checked. The fact that this feature has been checked,

and is destined for deletion, is indicated here by the strike mark. Note
that the LI *meet* is the head of the resulting phrase, because it is this LI
whose selectional feature was checked off when the two were merged.
Therefore the features of *meet* are used as the label of the phrase. Here
I use the categorial feature V as a convenient abbreviation for the full
list.

Next, following the Hierarchy of Projection, v is selected and merged
with the phrase, as shown in (A3).

(A3)

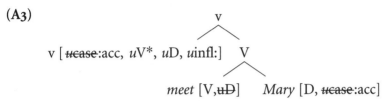

As soon as v is merged, the operation of Agree relates the feature of
[*u*case:acc] on v to the feature of [*u*case:] on *Mary*. Agree assigns the
value of acc to the unvalued [*u*case:] feature on *Mary*, and then marks
the [*u*case:acc] feature on both LIs as checked.

The strong feature [*u*V*] on v requires the establishment of a sisterhood relationship with a constituent of category V. This is a non-
selectional feature (because v assigns no theta role to the VP), and
therefore it will need to be satisfied by raising the V to v, rather
than simply by merging v with the VP (which happened anyway,
thanks to the Hierarchy of Projections). As discussed in the chapter,
the operation of Merge, by itself, cannot check off a non-selectional
feature.

The result after movement is shown in (A4). (To save space, adjunction is represented by "+", and the checked case-feature of v is sup-
pressed.)

(A4)

$$v\,[uD]$$

meet [V,u̶D̶] + v [u̶V̶*̶, *u*infl:]   V

<meet [V,u̶D̶]>   *Mary* [D, u̶case̶:acc]

The trace of the moved V takes the form of a copy, surrounded by angle
brackets.

The selectional feature [*u*D] of v has not yet been checked, and I therefore include it as part of the label of the entire phrase in (A4). This selectional feature is satisfied in the next step by selecting and merging the LI *John*, as shown in (A5).

(A5)

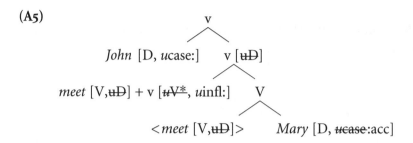

Again following the Hierarchy of Projections, T is now selected and merged, as in (A6).

(A6)

T [*u*D*]
┌──────┴──────┐
T [tense:past, ~~ucase~~:nom]   v
                          ┌────────┴────────┐
                 John [D, ~~ucase~~:nom]   v [~~uD~~]
                                      ┌──────┴──────┐
                        meet [V,~~uD~~] + v [~~uV*~~, ~~uinfl~~:past]   V
                                                          ┌────────┴────────┐
                                              <*meet* [V,~~uD~~]>   *Mary* [D, ~~ucase~~:acc]

The operation Agree immediately applies and values the case feature of *John* as nom. Agree also marks the [*u*case:nom] features on both T and *John* as checked. Similarly, Agree matches the [tense:past] feature on T to the general "inflectional" feature [*u*infl:] on v, yielding [~~uinfl~~:past].

Agree could also check the EPP feature [*u*D*] on T against the [D] feature on *John*, but this would not be sufficient, because [*u*D*] is strong and requires the establishment of sisterhood between the checker and check-ee. Therefore the DP *John* moves up and becomes the specifier, as in (A7). Note that the DP that raises is the closest to T, in terms of c-command.

(A7)

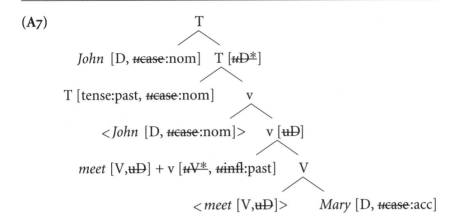

At this point we have used all the LIs in the numeration, and have checked all the uninterpretable features of those LIs. Hence, spell-out applies and sends the structure away (ultimately) to the A-P systems, for pronunciation. Along the way from spell-out to the A-P systems, operations of morphology and phonology will apply. In particular, the LI *meet* will be combined with its sister, the LI v, which has gained the feature-value of [*u*infl:past] during the derivation. The morphological and phonological components will ensure that this combination is pronounced as the word *met*.

Another major operation that occurs on the way from spell-out to the A-P systems is linearization, at least in strictly orthodox Minimalism (see Section 2.2.2 for discussion). I have included left–right order information in the trees of (A1–A7), but this is merely for the reader's (and my own) convenience. Strictly speaking, linear order is left unspecified, and can play no role, during the syntactic derivation.

3

The View from Phonological Theory

This chapter surveys the ideas on cross-linguistic variation that are prominent in contemporary phonological theory. Two major frameworks are considered: Optimality Theory (OT) and Government Phonology (GP). Much as in the previous chapter, I provide a brief overview of each framework and consider an example of how cross-linguistic variation is treated. Specifically, for both OT and GP I will focus on cross-linguistic variation in phonotactics. My principal question will be the extent to which each framework is compatible with grammatical conservatism on the part of the learner (see Section 2.1.3). Differences on this point have consequences for the types of errors that are predicted to occur during language acquisition.

3.1 Optimality Theory

3.1.1 Overview

The most widely adopted framework in current phonological research is Optimality Theory (OT); (Prince and Smolensky 1993, 2004; McCarthy and Prince 1993). I should begin by observing that OT itself is more properly a technique than a theory, in the sense of being a very general mechanism for constraint interaction, one that is strikingly independent of the domain to which the constraints apply. Alongside OT phonology one finds, for example, OT syntax (e.g. Grimshaw and Samek-Lodovici 1998) and OT semantics (e.g. Hendriks and Hoop 2000), both of which use the same basic machinery.

Here I will attempt a very brief sketch of OT phonology. As a concrete example I will use the Basic CV Syllable Structure Theory of Prince and Smolensky (2004, ch. 6). This choice will provide a convenient point of comparison with Government Phonology (in Section 3.2

below). Moreover, Tesar and Smolensky (2000) use the same example to illustrate their proposed OT learning procedure, Error-Driven Constraint Demotion (EDCD). Presenting the Basic CV Theory now will facilitate discussion of Tesar and Smolensky's proposal later in this section.

In phonology and elsewhere, the OT mechanism is non-derivational. It takes a single input (the underlying representation) and, in a single step, generates a potentially infinite number of outputs ("candidate parses"). The optimal parse is selected as the winner, and is predicted to be the grammatically well-formed output for the given input. The losers are all predicted to be ungrammatical, at least with respect to that input. Two parses can both be grammatical options for the same input only if they are in a perfect tie for the position of winner.

The evaluation of a parse is based on how well it satisfies the phonology of the language in question. Surprisingly, however, in OT the phonology of every language contains exactly the same set of constraints, called "CON". Grammatical differences between languages result from differences in the ranking of these constraints: the grammar for a given language is simply the particular ranking it employs. The winning parse usually violates some of the constraints, but less prominent ones than its competitors violate.

More precisely, the evaluation procedure ("Eval-H") works as follows. Suppose that the input is an expression I. The generation of candidate parses is accomplished by a function called "GEN". GEN(I) is the complete, and usually infinite, set of candidate parses. Suppose that p_1 and p_2 are both parses contained in GEN(I), and suppose that C_1 through C_3 are all constraints included in CON. If p_1 violates C_1, then it receives a "mark", $*C_1$. The complete set of marks for p_1 is the multiset, marks(p_1). For example, if p_1 violates C_1 once, and violates C_3 twice, but violates no other constraints, then marks(p_1) = $\{*C_1, *C_3, *C_3\}$. (Note that the two instances of $*C_3$ are distinct because marks(p_1) is a multiset, rather than an ordinary set.)

Evaluation of parses is always pairwise. For parses p_1 and p_2, we can determine the multiset of marks that p_1 receives but that p_2 does not. This is called marks'(p_1). Likewise, we can compute marks'(p_2), the multiset of marks that p_2 receives but p_1 does not. At this point the constraint ranking for the given language comes into play. Parse

		Onsets	
		Required	*Optional*
	Forbidden	CV	(C)V
Codas			
	Permitted	CV(C)	(C)V(C)

FIGURE 3.1 Basic CV syllable-types

Source: Jakobson (1962).

p_2 is preferred over p_1 if, and only if, the highest-ranked constraint in marks′(p_1) is ranked higher than the highest-ranked constraint in marks′(p_2). The grand winner, out of GEN(I), is a parse that is preferred over each and every other candidate.

The only way that a tie can occur is if the two winners have exactly the same multiset of marks. Note that the grammar itself, unlike the evaluation procedure, does not permit ties. In OT, the grammar is always a "total" ranking, one in which every constraint is ranked either higher or lower than each of the other constraints in CON.

Now let's see all of this in action. As an example, let's take Jakobson's (1962) four-way typology of languages, illustrated in Figure 3.1. Certain languages, corresponding to the upper left cell, allow only CV syllables. Other languages make the onset optional, and/or permit the addition of a coda.

Prince and Smolensky (2004) propose an OT account of this typology. In OT, a grammatical analysis includes a characterization of the relevant inputs to GEN, a characterization of the outputs that GEN will produce in response, a list of the relevant constraints, and a ranking of those constraints for each of the languages under discussion. In Prince and Smolensky's analysis, which they call the "Basic CV Syllable Theory", the relevant inputs to GEN are strings of arbitrary, finite, nonzero length, composed entirely of the characters V and/or C. The relevant outputs are the possible syllabifications of those strings.

Syllabification is represented by means of the dot notation: the dots in the string .X. mean that X is a syllable. The angle brackets in the string <X> indicate that X is underparsed. The box in .□V. indicates an epenthetic consonant, and the accented box in .C□́. indicates an epenthetic vowel.

TABLE 3.1 Constraints of the Prince–Smolensky Basic CV Syllable Theory

ONSET	The syllable must have an onset
NoCODA	The syllable must not have a coda
PARSE	Every segment in the input must occur in the output
FILL^{Ons}	Any onset in the output must have a counterpart in the input (No epenthetic consonants)
FILL^{Nuc}	Any nucleus in the output must have a counterpart in the input (No epenthetic vowels)

Prince and Smolensky propose that CON includes the set of five constraints summarized in Table 3.1.[1] The bottom three constraints are called "faithfulness" constraints, because they evaluate how faithfully the output reflects the input. (Note that OT constraints evaluate the output, but in order to do so they sometimes require access to the input.) PARSE is so called because it disallows underparsing. An underparsed segment is not included in any syllable, and is deleted before pronunciation. In contrast, the FILL constraints prevent the insertion of extra, epenthetic material in the output.

Now consider the input /VC/, in a language L_1 whose grammar ranks the five constraints from Table 3.1 as follows: ONSET $\gg$ NoCODA $\gg$ FILL^{Nuc} $\gg$ PARSE $\gg$ FILL^{Ons}. The symbol "$\gg$" means that the preceding constraint outranks the following constraint. The leading parses of /VC/, and the marks assigned to each parse by the constraints, can be conveniently summarized in an OT "tableau", as shown in Table 3.2. Note that the left-to-right order of constraints across the top of the tableau reflects their ranking in L_1.

The winning candidate, .□V.<C>, is indicated by the manual symbol, ☞. This parse results from insertion of an epenthetic consonant as onset, and underparsing (i.e. deletion) of the coda. The nearest competitor is <VC>, the result of underparsing both V and C. The marks of these parses are as follows: marks (.□V.<C>) = {*PARSE, *FILL^{Ons}}, and marks(<VC>) = {*PARSE, *PARSE}. The next step is to cancel the marks that are shared. This yields marks'(.□V.<C>) = {*FILL^{Ons}}, and marks'(<VC>) = {*PARSE}. Note that one, but only one, of the two PARSE violations for <VC> is canceled. Given that PARSE $\gg$ FILL^{Ons} in L_1, the candidate .□V.<C> is preferred.

[1] In fact a somewhat larger set of constraints is proposed in Prince and Smolensky (2004), but the list in Table 3.1 is sufficient for present purposes. Also, the constraints in this list go by several, slightly different names in the OT literature. Here I use the same, relatively transparent names adopted by Tesar and Smolensky (2000).

TABLE 3.2 (Partial) OT tableau for input /VC/ in language L_1

Candidate	ONSET	NoCoda	FILL^{Nuc}	PARSE	FILL^{Ons}
.VC.	*	*			
.□VC.		*			*
.V.Cĺ.	*		*		
.□V.Cĺ.			*		*
.V.<C>	*			*	
<VC>				**	
☞.□V.<C>				*	*
<V>.Cĺ.			*	*	

Indeed, the candidate .□V.<C> is preferred over each of its com-petitors in Table 3.2. Note that the list of parses in Table 3.2 is not exhaustive. Indeed, GEN(/VC/) is actually an infinite set, because there is no limit to the amount of overparsing (i.e. epenthesis) that can occur: .VC.□ĺ., .□ĺ.VC.□ĺ., .VC.□ĺ.□ĺ., and so on. Yet, these additional candidates will necessarily lose out to the parse .□V.<C>, because they will always correspond to one of the candidates in Table 3.2, with additional violations of the FILL constraints.

Finally, note the tight connection in OT between the proposed list of constraints and the predictions for cross-linguistic variation. In the present case, the set of total rankings of the constraints in Table 3.1 amounts to a prediction about the complete inventory of syllable-structure systems found in the world's languages. The pre-dicted language-types can be checked against descriptive surveys. Prince and Smolensky note that the theory requires various extensions in order to handle the full range of attested cross-linguistic variation. Nonetheless, they claim, the basic mechanisms remain the same and work quite well.

3.1.2 Learnability of an OT phonology

The next question is learnability: Can the child possibly acquire an OT phonology? If we grant that CON and GEN are innate (which is by far the best option, for purposes of learnability), then there are two main parts to the question: Can the child discover the underlying representa-tions (the inputs to GEN) for her language? And can she work out the particular ranking of CON that her language employs? These questions are tightly interconnected, because the inputs that could have given rise to what the child actually hears will vary, depending on the particular constraint ranking that is operative in the language.

Tesar and Smolensky (2000) discuss both parts of the learnability problem. Here I will focus on the second: How can the child discover the correct ranking of CON for her language?

I will follow Tesar and Smolensky (2000: 31–2) in simplifying the problem somewhat. Specifically, I will assume that the child can take the form that she actually hears and reconstruct the linguistically structured representation that GEN must have produced. Moreover, I will assume that the child can reconstruct, on the basis of that output, what GEN's input must have been.

This is clearly an oversimplification, especially when portions of the input have been deleted before pronunciation (e.g. as a result of underparsing, in the Basic CV Syllable Theory): the child receives no (immediate) information about the deleted material. Nonetheless, the simplified learning problem is by no means trivial.

Tesar and Smolensky propose a learning strategy that they call "Constraint Demotion" (CD). CD operates step by step, using one observed form (or "learning datum") at a time. At each point it keeps track of its current best guess, in the form of a partial ranking of the constraints in CON. For each datum that it receives, it requires the following information: an appropriately structured representation of the parse for that datum, and the input to GEN that gave rise to it. Furthermore, CD focuses on one pair of parses at a time: the (observed) winner, and one of its losing competitors. At all times it acts to ensure that its hypothesized ranking does not cause the loser to be preferred over the winner.

The mechanism is straightforward. CD calculates marks' (winner) and marks' (loser), according to its currently hypothesized ranking. If the highest-ranked constraint C_W that is violated in marks' (winner) outranks the highest-ranked constraint C_L that is violated in marks'(loser), then C_W is demoted to a new rank, immediately below C_L.

Interestingly, what CD produces is not, itself, a possible grammar. Recall that in OT a grammar is a total ranking of the constraints in CON. CD instead yields a partial ranking, in which some of the constraints are tied. Moreover, partial rankings are not necessarily learnable by CD (Tesar and Smolensky 2000: 48). The authors suggest (2000: 49) that the partial ranking from CD gets converted into one of the compatible total rankings by the time the child becomes an adult. They leave it as an open question whether it matters which total ranking the child chooses. In any case, though, CD is provably successful (at least) in the sense of yielding a partial ranking that accounts for all the data the learner has encountered.

Tesar and Smolensky then propose a refinement to CD that they call EDCD, or Error-Driven Constraint Demotion. The motivation is to address the following problem: for any given learning datum, there is a potentially infinite set of winner–loser pairs to choose from (given that GEN(I) can be infinite). Frequently these pairs are uninformative, because the winner is already preferred over the loser by the learner's current constraint ranking. How then should the learner proceed?

The strategy of EDCD is to take the input for the current learning datum and calculate the winning parse, according to the current constraint ranking. If this predicted winner matches the observed datum, then EDCD does nothing (since it has nothing to learn from that datum), and goes on to the next one. If the predicted winner differs, however, then EDCD constructs its winner–loser pair from the observed winner and the predicted winner, respectively. This is guaranteed to be an informative pair.

3.1.3 Acquisitional predictions of an OT phonology

From the parametric perspective, the first question is whether OT Phonology actually posits anything that could be considered a parameter, even in the broader sense of the term: a point of abstract grammatical variation. The answer is yes.

Tesar and Smolensky (2000: 45–6) note that an OT grammar is equivalent to a collection of (binary) "dominance parameters": each constraint either dominates, or is dominated by, each of the other constraints in CON. Hence, if CON contains n constraints, then a total ranking is equivalent to $n(n-1)/2$ dominance parameters. Furthermore, each constraint is (normally) an abstract grammatical statement, and its dominance relation to another constraint is a correspondingly abstract point of grammatical variation.

Note, however, that the dominance relations are not independent of one another. For example, if constraint C_1 dominates C_2, and C_2 dominates C_3, then C_3 cannot dominate C_1. The consequence for language acquisition is considerable: The child cannot set any parameter (i.e. dominance relation) independently of the others. This is not a problem for learnability (as we saw in the previous subsection), but in principle it makes it difficult for the child to be grammatically conservative.[2]

To see this, suppose that CON includes our three constraints C_1 through C_3, and the child's initial hypothesis is that they are unranked: $\{C_1, C_2, C_3\}$. Suppose further that the ranking in the target grammar is as follows: $C_1 \gg C_2 \gg C_3$. For the sake of concreteness let's assume that the child's learning strategy is EDCD (although my point does not depend on this), and that the first datum she encounters requires her to demote C_2 below C_1. Her new hypothesis will be $\{C_1, C_3\} \gg C_2$. This has the desired effect of moving C_2 below C_1, but it has the "collateral" effect of ranking C_2 below C_3. This is the exact opposite of their dominance relation in the target grammar. Eventually the problem will be corrected (C_3 will be demoted), but for some period of time the child will have an incorrect ranking, $C_3 \gg C_2$. Whether this will lead the child to produce errors of comission depends on the actual content of C_3 and C_2, but in principle it certainly could.

Let us consider a more concrete example, within the Basic CV Syllable Theory. The relevant example is actually difficult to construct, because there is remarkably little interaction between the constraints of this theory. As noted by Prince and Smolensky (2004: 115), the constraints affecting onsets (ONSET, FILL^{Ons}, PARSE) and the constraints affecting codas (NoCoda, FILL^{Nuc}, PARSE) have only one point of overlap (PARSE), and can therefore be ranked completely independently of one another. Nonetheless, the fact that PARSE affects both onsets and codas means that its demotion to handle a fact about onsets can (temporarily) have undesired effects on the treatment of codas, and vice versa.

Suppose that the child initially places all five constraints in a single stratum, without any relative ranking: $\{$ONSET, NoCoda, FILL^{Nuc}, PARSE, FILL$^{Ons}\}$. (Tesar and Smolensky 2000: 46, treat this as a natural starting point in a similar example.) Suppose further that the child's target is the same language, L_1, discussed above in Subsection 3.1.1 (cf. Table 3.2).

The first datum that the child encounters might be one with an input of /CVC/. Given that the constraints are unranked in the child's current hypothesis, her predicted parse for this input is chosen arbitrarily from among the following candidates, each of which incurs a

---

[2] Here I assume that the child's current hypothesis about the constraint ranking in the target language is what she uses to generate her own productions. To my knowledge, no alternative has been proposed.

TABLE 3.3 (Partial) OT tableau for input /CVC/, with constraints unranked

Candidate	ONSET	NoCoda	FILL^{Nuc}	PARSE	FILL^{Ons}
.CVC.		*			
.CV.\<C>				*	
.CV.CÓ.			*		

single mark (cf. Table 3.3): .CVC., .CV.\<C>, .CV.CÓ. (Note that the vertical lines separating the five constraints in Table 3.3 are dotted, not solid, to indicate that the constraints all belong to a single, unranked stratum.)

Suppose that the child selects .CVC. (which violates NoCoda), but the datum's structured representation is actually .CV.\<C> (which violates PARSE). In this case the child will be required to demote PARSE below NoCoda. According to EDCD, her new hypothesis will be {ONSET, NoCoda, FILL^{Nuc}, FILL^{Ons}} ≫ PARSE.

Crucially, the child has arrived at a working hypothesis in which FILL^{Ons} ≫ PARSE, but this is the opposite of the dominance relation in the target grammar. A consequence of this erroneous ranking is the following: on an input of the form /VCV/, the child's grammar will prefer \<V>.CV. (with the initial V deleted), but the target grammar L$_1$ will instead prefer .□V.CV. (with an epenthetic onset in the first syllable).

In sum, changing one aspect of the grammar (the dominance relation between PARSE and NoCoda) disrupted an unrelated part of the grammar (the dominance relation between PARSE and FILL^{Ons}). The resulting error type is one of omission, not comission, but this is accidental: the crucial constraint happens to be PARSE, and the effect of ranking PARSE too low in the hierarchy happens to be an error of omission. In the general case, though, errors of comission can come about in exactly the same way. Hence, the more general prediction is the following: when the grammar that the child is acquiring takes the form of an OT constraint ranking, we should expect to find errors of comission in her spontaneous speech. All else equal, grammatical conservatism is unexpected.

One might have thought the child's use of a partial ranking (e.g. in the EDCD algorithm) would make grammatical conservatism easier to accomplish. The child can reserve judgement about the relative ranking of two constraints by keeping them in a single, unranked stratum. Yet, in the example above, it was precisely the demotion of a single constraint from an unranked stratum that led to the problem.

Moreover, keeping constraints together in a single stratum can lead even more directly to violations of grammatical conservatism. Consider the situation in Table 3.3, where an input of /CVC/ is evaluated with the constraints unranked. The child is left to choose arbitrarily among three tied outputs: .CVC., .CV.<C>, and .CV.CÓ. If the target grammar happens to prefer .CV.<C>, and the child happens to choose .CV.CÓ., the result is the child's production of two syllables where the adult would produce only one, a highly salient violation of conservatism.

In Section 3.3 I will return to the question of whether grammatical conservatism is compatible with an OT approach to phonology. The big question, then, will be whether children are actually grammatically conservative in the domain of phonology. Indeed, I propose that this is the core acquisitional test of an OT analysis: What types of comission errors does the analysis predict, and are these errors robustly present in children's data (especially their spontaneous speech)?

In Chapter 7 I will present a study of children's acquisition of Dutch syllable structure, where the findings will be fully consistent with grammatical conservatism. Nonetheless, I believe that children may be less conservative in certain areas of phonology than they are in syntax. I will return to this point in Chapter 8. I will discuss the evidence, and some possible explanations, in Section 8.2. To the extent that children are found to be grammatically conservative in their phonology, however, this could in principle require some adjustments to the OT framework. In Section 8.5, I will provide a broader discussion of the implications of grammatical conservatism, to the extent that children exhibit it, both for constraint-ranking approaches and for other approaches to cross-linguistic variation.

3.2 Government Phonology

A prominent alternative to the constraint-ranking approach of OT is the Principles-and-Parameters framework of Government Phonology (GP; e.g. Kaye, Lowenstamm, and Vergnaud 1990; Kaye 1990, 1995; Charette 1991). I should say at the outset that the distinction between OT and GP need not be great, because GP analyses can usually be translated into OT terms (see Harris and Gussmann 2002 for an example). In

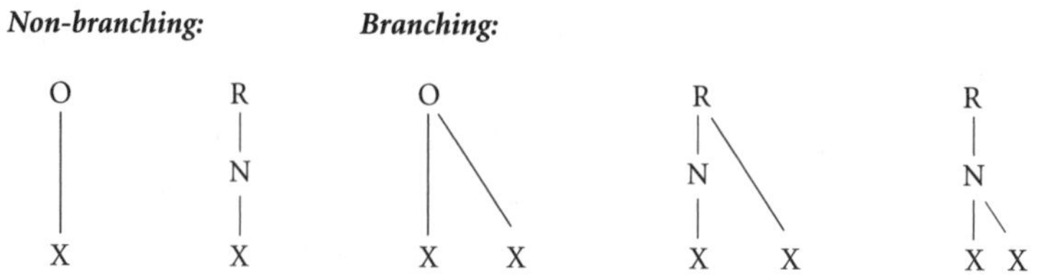

Non-branching: *Branching:*

FIGURE 3.2 Constituents in GP

contrast to the OT framework, however, orthodox GP posits constraints that are inviolable. Moreover, GP assumes a set of parameters that can, in principle, be set independently of one another, while OT constraint rankings have a natural tendency to create interdependencies, as discussed in the previous section.

In this section I will attempt a very brief sketch of GP. My emphasis will be on syllable structure, and I will closely follow the clear exposition of (Charette 1991). The technical details remain similar, if not always identical, in more recent GP analyses.

GP posits a highly restrictive theory of syllable structure. Interestingly, the notion of "syllable" is not among the theory's primitives. Instead, GP posits just three types of constituents: onsets (O), rhymes (R), and nuclei (N). What is traditionally considered a syllable is simply an onset followed by a rhyme. Moreover, each constituent is maximally binary, as illustrated in Figure 3.2.

In GP, syllabification is determined by government relations. The possibilities for government, in turn, are constrained by Charm Theory (Kaye et al. 1985, 1990), which I will only touch on here. The main idea is that any given segment has positive, negative, or neutral charm. Vowels typically have positive charm, and consonants typically have negative charm. Sibilants, nasals, liquids, and glides, however, have neutral charm. A segment with negative charm may not appear in the nucleus, and a segment with positive charm may not appear outside the nucleus. Normally a segment with positive or negative charm is a governor, and a segment with neutral charm is governed.

To take an example from Charette (1991), in French the word *patrie* is necessarily syllabified as *pa.tri*, while the word *parti* is syllabified as *par.ti*. In both cases the syllabification follows from the fact that the segment [t] is an obstruent (and has negative charm), while the segment [r] is a liquid (and has neutral charm). Hence, [t] must govern [r] in both words. The resulting structures are shown in (1).

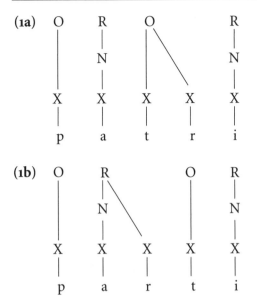

In (1a), [t] governs [r] because both segments are contained in a single constituent (O). Within a constituent, government always proceeds from left to right. In (1b), [t] again governs [r], but this time the relation is one of interconstituent government, which always proceeds from right to left. The government is "interconstituent" because [r] appears in the postnuclear position of a rhyme, while [t] appears in the following onset.

Government is subject to a requirement of locality. The governing and governed elements normally need to be adjacent on the skeletal tier (represented by Xs) or the level of nuclear projection (the Ns). The principal configurations for constituent government involve a branching onset, branching rhyme, or branching nucleus, as illustrated in Figure 3.3. The principal configurations for interconstituent government, shown in Figure 3.4, involve an onset and a preceding (postnuclear) rhymal position, two nuclei that are contiguous at the level of nuclear projection, or the nucleus of a rhyme and its preceding onset.

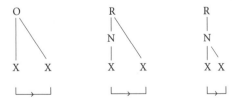

FIGURE 3.3 Principal configurations for constituent government

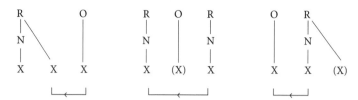

FIGURE 3.4 Principal configurations for interconstituent government

Government also plays an important role in the licensing of empty nuclei, which are used extensively in GP and are subject to the Empty Category Principle (cf. Kaye 1990: 314):[3]

(2)   EMPTY CATEGORY PRINCIPLE

    i.   A licensed empty nucleus has no phonetic realization.

   ii.   An empty nucleus is licensed if (a) it is properly governed or (b) it is final, in a language that licenses word-final empty nuclei.

Proper government is simply a special case of ordinary government, and all the usual requirements (directionality, locality, appropriate charm) still apply. The principal difference is that in the case of proper government, the governor must not itself be licensed.[4] Also, Kaye and his associates propose that an unrealized segment can be governed (hence properly governed) by any segment with a phonetic realization, regardless of its charm.

An example discussed in (Kaye 1990) comes from Moroccan Arabic.[5] In (3a), the singular form of the verb for 'write' contains three nuclei, all of which are empty. The final nucleus is licensed by word-final licensing (which is available in this language), and is therefore left uninterpreted. The final nucleus governs the middle nucleus, because the two are adjacent at the level of nuclear projection. Proper government is absent, however, because the final nucleus is licensed. Hence, the

---

[3] In this statement of the Empty Category Principle I refer to "word-final" licensing. Strictly speaking I should say "domain-final", so as to include morphophonological domains other than the word. In the examples that will be discussed here, however, the relevant domain is always the word.

[4] A further restriction on proper government is the following: the domain of proper government may not include a governing domain. This restriction will not, however, play any role in the examples discussed here.

[5] In the examples from Moroccan Arabic I include a word-final empty nucleus when there is a stem-final consonant. As Charette (1991: 216, n.4) observes, the presentation in (Kaye 1990) is somewhat inconsistent on this point.

middle nucleus is interpreted as the epenthetic vowel, which is [ɨ] in Moroccan Arabic. The fact that the middle nucleus is unlicensed means that it can serve as the licenser for the first nucleus, which therefore remains uninterpreted.

(3a)   tan ktɨb "I write"

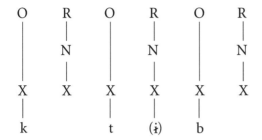

(3b)   tan kɨtbu: "we write"

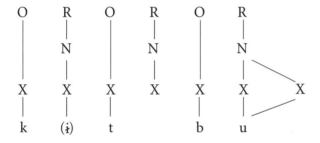

In (3b) the final nucleus is branching, and contains the long vowel [u:]. This nucleus is unlicensed, and therefore is eligible to properly govern the middle nucleus, which remains uninterpreted. The middle nucleus is thus licensed, and ineligible to properly govern the first nucleus, which is interpreted as an epenthetic vowel.

Note that the Empty Category Principle is parameterized: some languages allow word-final licensing, and others do not. This parameter captures a portion of the cross-linguistic variation described by Jakobson (1962): some languages allow CVC syllables, while others do not. More precisely, the sequence CVC will be possible as the phonetic realization of a *word* only if the language permits word-final licensing.

Concretely, the GP structure for such a word is shown in (4).

(4)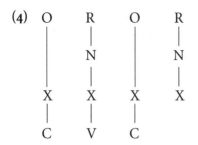

As usual, onsets and rhymes come in pairs. Thus, (4) contains a final rhyme, with a nucleus that is phonetically uninterpreted. The Empty Category Principle tells us that the uninterpreted nucleus is permitted if it is licensed, either by proper government or by word-final licensing. Proper government is not an option in (4), because the empty nucleus is not followed by another constituent. Hence, there is no possibility of interconstituent government. On the other hand, if word-final licensing is available in the language, then it will apply in (4) and license the empty nucleus.

Word-internally, GP provides a different way to obtain a coda (to use the traditional, non-GP term): one can place the final consonant in the postnuclear position of a rhyme. This postnuclear position is available only when it is licensed by a following onset. Hence, such a structure cannot be word-final. Moreover, the availability of branching rhymes is itself taken to be a point of parametric variation (Kaye 1989; Harris 1994; Pan and Snyder 2004, 2005*b*), as will be discussed in Chapter 7. Together, the parameters controlling word-final licensing and branching rhymes allow GP to account for cross-linguistic variation in the availability of codas.

Note that the Jakobsonian syllable typology discussed in Section 3.1 collapses word-internal and word-final CVC sequence into a single category. GP makes a sharp distinction, and the resulting typological prediction is well-supported: as discussed in Harris and Gussmann (2002: 5), languages such as Italian and Telugu permit CVC sequences word-internally, but not word-finally. Other languages, such as Luo and Yucatec Maya, permit CVC sequences word-finally but not word-internally. On the GP approach, Italian and Telugu have branching rhymes but no word-final licensing. Luo and Yucatec Maya have word-final licensing but disallow branching rhymes.[6]

---

[6] Harris and Gussmann (1998: 23) take this approach, and attribute the absence of word-internal codas in Luo and Yucatec Maya simply to the lack of branching rhymes.

The languages that Jakobson classified as "onset optional" can be analyzed within GP as languages that permit an empty category in onset position. In general, the principles of phonological government will always permit a phonetically realized nucleus to license a preceding empty onset (cf. Charette 1991: 92). Yet, as Jakobson observed, not all languages permit this. Pan and Snyder (2005*a*, 2005*b*) have proposed an Empty Onset Parameter to capture this variation: this parameter simply allows or disallows empty onsets in general, without regard to government relations.[7]

3.3 Acquisitional predictions of GP versus OT

The acquisitional predictions of a GP analysis can be derived in exactly the same way as they are for an analysis in P&P syntax. A prediction of concurrent acquisition exists for any two constructions with identical grammatical and lexical pre-requisites, and a prediction of ordered acquisition exists whenever the pre-requisites for one construction are a proper subset of the pre-requisites for the other.

An important question is whether grammatical conservatism, on the part of the child, is compatible with the GP framework. Indeed, the same question arises for P&P syntax: To what extent can the child actually speak, without making unwarranted commitments to particular parameter-settings? I will delay full consideration of this question until Chapter 8, Section 8.5. Here it is sufficient to note that grammatical conservatism is quite easy to achieve if the parameters obey Wexler and Manzini's (1987) Subset Condition:

In principle, though, a word-internal coda could also result from the presence of a word-internal empty nucleus, as seen above in the Moroccan Arabic example *kɨ tbu* "(we) write". Perhaps word-internal empty nuclei are independently blocked in Luo and Yucatec Maya, or perhaps the words in which they would have been possible were excluded from consideration. In languages that do allow word-internal codas, however, it will be necessary to decide whether they result from branching rhymes, word-internal empty nuclei, or a mixture of the two. If a given language exhibits positional restrictions on consonants, then the potential sources of codas can be distinguished by checking whether the codas are chosen from the set of consonants found in onset position, the set found in postnuclear rhymal position, or the union of those two sets.

[7] The separation of the Empty Onset Parameter from considerations of government is motivated by the widespread assumption in GP that empty onsets are available extremely freely in languages such as English and French. For example, Charette (1991: ch. 4) proposes that licensing is necessary only if the empty onset dominates a skeletal point (i.e. an "X"), and that most empty onsets (in French, at least) do not dominate such a point. Under such a view, cross-linguistic variation in the availability of empty onsets is difficult to derive from cross-linguistic variation in the mechanisms available for government.

(5)   THE SUBSET CONDITION (Wexler and Manzini 1987: 60):

> For every parameter p and every two values i, j of p, the languages generated under the two values of the parameter are one a subset of the other, that is,
>
> $$L(p(i)) \subseteq L(p(j)) \text{ or } L(p(j)) \subseteq L(p(i)).$$

In other words, suppose that for each parameter there is a subset option that simply precludes a particular class of linguistic constructions, and a superset option that allows them. Suppose further that the effect of this parameter is independent of how other parameters are set. In this case the child can be grammatically conservative simply by choosing the subset value of the parameter, and waiting for evidence that might require her to switch to the superset value.

My point in bringing this up is that many of the parameters proposed in the GP literature have a subset/superset character. For example, the Empty Category Parameter from (Kaye 1990) is parameterized so as to either allow or disallow word-final licensing of an empty nucleus. The option permitting word-final licensing leads to a language in which the possible words are a proper superset of the word-types allowed without word-final licensing. The same situation holds with proposals to parameterize branching rhymes and magic empty nuclei, as will be discussed in Chapter 7.

An exception to this pattern can be found in Charette's (1991: ch. 6) proposal to parameterize the directionality of interconstituent government. As noted in the previous section, the standard assumption in GP is that interconstituent government is universally right-to-left. If Charette is correct in her proposal that certain languages instead employ a left-to-right version, and that the directionality is a basic point of parametric variation, then this is a place where grammatical conservatism will be more difficult to achieve.

For example, if a language does not provide word-final licensing of empty nuclei, and it chooses the right-to-left direction for interconstituent government, then (phonetically) word-final consonants will be impossible, but word-medial geminate consonants will be readily available. This is because the process of gemination in GP requires an onset to govern the preceding postnuclear rhymal position. If the language chooses the left-to-right direction, phonetically word-final consonants will be possible (through rightward, nucleus-to-nucleus government of a word-final empty nucleus), but the word-medial geminates will be unavailable.

Hence, neither option results in a subset language. In order to be conservative the child will need to avoid producing linguistic constructions that require a commitment to either parametric option, until she discovers the correct choice. This is parallel to the situation for the Head Parameter in P&P syntax, as will be discussed in Chapter 8, Section 8.5.

To the extent that most of the proposed GP parameters have a subset–superset character, however, and to the extent that this subset–superset character is independent of the settings of other parameters, grammatical conservatism is quite easy to achieve. Recall that OT phonology, in contrast, captures cross-linguistic variation by means of a single ranking of all the available grammatical constraints. As we saw earlier in Section 3.1.3, this approach leads naturally to interdependencies: demotion of constraint A to a position below constraint B routinely causes "collateral" changes in the dominance relations between A and other constraints.

Whether the increased interdependencies in OT actually preclude grammatical conservatism is a complex question. For one thing it depends on the nature of the constraints. If most of the constraints are independent of one another, in the sense that their pairwise dominance relations have no detectable consequences, then an OT analysis may turn out to be simply a notational variant of the corresponding principles-and-parameters analysis. In this case, of course, the possibilities for grammatical conservatism will be the same for the OT and GP versions of the analysis.

Another relevant question is whether it is practically feasible for the child simply to reserve judgement on the dominance relation between two given OT constraints. In other words, is it possible for the child to limit herself to utterances that have the same surface realization, regardless of the dominance relation between these constraints? As shown in Section 3.1.3, this cannot be achieved simply by placing the two constraints in an unranked "stratum" of the dominance hierarchy. The reason is that in OT, the lack of a dominance relation can have detectable consequences, and these consequences may constitute errors of comission,[8] from the perspective of the target language.

Instead, the child will need to check whether there is any difference in the winning parse for the input, depending on the unknown

---

[8] "Comission" is a technical term in the language acquisition literature, pronounced to rhyme with "omission".

dominance relation. This is clearly feasible for a single pair of constraints, but the actual problem is much larger: if CON includes n constraints, then (as noted in Section 3.1.3) there are $n(n-1)/2$ pairwise dominance relations to consider. Early in the acquisition process, most of these dominance relations will be unknown. The child will need to check whether each prospective utterance is affected by any of the unknown relations, before she produces it.

Hence, the OT framework makes grammatical conservatism unlikely, at least to the extent that the dominance relations between different constraints in CON actually matter. (To the extent that they do not matter, OT is simply a notational variant of P&P.) This leads to the question of whether children are actually grammatically conservative in the domain of phonology. I will return to this question in Chapter 8, Section 8.2.

TABLE 4.1 Principal longitudinal corpora for English

Child	Main investigator	# Child utterances	Age span	Mean gap between recordings (in Days)
Adam	Roger Brown	45,555	2;03–4;10	19.5
Anne	Manchester Group	19,902	1;10–2;09	9.9
Aran	Manchester Group	17,193	1;11–2;10	10.6
Becky	Manchester Group	23,339	2;00–2;11	10.1
Carl	Manchester Group	25,084	1;08–2;08	10.8
Dominic	Manchester Group	21,180	1;10–2;10	10.5
Eve	Roger Brown	11,563	1;06–2;03	13.7
Gail	Manchester Group	16,973	1;11–2;11	10.3
Joel	Manchester Group	17,916	1;11–2;10	10.1
John	Manchester Group	13,390	1;11–2;10	10.7
Liz	Manchester Group	16,569	1;11–2;10	10.1
Naomi	Jacqueline Sachs	15,960	1;02–4;09	13.8
Nicole	Manchester Group	16,950	2;00–3;00	10.3
Nina	Patrick Suppes	31,505	1;11–3;03	8.8
Peter	Lois Bloom	26,891	1;09–3;01	25.0
Ruth	Manchester Group	20,419	1;11–2;11	11.2
Sarah	Roger Brown	37,012	2;03–5;01	7.4
Shem	Eve Clark	17,507	2;02–3;02	8.8
Warren	Manchester Group	16,651	1;10–2;09	10.3

as well as the age span covered and the frequency of recording (e.g. once a week, twice a month, once a month). As a result, the researcher needs to decide at the outset which corpora are suitable for the research question at hand. In the present case I will take the corpus in Table 4.1 that has the smallest mean gap between recordings: that of Sarah. This high frequency of recording, together with the large size of the corpus (over 37,000 child utterances), should provide the finest-grained picture available of how the child's speech changes over time.

In addition to differences in the size, age span, and recording frequency of these corpora, one needs to consider differences in the approach to transcription. Unfortunately for researchers, children's

advantage of distinguishing clearly between "2,25" (two months, 25 days) and "2.25 months" (two-and-a-quarter months), for example.

Table 4.1 lists only those CHILDES corpora available in July 2004 that follow monolingual English-acquiring children without any known developmental abnormality, that are based on audio- or videotape recordings of spontaneous speech (rather than simple diary notes, or recordings of controlled experiments), that cover a time span of at least nine months, that begin when the child is no older than 2;03, that have an average gap between recordings of no more than one month, that contain at least 10,000 child utterances, and that are described in the available documentation as being in a finished state.

speech is seldom perfectly clear. A major challenge in transcription is therefore to render the child's utterances in a way that is both theoretically neutral and maximally informative. To make matters worse, these two goals often conflict.

In particular, an investigator might choose to transcribe the child's utterances in phonetic symbols, or in the standard orthography of the adult language. The latter option is much more informative, in the sense that it encodes the transcriber's best guesses as to the particular words (and meanings) that the child intended. Yet, this benefit comes at the cost of theoretical neutrality: by choosing one possible interpretation from among all the interpretations compatible with the phonetics of the child's utterance, the transcriber is imposing his or her opinion of what the child could most plausibly have said at the given point in her development.

To address this conflict, some investigators include not only a transcription in standard orthography, but also a phonetic transcription, at least for utterances that differ markedly from the adult pronunciation.[2] Other investigators limit themselves to standard orthography, but they note phonetically unclear utterances with a symbol such as "[?]" (i.e. "transcriber's best guess").[3]

To assess the appropriateness of a corpus for a particular research project, one should begin with the database documentation provided in CHILDES. In some cases it will also be necessary to examine the

---

[2] At present the only longitudinal English corpora in CHILDES that include a phonetic transcription for *every* child utterance are three smaller corpora contributed by Roy Higginson.

For Dutch, CHILDES at one time included the Fikkert–Levelt corpora (Fikkert 1994; Levelt 1994), which provide highly useful data for phonological research. Each of the twelve children in this collection was recorded regularly (up to once every two weeks) for a period of approximately one year, beginning at an age between 1;00 and 1;11. For each recording, the transcript takes the form of an alphabetical list of the words the child produced. Each word is presented in the standard Dutch spelling, followed by information including a phonetic rendition of the child's pronunciation. At present (2006) these corpora are not available through CHILDES, in part because of difficulties with efforts to link them to audio files, but eventually they may become available again (Brian MacWhinney, p.c., 3 September 2006). A version of the corpora that was available previously from CHILDES will be used in the first case study presented in Chapter 7.

Yvan Rose and Brian MacWhinney are currently working on a project called PhonBank, which should make a much larger volume of child phonology data, for English and a number of other languages, available through CHILDES in the coming years.

[3] For detailed discussion of the options for treating unclear words in CHILDES transcripts, and the use of the %pho tier for phonetic renditions, see Chapters 4 and 11 of MacWhinney (2000).

original investigator's related research publications. If the corpus is indeed suitable, then the information one gathers at this stage may play an important role in planning computerized searches of the child's transcripts.

In the case of Sarah's corpus, there is no systematic phonetic transcription, but the orthography is not entirely standard either. For example, the determiner *this* is often rendered as *dis*, in a compromise between standard orthography and the phonetics of the child's actual utterance. Below I will focus on a point of syntax, rather than phonology, and the lack of systematic phonetic information in Sarah's corpus will therefore be acceptable. The search for relevant lexical items will be assisted by the CLAN program "Freq", which will be used to obtain a complete, alphabetical list of the lexical items, including nonstandard words and spellings, that occur in the child's utterances.

The lack of a separate phonetic representation, or "phonetic tier", in Sarah's corpus means that one cannot directly evaluate the plausibility of the transcriber's interpretation. To compensate, I will simply exclude from consideration any utterance that is marked by the transcriber as mumbled, unclear, or overlapping with another person's utterance. These are the cases when transcription is generally the least reliable.

I will also exclude any utterance that appears to be a memorized "routine" (e.g. *Now I lay me down to sleep*), an "imitation" of another speaker's utterance, or an exact "repetition" of one of the child's own utterances from earlier in the same transcript.[4] Such utterances will be excluded on the grounds that they do not reliably indicate a novel use of the child's own grammatical knowledge. Indeed, the words *routine*, *imitation*, and *repetition* have become technical terms for researchers working with spontaneous-speech data, and all three types of utterance are usually excluded from analysis.

4.4 Example: the English verb–particle construction

Without further ado, let's return to our research questions: What types of errors do children make, how often do they make them, and how

---

[4] More precisely, an utterance will be coded as a *repetition* if the same words (including their inflectional morphology, if any) occurred in the same order in one of the child's earlier utterances, within the same transcript. Thus, the utterance might be an exact repetition, or might contain only a proper subset of the words that occurred in the previous utterance. On the other hand, the child will receive credit for a *novel* utterance (not a repetition) if the utterance contains a new word, a change in word order, or a change in morphology (e.g. in the number marking on a noun, or the tense marking on a verb).

does children's behavior change upon the acquisition of new grammatical information? To address these questions, I will examine the English verb–particle construction. This will provide a representative case study of the child's acquisition of syntax, and will also provide useful background for several of the parametric studies in later chapters.

The verb–particle construction, as in "Mary *lifted* the box *up*" or "Jane *threw away* the newspaper", involves a particle that is typically (although not always) prepositional, and that can be separated from the verb by a direct object, if the verb has one. The construction is an idiosyncratic feature of English, unavailable in the major Romance and Slavic languages, for example. Hence, the child must acquire something about English in particular, in order to know that the verb–particle construction is available.

Further, the verb–particle construction is used with high frequency in spoken English. Children receive numerous examples in their input, and older children, like adults, use the construction frequently. The frequency is a crucial consideration in studies of spontaneous speech, because one has to rely on the child to *choose* the construction of interest. High-frequency constructions will reliably occur once they become available, but lower-frequency constructions might, by simple luck of the draw, never be sampled in the child's speech.

Now, to assess the child's errors with the verb–particle construction, I first need to decide what error types might occur in principle, and then design a computerized search that will catch as many of them as possible, if they do in fact occur. One aspect of adult English verb–particle constructions is word order. Examples (1a–1b) are grammatically well formed, but (1c–1g) are clear errors.

(1a)   Sue finished her dinner up.

(1b)   Sue finished up her dinner.

(1c)   * Sue finished up it.

(1d)   * Sue upped her dinner finish.

(1e)   * Sue up-finished her dinner.

(1f)   * Sue finished up her dinner up.

(1g)   * Sue finished off her dinner up.

Note that word order is more narrowly constrained with pronouns (1c) than with full noun phrases (1b). Also, while the verb and the particle are often viewed as forming a conceptual unit, they are not interchangeable (1d), nor can the particle be prefixed to the verb (1e) or be mentioned more than once (1f). The possibilities for including two different particles, as shown in (1g), are also limited. Notice that prefixation of a prepositional particle to the verb, as in (1e), is ungrammatical in adult English but is attested in related languages like German and Dutch. This makes it an especially interesting error type if it occurs in children's English.

The error types in (1c–1g) are not the only ones to consider. Another possible error would concern the placement of tense and aspect morphology, as in (2b, 2c).

(2a)   Bob might throw up his dinner.

(2b)   * Bob throw-upped his dinner.

(2c)   * Bob is throw-upping his dinner.

Once again these error types might be expected, given the tight conceptual connection between the verb and its particle.

Still another error type that might occur is an incorrect choice of verb or particle, as in (3c, 3e).

(3a)   Toni picked her glass up.

(3b)   Toni set her glass down.

(3c)   * Toni picked her glass down.

(3d)   José threw back the ball.

(3e)   * José threw there the ball.

Error type (3c) is quite plausible, given that the particular combination of verb and particle used in the English verb–particle construction can be partially or totally idiosyncratic (much to the chagrin of the adult second-language learner!). In this example, the fact that the particle *up*, but not *down*, can occur with the verb *pick* is unpredictable from the lexical meanings of the individual words. In (3e), the word *there* has been incorrectly analyzed as a particle, when in fact it is a locative proform. The error is evident because this pro-form lacks the particle's privilege of intervening between a verb and its direct object.

Perhaps the likeliest error type to occur in children's early use of the verb–particle construction is omission of words. This is so because omission errors in general are extremely common in children's early speech. As in (4b–4c), the child might well omit some portion of the verb–particle construction that is obligatory in adult English.

(4a)   Mary threw her dinner away.

(4b)   * Dinner away.

(4c)   * Threw dinner.

In the case of (4c) there is no particle, and it becomes difficult to recognize that a verb–particle construction is even intended. Example (4b), in contrast, will be retrieved if I search for all utterances containing a potential particle.

Indeed, my strategy will be as follows. I will search for all child utterances in Sarah's corpus that contain particles. I will begin by using the CLAN program "Freq" to obtain a complete list of the words she produces. I will then hand-search this list to identify all the words that could be used as particles, or that possibly contain a particle (as in "upfinished" from (1e), or "upped" from (2b)). Lastly, I will use the CLAN program COMBO to obtain the child utterances that in fact contained these words, together with their immediately preceding context. This information will be examined by hand to determine which utterances are relevant.

Note that one type of error, namely omission of the particle as in (4c), will not be detected by this approach, but the other error types (1c–1g, 2b–2c, 3c, 3e, 4b) will be caught if they occur. Moreover, errors of the type in (4b), where the particle is present but other portions of the sentence are omitted, can be used as an approximate index of the frequency of omission errors more generally. To capture errors of the type in (4c) directly, I would need to examine every child utterance and try to judge whether a particle was plausibly omitted. This would be not only time-consuming but unreliable, given that an utterance like (4c) might be an abbreviation of "Mary threw her dinner away", "Mary threw her dinner at her brother", or simply "Mary threw her dinner". Only in the first case was a particle even intended.

4.4.1 Computerized searches

This section and the following one will discuss the mechanics of transcript research in considerable detail. Interested readers may try out the computerized searches for themselves, using software that is available to the public from the CHILDES website (http://childes.psy.cmu.edu). Other readers may wish to skip ahead to Section 4.4.3, for the results.

When working with materials from CHILDES, one should always record the date when the materials were downloaded from the website.

This is because errors in the transcripts are occasionally discovered and corrected, and the format of the transcripts is occasionally modified for the sake of compatibility with new software tools. Such changes can affect the fine details of one's results and may lead to considerable confusion, if the download date of the materials is not clearly indicated when reporting one's results. In this section I use a version of the "Sarah" corpus that was downloaded from the CHILDES website on 1 July 2004. The corpus available from the CHILDES website has since undergone a number of changes. To replicate the exact results that are reported here, the reader should download the 01-JUL-04 version of the corpus from the following website: http://web.uconn.edu/snyder/parametric.

The first step is to obtain a lexicon of the words that Sarah produced. If the transcripts are in a computer directory called "Sarah", and the CLAN software package is installed on the computer, then one can simply click on one of the transcripts (say, SARAH001.cha), and the editing program "CED" should launch to open the file. The next step is to click on the drop-down menu "Window", and select "Command". This will open the CLAN command window. To set the working directory, one should click on the tab "Working", choose Sarah's directory, and then click on "Select directory".

In the command window, the next step is to type the following:

freq +t"SAR" +u *.cha > sarah.freq

Clicking on the tab "Run" creates a file called "sarah.freq" in Sarah's directory. In the file is a list of some 3,937 words, in alphabetical order, that Sarah produced at least once in her corpus. These include some nonstandard words such as *stoppity+sloppity@c*, where the symbol "@c" indicates that this is a word invented by the child. (The "+" symbol indicates that the two parts *stoppity* and *sloppity* seem to function together as a compound.) Other special words include *upsie@f*, where "@f" indicates that the item is a nonstandard word used by the child's family; *inen@b*, where "@b" indicates that the child was engaged in babbling or word-play; and *downed@n*, where "@n" indicates that the form is a neologism created by the child.

A careful examination of the file sarah.freq yields the list in Table 4.2 of words that might serve as, or contain, particles. Notice that I have "cast a wide net", and taken all the words that might conceivably be relevant, even if they are unlikely to be. Thus, I have included all of Sarah's prepositions, on the grounds that English particles are predominantly prepositional, even though not all prepositions can function as particles in adult English. I have likewise included all spatial adverbs such as *ahead* and *forwards*, even though the latter, for example, cannot function as a particle in adult English. I have also been generous in allowing that a form such as *backs*, for example, might conceivably have resulted from combining the particle *back* with the third-person singular present-tense suffix *-s*, even though it seems likelier to be a plural noun. Only in this way can I be confident of finding Sarah's errors with particles, when and if they occur.

Notice also that I have included in Table 4.2 some words (e.g. *hear, long, weigh*) that are exact or near homophones of possible particles (*here, along, away*). This is because a transcriber who encounters a particle used erroneously might well transcribe it as some homophonous word that feels more appropriate, from an adult-English perspective. My chances of identifying the child's errors with particles are greatest if I take into account all the ways they could plausibly have been transcribed. This is especially true for the morphological mistakes in Part D of Table 4.2, where for example an inflected particle *through+ing*, if it occurred, might well have been perceived as the existing English word *throwing*.

The next step is to search for Sarah's utterances that contain one or more of the words in Table 4.2. I first create a text file that contains each word in Table 4.2 on a separate line; I call it "particles.txt", and save it in Sarah's directory. To perform the search I will use the CLAN program COMBO. In words such as *look+it*, the "+" symbol has to be replaced by a "^" symbol in the file particles.txt. Otherwise, the Combo program will interpret the "+" as a logical "or", and return all of Sarah's utterances that contain either *look* or *it*. The "^" symbol, in contrast, is interpreted as "immediately followed by". Similarly, wherever the word contains an "@" symbol (as in *upsie@f*) a backslash must be inserted (*upsie\@f*) in order to prevent COMBO from interpreting the "@" as a special instruction. For the reader's convenience, the file particles.txt is included with the 01-JUL-04 version of Sarah's corpus that I have provided on the web.

I now return to the command window and run the following command:

combo +t"*SAR" +s@particles.txt -w2*.cha > sarah.particles

This command instructs COMBO to create a new file in Sarah's directory, "sarah.particles". The file will contain, for each of Sarah's transcripts, a

TABLE 4.2 Sarah's words that might function as, or contain, particles

A. Prepositions

about	down	onto	up
across	except	out	with
after	for	round [= around?]	within
along	in	through	without
around	inside	throw [= through?]	
at	into	to	
before	long [= along?]	toward	
behind	of	towards	
between	off	until	
cross [= across?]	on		

B. Spatial adverbs

ahead	downtown	shut	upon
apart	forth	sidewards	upside
away	forwards	standing	upside+down
back	from	there	upstairs
backwards	hear [= here?]	together	way
close	here	under	weigh [= away?]
dere	open	untangled	
downstairs	outside	untied	

C. Possible prefixed or suffixed particles

backbend [back]	forehead [for]	forgot [for]	make+up [up]
cook+out [out]	forget [for]	look+it [at]	
merry+go+round [around]	runway [away]		

D. Possible inflected particles

backs [= back+s?]	hearing [= here+ing?]	one's [= on+s?]	throwed@n [= through+ed?]
dere's [= there+s?]	here+ing?]	one-'s [= on+s?]	through+ed?]
downed@n [= down+ed?]	here's [= here+s?]	ones [= on+s?]	throwing [= through+ing?]
ford [= for+ed?]	inen@b [= in+ing?]	outen@b [= out+ing?]	twos [= to+s?]
fours [= for+s?]	office [= off+s?]	there's [= there+s?]	ups [= up+s?]
heared@n [= here+ed?]	opened [= open+ed?]	throwed [= through+ed?]	upsie@f [= up+s?]
	opens [= open+s?]		
	once [= on+s?]		

list of the child's utterances that contain one or more of the words in the file "particles.txt". For each matching utterance, the program will include two lines of preceding dialogue (as a result of the "-w2" in our command line). These lines will help me to quickly identify most of the child utterances that were a direct imitation of another speaker's previous utterance.

The resulting file, sarah.particles, contains some 7,272 of Sarah's utterances. Do I need to examine all of them? Not necessarily. The reason is that particles, as well as some of the other words included in our search, are extremely frequent in spoken English. A great many of Sarah's utterances will include these words even after the period of interest, when she is first acquiring the verb–particle construction. A sensible strategy will be to determine a point at which I can reasonably say that Sarah has acquired the construction, and to end the case study there.

One simple indication of competence with the verb–particle construction is for the child to make productive use of the word order V–NP–Particle. Productive use would crucially involve the use of contextually appropriate noun phrases between the verb and the particle. A child whose grammar does not yet permit the verb–particle construction might memorize an intransitive verb and its particle together as a frozen "chunk", and successfully insert them as a unit into seemingly adult-like sentences. Yet this tactic will not work in the case of a discontinuous verb–particle combination. A direct object, especially if it contains a lexical noun rather than a pronoun, will inevitably be anomalous in most contexts if it is used as part of a frozen V–NP–Particle unit.

For present purposes, then, I will plan to end my examination of Sarah at a point in her corpus four months later than the transcript in which she first demonstrates that she can produce discontinuous verb–particle constructions, separated by a direct object appropriate to the context. The four-month window should give me a sizable sample of Sarah's speech during a period when she is still working to master the construction, but keep my own workload within reasonable bounds.

Note that these steps will by no means eliminate the workload. The hand coding of the data, to be described in the next section, will require about two weeks of solid work. The reader who is following along at the computer will probably want to forego actual data coding, but may wish to examine first-hand the particular examples that are mentioned later in Section 4.4.3.

One final point before concluding this section: Please notice what I have NOT done. I have not yet opened any of the transcripts! Instead, I have begun by establishing my research questions: the nature and frequency of errors, and the pattern of change as verb–particle constructions become part of the child's grammar. Next I have considered the possible error types that might occur in principle, and planned a computerized search that will yield a large volume of relevant utterances, with and without possible errors. Finally I have made a decision about how to limit the scope of my analysis to a subpart of the child's data, so as to ensure that the project is practically feasible.

None of these steps has required me to examine the child's actual utterances, and this is good, because sifting through the child's utterances looking for "interesting" examples would have seriously compromised the scientific integrity of my investigation. Recall that a shortcoming of old-fashioned diary studies was that they grossly misrepresented the frequency of errors. To avoid making the same mistake in a corpus-based study, I must refrain from sifting idly through the data and noting down the utterances that catch my attention. Instead, I need to carefully plan my project in advance of looking at the child's data. In the present case it is vital to identify the error types that do not occur, as well as those that do. If I peruse the child data first, before pinning down the error types that I will look for, I am quite likely to focus on whatever error types I have already noticed, and to forget about other error types that could in principle have occurred.

4.4.2 Plan for data analysis

Before I open the file sarah.particles, I need to complete one more step: I need to decide exactly how the data will be analyzed. The four basic steps of my procedure will be as follows:

(i) For each successive utterance in sarah.particles, I will determine whether the potential particle was plausibly functioning as part of a verb–particle construction.

(ii) If so, I will check whether the utterance is an imitation, repetition, or routine. If it is, I will add a label of the form "&&& imit/rep/routine" immediately after the utterance, in the file sarah.particles. (The sequence of characters "&&&" does not normally occur in CHILDES transcripts, and will therefore be easy to locate with the "find" function in a word processor.)

(iii) If the utterance is relevant (i) and novel (ii), then I will classify it as belonging to one of the following two categories: **Adult-like** (verb, particle, and direct object (if any) all used appropriately), or **Erroneous.**

- Utterances that fall into the category of **Adult-like** will be further classified into one of the following subcategories:
  — intransitive V–Particle (e.g. *stand up*, labeled "&&&* v-p"),
  — V–Particle–NP (e.g. *lift up the box*, labeled "&&&* v-p-np"),

> — V–Full NP–Particle (*lift the box up*, labeled "&&&*
> v-np-p"), or
> — V–Pronoun–Particle (*lift it up*, labeled "&&&* v-pro-p").
> - Utterances that fall into the category of **Erroneous** will be
> further classified as belonging to one or more of the following
> subcategories:
> — Errors of Word Order (as in *lift up it, up the box lift, up-lift
> the box, lift up the box up, lift up the box out,* labeled "&&&*
> order"),
> — Errors of Morphology (as in *lift upped* or *lift upping,*
> labeled "&&&* morph"),
> — Errors of Lexical Item (as in *raise the box down,* labeled
> "&&&* lex"),
> — Errors of Omission (where the verb and/or the direct
> object is omitted, as in *lift up* or *box up,* labeled "&&&*
> omit (XX)," where XX is the word or phrase that seems to
> have been omitted), and
> — Other errors (labeled "&&&* error").
>
> (iv) When items of the type V–Particle–NP begin to appear, I will
> set the endpoint for the analysis four months later in the
> corpus.

The procedure above is still somewhat schematic, in that I have not
yet specified how I will identify a sequence of words as an actual
verb–particle construction. The following guidelines will apply to many
cases:

- Reversal Test: Transitive verb–particle constructions can be recognized by the possibility of reversing the order of the object and
the particle (*lift the box up* ↔ *lift up the box*) without rendering
the phrase ungrammatical. An exception is when the object is a
pronoun (**lift up it*).
- Intransitive verb–particle constructions can often be recognized by
the presence of a preposition (i.e. a prepositional particle) without
an object (*walk up*). Non-prepositional particles (e.g. *back, forth,
together, apart,* as in *come together*) may be recognized by the fact
that they also participate in transitive verb–particle constructions
(as in *bring together the class, bring the class together*).
- In the case of an erroneous utterance, if the child's target was a
verb–particle construction, then it should be possible to obtain a
well-formed phrase by "undoing" the error. For example, if the
child produces **lift-upped the box,* this is plausibly an error of

morphology precisely because moving the tense morphology onto the verb (*lift-ed up the* box) yields a well-formed verb-particle construction (in this case, one that passes the reversal test).

As I make decisions on ambiguous cases, it will be important to note them and apply the decisions consistently. For this purpose I will keep all such notes together in a text file called *coding_notes.txt*, stored in Sarah's main directory.

In general, if an utterance was plausibly an attempt at a verb–particle construction, then I will count it as such, even if an alternative analysis is available. This strategy will assure me of a comprehensive picture of the error types that Sarah produced. Importantly, if Sarah's grammar at some point yielded an erroneous form, then the form can be expected to occur repeatedly in her corpus, with different lexical items. This is especially clear for Sarah, because her corpus contains such large numbers of her utterances and has such a high frequency of recording. Therefore, if I am lenient in my criteria for the category of "erroneous verb–particle construction", and a given error type was indeed part of Sarah's grammar at some point, then I will find more than one or two examples. If the given error type was never in fact permitted by Sarah's grammar, however, then I should find only isolated examples, even with my lenient criteria.

Once my data coding procedure has been completed, I will need to tabulate my results and generate charts to represent them graphically. The tabulation is best conducted using a computer spreadsheet program such as Microsoft Excel®. This makes it easy to compare the relevant utterances from a given transcript (to confirm that all repetitions have been detected, for example), to calculate total numbers of the various utterance types during a given age-range, to calculate the frequency of a given utterance type per 1,000 child utterances, and to generate suitable graphs. An excerpt from my Microsoft Excel® spreadsheet for Sarah's data is shown in Figure 4.1.

Finally, while the practice of leafing idly through a child's transcripts is strongly discouraged, it is sometimes necessary to go back to the original transcript and examine more of the context for a given utterance than the two or so preceding lines obtained with the COMBO program. In general it is best to start by reading the "header" at the very beginning of the transcript. The header includes a list of the speakers in the transcript, often with an indication of their relationship to the child, and may also include a sentence or two describing the situation at the time of recording (e.g. eating breakfast, playing a game). Next

Transcript	Line	Utterance	Code	Age	# Utt.	# v-np-p	f(v-np-p)	#v-pro-p	f(v-pro-p)	#v-p	f(v-p)
20 to 23				2;7	1067	3	0.003	0	0.000	4	0.004
20				2;7,5	269	1		0		1	
	621	I took eye out.	v-np-p								
	713	I fall down.	v-p								
	469	I cut off.	omit-TR								
	815	I throw (a)way?	omit-TR								
	818	Daddy throw (a)way?	omit-TR								
21				2;7,12	355	2		0		2	
	389	I got swing out.	v-np-p								
	649	I poke my eye out	v-np-p								
	90	come on -: Mommy.	v-p								
	407	I fall down boom.	v-p								
	84	you through?	omit-IN (are)								
	682	he hat on.	omit-TR								
	759	a hat on.	omit-TR								
22				2;7,18	170	0		0		0	
	409	no # mummy # you put way now.	omit-TR								
23				2;7,28	273	0		0		1	
	203	go ahead.	v-p								
24 to 26				2;8	1038	2	0.002	0	0.000	5	0.005
24				2;8,2	339	0		0		1	
	44	here my sit down. (=my place to....?)	v-p								
25				2;8,25	286	0		0		2	
	253	go away.	v-p								
	254	he go away.	v-p								
	123	Daddy took away.	omit-TR								
	327	put back.	omit-TR								
	380	ok I right back.	omit-IN								

FIGURE 4.1 Portion of spreadsheet containing coded data from Sarah

one should go directly to the utterance of interest and work backwards until the relevant aspects of the context become clear. In most cases it will suffice to go back a single page, because young children seldom stay long with any single topic of conversation!

4.4.3 Results

With respect to the types and frequency of errors, the principal finding is that Sarah's errors with verb–particle constructions were overwhelmingly errors of omission. Sarah began to use transitive verb–particle constructions with the order verb–NP–particle at age 2;06. As planned, the search of Sarah's corpus ended four months later, at age 2;10 (through the end of transcript 35). From the beginning of the corpus (at 2;03) through 2;10, Sarah produced a total of 10,233 recorded utterances. Among these were 32 erroneous particle constructions. The frequency of these errors, at any given age, ranged from 0.6 to 6.6 per thousand child utterances. Of the 32 errors, 29, or 90.6 percent, were errors of omission. These results are shown graphically in Figures 4.2 and 4.3, where the transitive and intransitive constructions are plotted separately.

The three "substantive" errors, those that went beyond simple omission, are listed in (5).

(5a)   Transcript 18, line 1082:   took my eye on.

(5b)   Transcript 26, line 97:   put back hm.

(5c)   Transcript 34, line 569:   I xx go downed@n.

In utterance (5a), the sole lexical-item error, the particle *on* is substituted for *out*.

The utterance in (5b) contains material transcribed as "hm", which could perhaps be the pronoun *him* or the contracted pronoun *'em* (= them). The transcriber's interpretation of this material as the interjection *hm* is equally plausible, but in the spirit of casting a wide net, I will accept it as a pronoun. In this case (5b) is an error of word order, because an unstressed pronoun cannot follow the particle in adult English.

Finally, utterance (5c) is the sole example of a morphological error: tense morphology is placed on the particle *down*, rather than the verb. The form *downed* was included in Part D of Table 3.2, because it occurred in the file sarah.freq and was potentially an inflected particle. The transcriber's use of the @n label supports this interpretation,

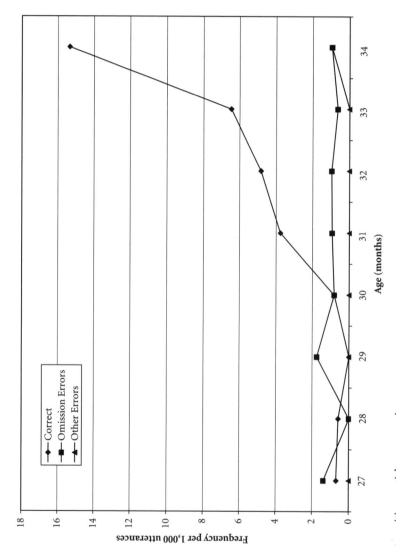

FIGURE 4.2 Sarah's intransitive particle constructions

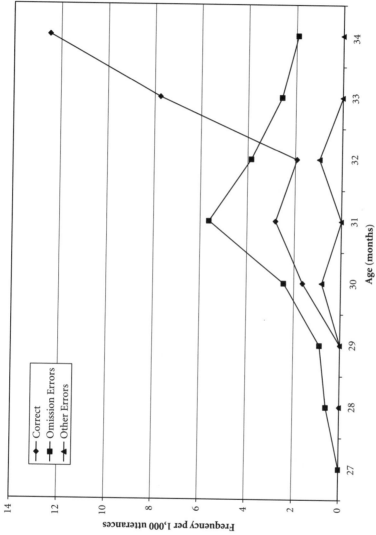

FIGURE 4.3 Sarah's transitive particle constructions

because @n is used principally for over-applications of regular morphology (e.g. *maked@n, winned@n, childs@n*) in Sarah's corpus. Most importantly, (5c) includes the tense-less verb *go* immediately before the particle, and this makes it especially plausible that the *-ed* ending was meant as a tense-marker. On the other hand, (5c) contains the symbol *xx*, which represents a word that the transcriber could not identify. One might in principle exclude the utterance on the grounds that part of it was unclear to the transcriber, but this would be inconsistent with my wide net approach. Moreover, the portion of the utterance that was marked unclear was strictly prior to the verb–particle construction.

In summary, then, Sarah made at most three substantive errors with the verb–particle construction in the space of 10,233 utterances. Let us turn now to the question of how the child's speech changes upon acquisition of the verb–particle construction. Figures 4.2 and 4.3 both show what I like to call a "geyser" effect: when a new, high-frequency construction enters the child's grammatical repertoire, we first see only a few examples, but these are followed soon after by regular use, and within a few months by an explosion of examples.

Also, as we have just seen, the child's grammatical errors during this period are predominantly errors of omission. Substantive grammatical errors are exceedingly rare in children's spontaneous speech. Thus the child moves in a relatively short span of time from never producing the adult construction, to using it with high frequency, all with a minimum of true grammatical errors.

Before closing this section, let us briefly consider some of the finer details of Sarah's data. Recall that in my coding I divided adult-like uses of the transitive verb–particle construction into three categories: v-np-p (where "np" is a full, non-pronominal NP), v-pro-p (where "pro" is a pronoun), and v-np-p. This three-way division is not indicated in Figure 4.3. In fact, Sarah's earliest transitive verb–particle constructions belonged to the v-np-p type, which first appeared in Transcript 18, at 2;06,20 (line 1082, *took my eye on*; line 1087, *pull my eye out*). Examples with a pronominal object (v-pro-p) did not appear until Transcript 28, at 2;09,06 (line 495, *put em (a)way*), and examples of the v-p-np type had not yet appeared by the end of Transcript 35, at 2;10,24.

Brown and Hanlon (1970) first noticed that the order V–NP–Particle tends to appear in children's speech earlier than V–Particle–NP. Indeed, Sarah was one of the children whose data they examined. This finding was replicated by Hyams, Schaeffer, and Johnson (1993). Snyder and Stromswold (1997) examined the CHILDES corpora for twelve

children, and found that four children acquired the two constructions at approximately the same time, but the remaining eight children
acquired them in the order observed by Brown and Hanlon. No child
has yet been found to acquire the order V–Particle–NP significantly
earlier than V–NP–Particle.

The ordering of v-np-p before v-pro-p has not, to my knowledge,
been noticed in the acquisition literature, and may be specific to Sarah.
It will be interesting to see whether the pattern holds up in additional
children.

A final point is the relationship between transitive and intransitive
verb–particle constructions. Before the first use of v-np-p, in Transcript 18, Sarah produced exactly two uses of v-p: one in Transcript 3,
at 2;3,19 (line 752, *go out*), and one in Transcript 7, at 2;04,10 (line 604,
xx baby xx fall down). The next use occurs in Transcript 18, at 2;06,20
(line 265, *I fall down!*). As can be seen in Figure 4.2, from the use in
Transcript 18 onward, the v-p construction rapidly enters regular use
and then (by age 2;9 or 2;10) enters frequent use. From this perspective,
the uses in Transcripts 3 and 7 appear anomalous: They did not lead
directly to regular use.

Moreover, one needs to be cautious in crediting Sarah with knowledge of the v-p construction, because unlike the discontinuous v-np-p
construction, the v-p combination can readily be stored in memory
as an unanalyzed "chunk". The uses in Transcripts 3 and 7 both lack
inflectional marking on the verb, and this makes it especially difficult
to judge whether they have been created by the grammar *de novo*, or
simply retrieved from memory as a unit.

Stromswold (1996) argues that researchers working with longitudinal corpora should credit the child with knowledge of a grammatical
construction at the point of first clear use, provided this is followed
soon afterwards by regular use with a variety of different lexical items.
This metric is highly correlated with other measures that have been
proposed in the literature, but is more sensitive: other, more conservative measures systematically delay the attribution of grammatical
knowledge to the child. I will therefore follow Stromswold and adopt as
my acquisition measure the age of "first clear use, followed soon after
by regular use".

In the case of Sarah's v-p constructions, this criterion requires us to
exclude the first two uses as "isolates", because they are not followed
rapidly by regular use. The result is that Sarah acquires the v-p construction at the exact same age (2;06,20) as the v-np-p construction. To

my knowledge the acquisition literature has not previously examined the relationship between transitive and intransitive verb–particle constructions. Thus, we once again have an interesting pattern in Sarah's data, but one that may or may not hold up when other children's corpora are examined.

4.5 Conclusion: grammatical conservatism

This chapter has presented the basic tools for corpus-based research on child language acquisition. The resources of CHILDES have been used to approach three foundational questions: What types of grammatical errors does a child produce as she acquires her native language? How frequent are such errors? And how exactly does the child's speech change, when a new point of grammar is acquired? These questions have been addressed through a highly detailed case study of Brown's longitudinal corpus for Sarah.

The principal findings are as follows: (1) At least in the case of the verb–particle construction, the syntactic errors found in a child's spontaneous speech are overwhelmingly errors of word omission. Substantive errors are vanishingly rare, even if one performs a search (as I did here) that is expressly designed to detect them. (2) When a high-frequency grammatical construction such as the verb–particle construction enters the child's grammatical repertoire, one finds a "geyser" effect: the child rapidly progresses from first clear uses to regular use, and then (within a few months) to high-frequency use. In Sarah's data this effect was seen more clearly for the transitive (v-np-p) construction, but was also evident with the intransitive (v-p) construction.

Crucially, the findings from the verb–particle construction provide us with clear evidence for grammatical conservatism in children's spontaneous speech. Of the nine potential error types in (1–3), *none* occurred more than once in the 10,233 child utterances recorded during the four months when Sarah was first beginning to use the verb–particle construction. This is extraordinary. If the child were trying out different grammatical possibilities (such as the versions of the verb–particle construction found in Dutch and German), and were saying the results aloud, we would surely know it: the error types in (1–3) include forms that are grammatical and indeed frequent in languages like Dutch and German. Moreover, if the child had used any conceivable "extra-grammatical" strategy for producing verb–particle constructions, then error types from (1–3) would almost certainly have been well attested.

The implication is that the child did not begin with an extra-grammatical strategy, or even a non-English grammar, as an early way to produce verb–particle constructions. Instead, she waited: She analyzed her input and worked out the adults' grammatical basis for the construction, before she ever attempted to produce it herself. To the extent that she needed to express ideas that might require some form of verb–particle construction in the adult language, she simply produced a telegraphic version, in which the verb or the particle was omitted. Thus we find errors of omission, but virtually no errors of "comission".

As discussed in Chapter 2, this property of grammatical conservatism in children's spontaneous speech is extremely valuable: it means that hypotheses about grammatical variation make powerful, testable predictions for child language acquisition. We will see in Chapter 6 that the predictions are stronger for studies of spontaneous speech than for studies of elicited production or comprehension, because with the latter methodologies, unfortunately, we often find clear exceptions to grammatical conservatism. It appears that children are grammatically conservative by preference, but that the demands of controlled experimental tasks (in contrast to passive observation) can overcome this conservatism. On the other hand, studies of elicited production and comprehension have special strengths of their own, as will be discussed in Chapter 6.

In the next chapter I will turn to methods for statistical hypothesis testing with longitudinal corpus data. The emphasis will be on analyses of correlation, including partial correlation, that can be applied appropriately when data are drawn from the corpora of at least ten different children; and non-distributional methods, such as frequency-based binomial tests, that can be applied appropriately in single child case studies. As a test case I will evaluate acquisitional hypotheses from some of my own past work (Snyder 2001), using new CHILDES corpora that have become available since that work was completed.

5

Statistical Methods for Longitudinal Studies

In this chapter I review some of the methods available for statistical hypothesis testing in a longitudinal study of spontaneous speech. I begin with methods to test a prediction of concurrent acquisition, and then turn to predictions of ordered acquisition. Finally I work through an example from some of my own research, testing the prediction that bare root compounding will be acquired prior to, or at the same time as, but never significantly later than, the English verb–particle construction.

5.1 Checking for concurrent acquisition

In Chapter 2 (Section 2.1.3), I introduced two main types of prediction that can be derived from a parametric hypothesis. The first of these was a prediction of concurrent acquisition, as in (1):

(1) If the grammatical knowledge (including parameter settings and lexical information) required for construction A, in a given language, is identical to the knowledge required for construction B, then any child learning the language is predicted to acquire A and B at the same time.

The next question is how to test this type of prediction.

One approach is based on the following reasoning: if A and B are used frequently in the speech of older children, then in a longitudinal corpus of spontaneous speech from any given child, we expect to see A and B appear at approximately the same time.

To assess whether A and B indeed appeared at "approximately the same time", we can use the Binomial Test, a very simple technique from probability theory. Here is the logic: suppose that A and B become available to the child at the same time. Even if both constructions are high in frequency, it would be unreasonable to expect that the first uses of A and B will occur in one and the same utterance. Rather, whichever construction has a higher frequency of use in the speech of slightly older children is likely to appear first, and perhaps even to appear several times before the first use of the other construction. Nonetheless, it would be surprising to find that the child made extensive use of one construction before trying out the other one. The Binomial Test allows us to quantify the degree of our surprise.

Suppose that the child's first use of A occurs in Transcript 20, and her first use of B occurs in Transcript 24. Suppose further that we find some 12 uses of A (in Transcripts 20–24) before the first use of B. What is the likelihood of this outcome, under the null hypothesis that A and B became available to the child concurrently?

To answer this question we need an estimate of the relative frequency of A versus B during a period when both are clearly available to the child. A reasonable approach is to count the uses of A and B in Transcripts 25–34, the ten transcripts immediately following the appearance of the second construction. Suppose that in these ten transcripts we find 19 uses of A, and 13 uses of B. We can then calculate the desired probability as in (2):

(2) $p = (19 / (19+13))^{12} = (.59375)^{12} = .00192$

In other words, under the null hypothesis that A and B became available to the child at the same time, and had the same relative likelihood of use that they have slightly later in the same child's corpus, the probability of finding 12 (or more) uses of A before the first use of B is less than one in five hundred (.002).[1]

The procedure we just followed is known as a Binomial Test, and is an example of a non-distributional method for statistical hypothesis testing. Distributional methods, such as *t*-test and Analysis of Variance, are much more widely used, primarily because they are more sensitive. Yet, distributional methods are valid only if we can argue that our sample of subjects is large enough to be representative of a larger population. This assumption clearly cannot be made for an in-depth case study of a single child, for example, because much about that child will surely be idiosyncratic and non-representative of children more generally. Moreover, distributional methods use the variability within the sample

---

[1] The method presented above is based on relative frequency. An alternative is to use the absolute frequency of one of the constructions. This latter approach will be explained in detail in Chapter 7, Section 7.1.

to estimate the variability in the larger population, and a sample of a single child provides no information whatsoever about between-child variability.

Nonetheless, if we are testing a theory that predicts that A and B will be acquired concurrently by *every* child acquiring the given language, then a detailed case study of a single child has the potential to yield a clear counterexample. In the example above, the single (hypothetical) child we examined turned out to be an example of a child who acquired A significantly earlier than B (at the significance level of $p < .05$ or $p < .01$).

Thus, if the theory being tested makes strong enough predictions, then even a case study of a single child or a small number of children can be highly informative, and the use of a non-distributional method such as the Binomial Test on each child's corpus is a reasonable approach to statistical hypothesis testing. A few caveats are in order, though. First, the *failure* to find a significant difference is always harder to interpret. Even if three or four children show no significant difference by Binomial Test, we do not have strong evidence that A and B are acquired concurrently. To support (rather than refute) a prediction of concurrent acquisition, a better method is a test of correlation, to be discussed below.

Second, if we analyze several different corpora looking for a child who acquires A and B at different times, then we need to make an adjustment to the p-value that we obtain for each child. The reason is that we need to control the experiment-wise risk of an error (i.e. the risk of concluding that A and B were acquired separately by at least one child, when in fact they were acquired together by all the children in the study). Even if A and B always become available to the child at the same time, there is a possibility that some particular child, just by chance, will use A a fairly large number of times before she makes her first use of B. The greater the number of children we examine, the greater the likelihood that we will encounter at least one such child.

A simple (and conservative) approach to this problem is to perform a Bonferroni correction on each child's p-value: we simply multiply the child's p-value by the total number of children being examined. For example, if the p-value obtained in (2) came from one of 12 children who were studied, then the adjustment would be as in (3):

(3)   Bonferroni $p = 12 \times .00192 = .0230$

This result is still significant at the .05 level, but no longer significant at the .01 level.

Let us turn now to another method of judging whether two constructions are acquired concurrently, namely by testing for a correlation. Here is the logic: if constructions A and B become available to any given child at the same time, and if we have a way to estimate the age at which a particular construction became available to a particular child, then across a sample of children, we should expect the estimates for A and the estimates for B to co-vary. Statistics provides us with good methods for testing the predicted correlation, if we can find a way to estimate the ages of acquisition.

In Chapter 4, I argued that children's spontaneous speech exhibits a remarkable property, namely grammatical conservatism: the child does not begin making productive use of a new grammatical construction in her spontaneous speech until she has determined that the construction is indeed permitted in the adult language, and she has identified the adults' grammatical basis for it.

Grammatical conservatism means that we can be relatively liberal in crediting the child with adult-like grammatical knowledge. If a grammatical construction is present in the child's spontaneous speech, if it occurs with a variety of different lexical items, and if the child's use of it appears to be fully adult-like, then grammatical conservatism implies that the child must have discovered the correct grammatical basis for the construction.

Furthermore, if the child exhibits a fairly rapid transition from never using a given construction to using it frequently and correctly, then we can surmise that the child acquired the final grammatical pre-requisite *at the point of the transition*. In the presence of such a transition we can apply a criterion for acquisition that I will call FRU, for "First clear use, followed soon after by Repeated Use" (or perhaps simply "First of Repeated Uses"). This measure combines the advantages of two criteria discussed by Stromswold (1996: 45): the criterion of First Use, which is the most sensitive measure available; and the criterion of Repeated Use, which permits greater confidence in the child's grammatical mastery of the construction.

Thus, to judge when a child acquired the final pre-requisite for a construction, we look for the child's first clear use of the construction in her longitudinal corpus. When we find a candidate, we next check the portion of the corpus immediately following the utterance (typically, the recordings made during the following month), and look for additional uses with different lexical items. If a potential first use of the construction is not followed soon afterwards by repeated use, then we cannot rely on it, and we need to exclude it as an "isolate".

One major source of isolates is transcription error, because transcribing child speech is a difficult and uncertain task. Another possible source is the child's use of a memorized routine, which might be grammatically unanalyzed. As noted in Chapter 4, we exclude any utterance that is obviously a memorized routine, or (for similar reasons) any utterance that is a direct imitation of an earlier adult utterance. These do not qualify as "clear" uses.

Note that identification of the FRU depends on a fairly rapid transition from zero use to regular use, and this type of transition cannot be expected if the construction is used only infrequently by older children and adults. In studies of spontaneous speech we observe a given construction only if the child chooses to use it. Low-frequency constructions will not reliably appear in the child's transcripts even if she has the requisite grammatical knowledge to produce them.

In contrast, if the construction is high-frequency, then we will normally see an abrupt "step-function" from zero use to frequent use. This is the best situation for inferring the point at which the child's grammar changed. Roger Brown and Camille Hanlon (1970) noted this type of transition when they were investigating the acquisition of English tag questions, and they also remarked on what they termed a "brief infatuation":

In the last two samples the TrNQ tags [WS: transitive-negative-question tags, as in *We saw Daddy, didn't we?*] jump from a long-term zero frequency level first to 16 instances and then to 32. These last output rates are 4 to 8 times adult rates. The children have often shown this type of brief infatuation with a construction when it was first learned; the frequency typically falls back within a few weeks to a level approximately that of adult speech. (Brown and Hanlon 1970: 33)

When we are fortunate enough to witness a brief infatuation, we get an especially clear transition point in the data.

Hence, if A and B are both used fairly frequently once they are acquired, then we can obtain a good estimate of when they were acquired by identifying their FRUs in the corpus. The next step is to test for a statistically significant correlation. The standard Pearson Correlation Test is an appropriate method, provided we have data from a sufficient number of children in our sample.

As a rule of thumb, the bare minimum of subjects needed for a meaningful analysis is five times the number of variables. For example, the age of FRU for construction A and the age of FRU for construction B are both counted as variables. If we are simply testing for a correlation between these two, then we will need data from at least $5 \times 2 = 10$ children. As discussed in Chapter 4, CHILDES currently provides at least nineteen excellent longitudinal corpora for English (and a considerable number of more limited corpora). Unfortunately, for languages other than English the number of longitudinal corpora is often much smaller, although the situation is gradually improving. Also, the number of corpora available for English is still relatively low. This means that a failure to reach statistical significance in a correlation analysis should not be given much weight: the number of subjects available is large enough to detect strong correlations when they are present, but not necessarily large enough to detect weaker effects.[2]

One final point on correlation: the investigator should also consider using the technique of partial correlation. Suppose that A and B are predicted to be acquired concurrently, but some other, non-grammatical factor, such as the child's ability to plan and execute long utterances (let us call this "processing capacity"), would also predict A and B to appear at roughly the same age. We can use partial correlation to assess whether an observed correlation between the FRU of A and the FRU of B is stronger than what we would expect if the requisite processing capacity were the *only* connection between A and B.

To do this, we need to determine the age at which each child's processing capacity reached some relevant level. One measure of processing capacity is the Mean Length of Utterance in morphemes (MLU_m). The MLU_m for a given child in a given transcript can be computed automatically by the CLAN program "MLU".[3] Furthermore, we can estimate the relevant level of MLU_m by taking an average of the MLU_ms for the transcripts in which we found the FRUs of construction A (for example). Perhaps this will be an average MLU_m of 2.7 morphemes. Then we can check each child's corpus to find the first transcript in which the MLU_m reached or exceeded 2.7 morphemes.

---

[2] Thanks to Len Katz for discussion of these issues.

[3] The capacity to compute MLU_m is a relatively recent advent in CHILDES, and is dependent on the presence of a "morphological tier" beneath each of the child's utterances in the transcripts. At present all of the main corpora for English include this morphological tier, but corpora for other languages may lack it. In such languages, the MLU_w, or Mean Length of Utterance in Words, is usually a fine substitute for MLU_m, and can also be calculated by the CLAN "MLU" program.

Conveniently, the bare minimum number of children for the partial correlation analysis is the same as it was for the regular correlation analysis. In the present case, we still need only ten children for an analysis on the FRU of A and the FRU of B, even if we "partial out" the age of the first transcript with $MLU_m \geq 2.7$ morphemes. If we obtain a significant partial correlation of A and B, "holding constant" the age of $MLU_m \geq 2.7$, then we may conclude that the concurrent acquisition of A and B is unlikely to have resulted simply from a similarity in processing demands. I will provide a concrete example of this procedure below, in Section 5.3.

5.2 Checking for ordered acquisition

The second main type of prediction that can be derived from a parametric hypothesis is a prediction of ordered acquisition, as in (3).

(3)   If the grammatical knowledge (including parameter settings and lexical information) required for construction A, in a given language, is a proper subset of the knowledge required for construction B, then the age of acquisition for A should always be less than or equal to the age of acquisition for B. (No child should acquire B significantly earlier than A.)

Once again, the question is how to test this type of prediction.

One option is to perform case studies on several individual children, using the Binomial Test. The prediction is that each child whose longitudinal corpus is examined will either show no significant difference between the FRU of A and the FRU of B, or will begin to use A significantly earlier than B. Any child whose FRU of B is significantly earlier than her FRU of A, even after we perform a Bonferroni correction, is a counterexample to the prediction.

As it is with predictions of concurrent acquisition, this technique is better for refuting, rather than supporting, a prediction of ordered acquisition. This is because the most relevant cases for supporting the predicted ordering are those where the FRU of B is *not* significantly earlier than the FRU of A. The absence of a significant difference is a weak basis for an argument. Nonetheless, one can attempt an indirect argument: if the FRUs for A and B are usually close together, in absolute terms, and if the sample includes children whose FRU of A is significantly earlier than the FRU of B, then it is (perhaps) noteworthy that no child's FRU of B was significantly earlier than her FRU of A.

An alternative approach is to use a distributional method, the paired *t*-test. If the FRU of A appears at approximately the same time as the FRU of B, or sometimes substantially earlier than B, but never substantially later than B, then we expect to see a significant difference between the FRUs of A and B in a paired *t*-test. A significant difference provides direct support for the predicted ordering effect. On the other hand, because the *t*-test is a distributional test, it requires a somewhat larger number of subjects, on the order of a dozen or more, before it becomes appropriate. Also, if A and B tend to be acquired close together, then even a small amount of "noise" in the FRU measure can make it difficult to reach significance.

Another method that can provide direct support for a predicted ordering effect is a correlation test. The strongest correlations are found in cases of concurrent acquisition, but a significant correlation can also result from an ordering effect. This is because the correlation test is really checking for predictive power: How accurately can we predict the value of one variable, if we know the value of the other one?

If there really is an ordering effect between A and B, then the later A is acquired, the later B will be acquired. The age of acquisition for one construction does not tell us exactly when the other one will be acquired, but it narrows down the range of possibilities, and a correlation test can often detect this. Recall that a correlation test with two factors can be applied appropriately whenever we have data from at least ten children. Also, the potential noisiness of the FRU measure is much less problematic in a correlation test than it is in a paired *t*-test.

5.3 Example: particles and compounds in English

In this subsection I provide a concrete example of the parametric approach to child language, drawn from my own research. The example will (eventually) serve to illustrate some of the statistical methods discussed above, but I begin by recounting the general history and goals of the research project.

5.3.1 History and goals

Let us return to the English verb–particle construction, discussed in Chapter 4, but this time we will consider it from a cross-linguistic perspective. When we look at languages other than English, we soon discover that the verb–particle construction is far from universal. For example, Spanish lacks any direct counterpart, as illustrated in (4).

(4a)   English: Mary lifted the box up.

(4b)   Spanish: María levantó la   caja (?*arriba).
             Mary lifted   the box   upwards

The adverb *arriba* "upwards" in (4b) is the best available counterpart to the English particle *up* in (4a), but it still sounds anomalous. Moreover, the use of a bare preposition (like English *up*) as a postverbal modifier is completely absent from Spanish.

   The parametric approach to child language now leads us to ask: What exactly does the child acquire, when she learns that English permits the construction in (4a)? This question was raised, but left open, in Snyder and Stromswold (1997). In Snyder (1995, 2001) I formulated and tested a partial answer:

(5)   A language permits the English-style verb–particle construction only if it allows speakers to freely create novel, endocentric root compounds.

This proposal requires some explanation: what does it mean, where did it come from, and how does it help?

   First recall that a "root compound" is a complex word that is composed of two or more bare roots, as in *alarm clock* or *art show jury*. The result is often a noun, but need not be, as we can see from examples such as *force-feed* and *age-old*. Crucially, a root compound contains nothing more than the bare roots. A form like French *verre à vin* "glass for wine" or Russian *prazdnik pesn-i* "festival song-Genitive.Singular" is excluded, because these require the addition of a preposition, or an equivalent declensional suffix, to express the meaning of English *wine glass* or *song festival*.

   A root compound is "endocentric" if one of the roots functions as the head of the compound. For example, the compound *off ramp* is endocentric because the root *ramp* is its head, determining that the compound is a noun (not a preposition) and that it names a type of ramp. In contrast, *redhead* is an example of an "exocentric" compound, because it names a type of person (i.e. a person with red hair), not a type of redness or a type of head.

   Most languages include numerous examples of endocentric root compounds in their lexicons, but a much smaller number of the world's

languages allow speakers to create root compounds at will. This difference can be seen from (6).

(6a)   English: frog man

(6b)   Spanish: hombre   rana
                 man   frog
                 "underwater diver"

In English, the compound *frog man* has a lexicalized meaning of
"underwater diver", but it can easily be used with a novel meaning, such
as "man who does scientific research on frogs" or "man who collects
statues of frogs", as long as the context allows the listener to see how
frogs are relevant.

   In contrast, Spanish (6b) has a lexicalized compound *hombre rana*
"underwater diver", but the meaning is fixed. For example it would be
jarring if a Spanish speaker suddenly began using this compound to
mean "man who studies frogs", even if such a person had already been
mentioned in the conversation. Use of the compound here would be
perceived (at best) as an attempt to coin a new word, and the listener
would expect the speaker to provide an explanation. Hence in Spanish,
to introduce a new meaning for an existing compound, or for that
matter, to introduce an altogether new compound, requires a conscious
act of word coinage. In English, however, novel root compounds can
be created freely and unconsciously, exactly like novel phrases and
sentences, with the expectation that the listener will understand their
meaning in the context.

   Thus, English is a language with a verb–particle construction, and is
also a language that allows speakers to create novel, endocentric root
compounds at will, exactly as required by the proposal in (5). The
next question is where the proposal in (5) came from. The idea first
occurred to me when I was reading the work of Ad Neeleman and Fred
Weerman (1993) on the verb–particle construction in Dutch. These
authors observe a surprising restriction on word order, as shown in (7)
(Neeleman and Weerman 1993: 436, ex.7).

(7)   ... dat Jan het meisje (vaak) op (*vaak) merkte.
             that John the girl   (often) up (*often) noticed
        "...that John noticed the girl."

The material in (7) is an embedded clause, following an introduction
like *Ik gelove* "I believe". The relevant point is that the adverb (*vaak*

"often") cannot intervene between the verb (*merkte*) and its associated particle (*op*), despite the usual flexibility of Dutch word order in the portion of an embedded clause immediately preceding the verb.

A similar observation can be found in LeRoux's (1988) work on Afrikaans. LeRoux observes that Afrikaans verb–particle combinations (e.g. *af+kyk*, literally "off+look", or "crib") behave as a unit in a variety of syntactic contexts, as for example when V-raising applies to an embedded clause in (8a–8b) (Le Roux 1988: 241, ex.9a).

(8a)   Hy sal nie [die antwoorde by   my e] kan af + kyk nie.
　　　he will not the answers   from me   can off   look not
　　　"He will not be able to crib from me."

(8b)   *Hy sal nie [die antwoorde by   my af e] kan kyk nie.
　　　he will not the answers   from me off   can look not
　　　"He will not be able to crib from me."

Both Neeleman and Weerman and Le Roux analyze the Dutch/Afrikaans facts as follows: the verb–particle combinations in these examples are morphological compounds. In other words, verb–particle combinations in Dutch and Afrikaans have not only the semantic properties, but also the morphological properties, of a single, complex word.[4]

The idea that there might be a grammatical connection of some kind between compounding and verb–particle constructions led me to the hypothesis in (5). In English, of course, the verb and the particle do not behave as a morphological compound at the point of spell-out. Nonetheless, I reasoned that they might form a compound at some earlier or later point in the syntactic derivation; or if not an actual compound, that they might bear a relationship to one another that is similar in some crucial way to the relationship between the parts of a compound.

Accordingly, I looked for a point of cross-linguistic variation in compounding that might plausibly correlate with availability of the verb–particle construction. Consider Spanish, which (as we have seen) disallows anything resembling the English verb–particle construction. Spanish is actually similar to English in having bare root compounds (e.g. *hombre rana*) in its lexicon. Moreover, in the domain of exocentric

---

[4] It should be noted that the verb necessarily separates from its particle when it moves to verb-second position in Dutch. Neeleman (1994) proposes that the verb is still generated as a part of a compound, but moves out of the compound (and leaves the particle behind) when it raises to verb-second position.

compounding, Spanish makes liberal use of at least one type that is unproductive in English, namely compounds like *lava+platos*, literally "wash(es)-dishes", for "dish-washer". On the other hand, the ability to create novel endocentric compounds distinguishes English from Spanish in the right way.

At this point I have explained what (5) means, and where it came from. The remaining question is how it helps. Recall that our objective is to gain a better understanding of what exactly the child acquires, when she determines that English allows its version of the verb–particle construction. The generalization in (5), if it holds up to empirical testing, will suggest an explanation along the following lines: one of the pieces of information that the child must acquire, before the English verb–particle construction becomes grammatically possible for her, is the same information that makes endocentric, bare-root compounding freely available in English.

Making this explanation more precise is an on-going area of my research. My current thinking is that languages of the English type permit the construction of compounds during the syntactic derivation. In Minimalist terms, the operation of Merge (or perhaps Adjoin) applies to combine two bare roots as syntactic sisters. What makes English different from Spanish is that English provides a mechanism of semantic composition that interprets the resulting structure as an endocentric compound. In Spanish, the syntax could always create a novel endocentric, bare-root compound, but the C-I systems would reject it as uninterpretable. Hence, when a Spanish speaker invents a complex word that superficially resembles an English endocentric compound, the word takes on a fixed meaning that has to be taught to other speakers in the same way as for any other coinage.

The idea, then, is that this same mechanism of semantic interpretation is crucial for composing the meaning of a verb with the meaning of a morphologically autonomous, directional particle. Sigrid Beck and I (Beck and Snyder 2001*a*, 2001*b*) proposed the idea of a semantic parameter (the Resultative Parameter) that would limit the cross-linguistic availability of the English-type verb–particle construction. The idea of generalizing the parameter, so that its consequences extend to both verb–particle constructions and novel endocentric compounds, is advanced in Snyder (2001), where I propose The Compounding Parameter (TCP). TCP is refined somewhat and extended to additional grammatical constructions in other work, including Snyder et al. (2001) and Snyder (2005).

5.3.2 Testing the proposal

The next step is to test the proposal empirically. The hypothesis in (5) makes testable predictions for both cross-linguistic variation and child language acquisition. Let us start with cross-linguistic variation: each language that has an "English-style" verb–particle construction should allow its speakers to freely create novel, endocentric root compounds.

The hypothesis seems straightforward to test, until we try to decide whether a language other than English permits an "English-style" verb–particle construction. The examples in (7) and (8) should make it clear that the verb–particle constructions of Dutch and Afrikaans differ from the English construction, for example in the fact that the particle can be "prefixed" (in some sense) to the verb. Yet, both LeRoux (1988) and Neeleman and Weerman (1993) argue, on the basis of in-depth syntactic research, that the Dutch and Afrikaans constructions have much in common with the English construction.

In languages for which such detailed research is unavailable, how can we decide which verb–particle constructions to count as "English-style"? My own strategy was to look for an easy-to-use surface diagnostic that might plausibly detect a distinguishing characteristic of the English construction. Of course, as mentioned in Chapter 2 this is dangerous, because a given diagnostic can often be satisfied by two or more grammatical constructions that are fundamentally different. With this caveat in mind, I began looking at the ways that English verb–particle constructions are translated into other languages.

What I found was that English is relatively unusual in allowing a particle to be "free-standing", that is, morphologically independent of the verb. In contrast, some languages have morphological affixes that appear on the verb and contribute a meaning similar to that of an English particle, but that cannot be detached from the verb under any circumstance (e.g. Russian _uletaet_ "flies away", _priletaet_ "flies in"). Still other languages, like Spanish, simply use distinct verbs (e.g. _entrar_ "go in", _salir_ "go out") where English might use a single verb and vary the particle.

Hence, I decided to examine a range of languages for which I had native speaker consultants available, and check whether the languages that employ morphologically separate (or separable) particles consistently permit the free creation of novel endocentric root compounds. Concretely, I asked my consultants about the ways they might express the meanings in (9).

(9a) lift the box up

(9b) set the box down

(9c) on a fishing trip, a can where you store worms, for use as bait

(9d) in the kitchen, a box where you store bananas

I counted a translation of (9a) or (9b) as an example of a separable-particle construction only if the direct object (*the box*) could intervene between the verb and a separate directional word. On the other hand, I decided to accept the directional word as a particle even if it was not a preposition. Khmer, Thai, and Mandarin all appear to use a second verb instead.

In (9c) and (9d) I expected the speaker of an English-type language to produce compounds corresponding to *worm can* and/or *banana box*. I accepted either order of the head and the modifier (cf. Khmer *kapong jole:n*, literally "can worm"), but I excluded any form that involved a preposition (cf. Russian *banka dlja chervej* "can for worms") or special "connective" morphology (cf. the Hebrew construct-state expression *kufsat tulaAim*, roughly "can-of worm"). In the case of Japanese, I eventually discovered that my consultants were unhappy with the form *esa kan* "worm can" because the word *kan* is used exclusively for containers of food, and the Japanese do not eat worms.[5] My consultants were quite happy, however, with *banana bako* "banana box" for (9d).

My findings are summarized in Table 5.1. The cross-linguistic evidence provides support for a one-way implication: languages with a separable-particle construction consistently allow the free creation of novel root compounds, as seen in the top group of languages in Table 5.1. Yet, not all the languages that allow the free creation of novel root compounds permit a separable-particle construction (as seen in the middle group of languages).

In sum, while my cross-linguistic survey has a number of limitations, it nonetheless provides *prima facie* support for the hypothesis in (5). The next step is to test the hypothesis with evidence from child language acquisition. The key prediction is an ordering effect: in a language like English, any given child will acquire the possibility of novel, endocentric, bare-root compounds prior to, or at the same time as, but never significantly later than, the possibility of the verb–particle construction.

---

[5] In Snyder (1995) I relied on the diagnostic in (9c) and mistakenly classified Japanese as disallowing the free creation of N-N compounds. Nobuhiro Miyoshi pointed out the problem in Miyoshi (1999), and the error was corrected in Snyder (2001).

TABLE 5.1 Cross-linguistic survey of particles and compounds

Language family: Language	Separable particles?	Novel, bare-root endocentric compounds?
Austroasiatic: Khmer	Yes	Yes
Finno-Ugric: Estonian	Yes	Yes
Germanic: Dutch	Yes	Yes
Sino-Tibetan: Mandarin	Yes	Yes
Tai: Thai	Yes	Yes
American Sign Language	No	Yes
Basque	No	Yes
Japanese	No	Yes
Afroasiatic: Egyptian Arabic	No	No
Austronesian: Javanese	No	No
Romance: Spanish	No	No
Slavic: Serbo-Croatian	No	No

As was discussed in Section 5.1, we expect an examination of children's longitudinal corpora to yield the following results: (i) no child acquires the verb–particle construction significantly earlier than the relevant form of compounding, when evaluated by a Bonferroni-corrected Binomial Test; (ii) the age of FRU for compounding is (perhaps) significantly earlier than the age of FRU for the verb–particle construction, when evaluated by paired *t*-test; and (iii) the age of FRU for compounding is (perhaps) significantly correlated with the age of FRU for the verb–particle construction, when evaluated by Pearson's Correlation Test. I include the qualifier "perhaps" in (ii) and (iii) because the presence of a significant effect could easily be prevented by small sample size or noisiness of the data, even if the hypothesis in (5) is correct.

Much as in the cross-linguistic survey above, a crucial first step will be to choose suitable diagnostics for the verb–particle construction and the relevant form of compounding. In Chapter 4 we saw that Sarah acquired the V–NP–Particle construction at approximately the same time as the intransitive V–Particle construction, and considerably earlier than the V–Particle–NP construction. The same acquisitional ordering of V–NP–Particle prior to (or at the same time as) V–Particle–NP has been a consistent finding in the literature on children's acquisition of English.

Hence, V–NP–Particle makes an attractive diagnostic: it is one of the earliest forms of the English verb–particle construction to appear in children's spontaneous speech. Moreover, the location of the NP means that the child's successful combination of the verb with the particle is highly unlikely to have resulted from an unanalyzed "chunk" of lexical material (as it might, in principle, when the verb is adjacent to the particle). This discontinuity of verb and particle was also a key criterion in my cross-linguistic survey. Lastly, V–NP–Particle is a high-frequency construction in the speech of adults and older children. For these reasons we can take the FRU of the V–NP–Particle construction as a highly appropriate diagnostic for the point when English-style verb–particle constructions first become grammatically available to the child.

In the case of compounding, the most important criterion is that the child's compound must be, as far as we can determine, a novel creation by the child. Simply producing a lexical compound, like *toothbrush* or *apple sauce*, does not indicate that the child knows how to create new compounds for herself. Likewise, the child's use of a new compound that was introduced earlier by an adult tells us only that the child's memory is functioning normally. Another important criterion is that the novel compound should be well formed from the perspective of adult English. For example, the word functioning as a modifier must precede the compound's head.

With respect to the measure of FRU, it is difficult to say in advance whether novel compounding will be frequent enough to yield a rapid transition from zero use to repeated use. For example, novel compounds are considerably less frequent than verb–particle constructions in the spoken English of adults. Nonetheless, to anticipate the results, we will be helped by a "brief infatuation" of the sort described in Section 5.1: when children discover the possibility of novel compounding, they use it much more frequently than adults do. The reason may be the great increase in expressive power afforded by compounding, given the child's small vocabulary size; or it may simply be that compounding is perceived as a new toy. In any case, the brief infatuation means that FRU provides us with a clear indication of when the child's grammar changed.

The next question is how to search the children's longitudinal corpora for each of our diagnostics. The bad news is that there is really no good way to computerize a search for novel bare-root compounds. The best we can do (as far as I can see) is to search for child utterances that include at least two words. Young children produce a great many single-word utterances, and excluding these makes the search go much faster.

In CHILDES, novel compounds are transcribed as a sequence of two words, separated either by a space or by a "+" symbol. The following CLAN command (formulated for use on the version of Sarah's corpus that we examined in Chapter 4) will catch either type of transcription of a novel compound, and will exclude most of the irrelevant, single-word utterances.[6]

combo   + t"*SAR"   + s_*^!.^!. *.cha   >   sarah.two

The results, sorted by transcript, will be sent to a new file "sarah.two" in the working directory.

The next step is to search this file by hand, and look for any utterance that could plausibly contain a root compound. If one has the benefit of a research assistant, then this assistant can be asked to search the file for all potential compounds. The investigator can then examine each utterance in the context of the transcript where it occurred, and pass judgement on whether the form is indeed a novel compound (i.e. sensible in context, and not used earlier in the corpus by an adult). This arrangement of research assistant as "proposer" and investigator as "disposer" has the advantage that the investigator can be somewhat shielded from the biasing effect of knowing at what point in the corpus verb–particle constructions begin to appear. The assistant will see all the child's verb–particle constructions, but the investigator need not. (This strategy assumes that the search for compounds precedes the search for verb–particle constructions.)

For purposes of identifying the FRU, it is important to find at least the first three or four clear uses of novel compounds by any given child. To count as the FRU, the first clear use should be followed soon after by additional uses. How soon is soon enough? As a rule of thumb, I suggest that the first clear use should be followed *within one month* by additional uses. If the construction does not exhibit the type of rapid transition that would yield multiple uses within the first month, then the age of first clear use is likely to be a rather noisy measure of when the construction was actually acquired.

The search for a child's first V–NP–Particle constructions goes much as described in Chapter 4, except that we no longer need to search for all the conceivable errors. In particular, the demands of the project can

---

[6] The search string following the "+s" switch tells COMBO to search for any utterance containing an arbitrary string of zero or more characters (_*), followed by a word boundary (^) and something other than a period (!.), followed by another word boundary (^) and something other than a period (!.).

be greatly reduced by searching specifically for those utterances that contain a word that is actually used as a particle in adult English. If desired, the list can even be limited to those words that are used as particles commonly, such as those in (10):

(10)   around, away, back, down, in, off, on, open, over, out, under, up

If we save the list of particles (one per line) as a text file "particles2.txt", then the following CLAN command (again formulated for use on Sarah's corpus) will yield each child utterance containing at least one of these potential particles, accompanied by the two preceding utterances (by any speaker):

    combo   + t"*SAR"   + s@particles2.txt   − w2   *.cha   >
        sarah2.particles

(In an effort to avoid confusion I have chosen file names— particles2.txt, sarah2.particles—that are distinct from the ones I used for the work on particles in Chapter 4.)

Our final step, before beginning the actual computer searches, is to decide on the longitudinal corpora that will be examined. Here I will use the principal longitudinal corpora for English that are currently available in CHILDES, namely the nineteen longitudinal corpora listed in Chapter 4, Table 4.1. The findings for these nineteen children have been reported previously in Snyder (2001) and Sloat and Snyder (2006). Table 5.2 collects together the FRUs. As mentioned earlier, many of the children exhibit a brief infatuation with bare-root compounding when they first begin to use it, and as a result, the FRUs in Table 5.2 for both bare-root compounding and V–NP–Particle are followed soon after by additional uses.[7]

---

[7] A few comments are in order regarding the information in Table 5.2. First, two minor errors in Snyder (2001) have been corrected: Peter's FRU for V–NP–Particle is taken here to be the utterance *I put them back* at age 1.94, rather than the next use of V–NP–Particle, at age 1.98. Also, Nina's FRU for novel compounding is taken here to be the utterance *rabbit book* at age 1.96, rather than *zoo book* at age 1.99. Second, the ages in years are calculated as follows. If the child's age is Y;M,D, then the age in years is $Y+(M+(D/30.4))/12$. In other words, the length of a month is standardized to 30.4 days.

Finally, a few of the FRUs for novel compounding, such as Peter's use of *tape+recorder button*, may appear to be lexical. Yet, careful examination of the context and the adult input (throughout the corpus) led to the conclusion that each such FRU was in fact an original creation of the child's. In the case of Peter's example, one of the investigators had actually taught him the words *tape recorder* and *button* during the first transcript, but the first (and almost only) time that the combination occurs in the corpus is when Peter puts them together in this utterance.

TABLE 5.2 FRU of a novel, endocentric, bare-root compound, and FRU of a V–NP–Particle construction

Child	Bare-root compound		V–NP–Particle	
	Age (years)	FRU	Age (years)	FRU
Adam	2.26	tatoo man	2.26	put dirt up
Anne	2.05	animals steps	1.93	put the monkey on
Aran	1.99	car noise	2.08	put sand up
Becky	2.08	Noddy car	2.08	ride his back
Carl	1.96	car bridge	1.95	take it off
Dominic	2.02	elephant trains	2.15	I take fence off
Eve	1.83	pig (=peg) toy	1.83	write it down # my pencil
Gail	2.01	Gromit tissues	1.99	turn it on
Joel	1.95	tiger shirt	2.07	put it back
John	2.00	seesaw lion	1.96	put colors away
Liz	2.04	spider book	1.96	Liz put clothes on
Naomi	1.92	bunny girl	1.90	take it out
Nicole	2.30	happy holiday day	2.30	put this one on
Nina	1.96	rabbit book	1.96	take it off
Peter	1.87	tape+recorder button	1.94	I put them back
Ruth	2.41	choo+choo brick	2.27	me throw baba out
Sarah	2.59	ribbon hat	2.56	pull my eye out
Shem	2.25	bunny+rabbit record	2.21	you can get it out
Warren	1.85	my baby drink	1.85	Warren put slippers on
Mean	2.07		2.07	

Let us begin by applying a paired t-test. If bare-root compounding is acquired earlier than, or concurrently with, but never substantially later than, the verb–particle construction, it is possible that we will see a significant difference by paired t-test. In fact, however, there is no difference: $t(18) = 0.29$, two-tailed $p = .775$. In fact, this is unsurprising given that the mean ages of FRU for the two constructions are identical: 2.07 years. If the mean ages are the same, there cannot be a significant difference by t-test.

This situation can arise in at least two ways: the ages of FRU for the two constructions might be completely independent of one another (and simply happen to have the same average); or the ages of FRU for the two constructions might be nearly identical to one another, for each child in the study. In either case, the sign of the difference between the two FRUs will vary, and the t-test will be non-significant. To determine which of these situations is present here, the next step is to run a correlation test.

The results of the Pearson Correlation Test are as follows: $r = 0.937$, $t\ (17) = 11.1$, $p < .001$. In other words, the ages of FRU for the two

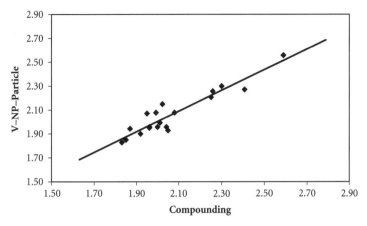

FIGURE 5.1 Scatter-plot of FRUs, with best-fit linear trend line

constructions are very closely associated. The coefficient of determination is $r^2 = 0.880$, indicating that fully 88.0 percent of the variation in the ages for either construction can be explained by the variation in the ages for the other construction.

The results are shown graphically in Figure 5.1. Note that the best-fitting linear trend line is very nearly an identity function. Hence, the absence of a significant effect by paired t-test is clearly the result of the two constructions being acquired concurrently. This suggests that the grammatical knowledge required for novel, endocentric, bare-root compounding is usually the *last*-acquired pre-requisite for the English verb–particle construction.

One last step is required, however. We need to evaluate the likeliest non-grammatical explanation for the correlation we have obtained: the explanation could simply be that the verb–particle construction resembles novel compound-formation in the general processing demands that it imposes on the child. When the child's processing capacity reaches a certain minimum level, both constructions enter the child's spoken repertoire. In this scenario, the grammatical pre-requisites for the two constructions might be completely irrelevant. For example, the grammatical pre-requisites might be acquired much earlier, at a point when processing limitations still make it impossible for the child actually to produce the constructions.

As discussed in Section 5.1, we can use MLU_m (mean length of utterance, in morphemes) as a convenient index of the child's processing capacity. Moreover, we can take the age of the transcript in which a child's MLU_m first reaches a given minimum, as the age at which the child first attains the corresponding level of processing capacity.

TABLE 5.3 MLU$_m$ control measure

| Child | V–NP–Particle | | First MLU$_m$ ≥ 1.919 | |
	Transcript of FRU	MLU$_m$	Transcript	Age
Adam	001	2.142	001	2.26
Anne	03b	1.745	23a	1.93
Aran	04a	1.911	04a	2.02
Becky	03b	1.455	08b	2.23
Carl	08b	2.041	01a	1.73
Dominic	10b	1.648	11b	2.19
Eve	09	3.011	03	1.58
Gail	01a	1.745	01b	1.99
Joel	06a	1.472	08b	2.11
John	01a	1.965	01a	1.96
Liz	02b	1.493	04b	2.04
Naomi	19	2.373	10	1.86
Nicole	09b	1.454	16a	2.53
Nina	01	2.067	01	1.96
Peter	04	1.278	05	1.97
Ruth	12a	1.757	14b	2.34
Sarah	018	1.983	008	2.37
Shem	01	3.083	01	2.21
Warren	01a	1.842	02b	1.87
Mean		1.919		

To estimate the minimum MLU$_m$ required for the V–NP–Particle construction, I will use the CLAN program "MLU" to calculate the MLU$_m$ for the transcript in which each child's FRU occurred. The results are shown in Table 5.3.[8]

To calculate a partial correlation, we first need the three overlapping correlation coefficients. Let us take x to be the age of FRU for a novel compound, y to be the age of FRU for a V–NP–Particle construction, and z to be age at which MLU$_m$ first reached 1.919 morphemes. Then, $r_{xy} = .9373$, $r_{xz} = .8150$, and $r_{yz} = .8690$. Note that the last of these, the correlation between the first V–NP–Particle and the first MLU$_m$ ≥ 1.919, is fairly strong, indicating that the MLU measure is (as intended) a reasonably good predictor of the age when the child begins using V–NP–Particle.

---

[8] To calculate the values of MLU$_m$ in Table 5.3, I used the 11-MAY-06 version of the CLAN "MLU" program, the 08-MAY-05 version of the American corpora (Adam, Eve, Naomi, Nina, Peter, Sarah, Shem), and the 24-JUL-06 version of the Manchester corpora.

The question is whether the age of FRU for novel compounding still accounts for a significant proportion of the variation in age of FRU for V–NP–Particle, after the contribution of the MLU measure has been "partialed out". In fact, the correlation remains robustly significant: $r_{xy.z} = .799$, $t(17) = 5.31$, $p < .001$. The coefficient of determination is $r_{xy.z}^2 = .638$. This means that compounding still accounts for 63.8 percent of the variation in V–NP–Particle, even when the age of first $MLU_m \geq 1.919$ is held constant, mathematically.

We should also check whether the MLU measure can account for any of the variation in the V–NP–Particle construction that is not explained by novel compounding. In fact, it can: $r_{yz.x} = .52$, $t(17) = 2.44$, $p = .0267$. The coefficient of determination is .271, indicating that 27.1 percent of the variation can be accounted for in terms of the control measure, if the age of FRU for novel compounding is held constant. Hence, it is plausible that limits on processing capacity may sometimes delay the child's FRU of V–NP–Particle, although the effect is relatively modest. Incidentally, there does not seem to be any meaningful association between novel compounding and the MLU measure, once the contribution of V-NP-Particle is partialed out: $r_{yz.x} = .003$, $t(17) = 0.01$, $p = .992$ NS.

5.3.3 Conclusions

The hypothesis in (5) is now supported by converging evidence from two, quite different sources: a cross-linguistic, typological survey, and a longitudinal study of children acquiring English. The cross-linguistic survey has the disadvantage that it is based on a relatively small sample of languages, by the standards of linguistic typology. On the other hand, the sample does include representatives of some ten distinct language families, and of three different branches within the Indo-European family.

The acquisitional support for the hypothesis comes mainly from a correlational analysis. This included the use of partial correlation to control for the "nuisance variable" of the child's processing capacity. The use of a paired t-test contributed relatively little in the end, because the children always acquired the two constructions of interest, root compounding and verb–particle combinations, more or less concurrently. The method of the Binomial Test was not applied here, but it will play an important role in Chapter 7, in the discussion of noun-drop in Spanish.

6

Experimental and Statistical Methods for Cross-Sectional Studies

In this chapter I discuss two of the main experimental methods used with children in a laboratory setting. I then review statistical methods for testing a prediction of concurrent or ordered acquisition with the resulting cross-sectional data. Finally I provide a real life example from Kang's (2005) work on case-marking and scrambling in children acquiring Korean.

6.1 Experimental methods

Two of the most widely used experimental methods for assessing a child's grammar are elicited production and truth-value judgement. Good overviews can be found in McDaniel, McKee, and Cairns (1996). In this section I will focus on the more specific issues that arise when using these methods to evaluate a parametric hypothesis. In particular, I will argue that each method has its own special strengths and weaknesses, which need to be kept in mind when interpreting the resulting data.

6.1.1 Elicited production

Recall that elicited production refers to the technique of placing a child in a situation designed specifically to elicit a particular grammatical form. Where naturalistic observation of spontaneous production requires the researcher simply to wait for the child to use whatever grammatical forms she chooses, elicited production "stacks the deck".

In fact, the mildest forms of elicitation are normally considered to fall within the bounds of naturalistic observation. For example, the researcher collecting spontaneous-production data might instruct the adults participating in the recording session to do whatever they can to keep the child talking, on the grounds that long periods of silence are uninformative. Moreover, a researcher who is interested in the child's knowledge of spatial prepositions, for example, might go to a recording session armed with a set of toys that can be arranged in a variety of different spatial configurations, and hope that this will create natural opportunities for the child to use whatever spatial prepositions she has at her disposal.

The term "elicited production" is normally reserved for more aggressive interventions. Thornton (1996) provides the following example. The researcher's objective is to discover what a given child knows about passive constructions in English. The child is invited to play a game, involving a puppet and some toys, and the researcher begins by using the toys to act out a scenario. In a typical trial, there are two toy zebras and one toy crane, and the crane is using a feather to tickle one of the zebras. At this point the researcher summarizes the context and directs the child to ask the puppet a question (Thornton 1996: 77):

(1)   *Experimenter:* In this story, the crane is tickling *one* of the zebras. Ask the puppet which one.
       Child: Which zebra is getting tickled by the crane?

Notice that the researcher scrupulously avoids using a passive construction in the prompt.

On the other hand, the prompt focuses the child's attention on the logical object (a zebra). Moreover, the prior context de-emphasizes the logical subject (the crane), because there is only one agent of tickling in the scenario. The result is that a passive construction is favored, if it is grammatically available to the child.

The elicitation of English passives, as in this example, does not typically succeed until the child is relatively old. O'Brien, Grolla, and Lillo-Martin (2006) have recently reported success with (older) three-year-olds, and this is unusually early by the standards of the literature. Yet, this situation is specific to the passive, and does not apply to elicited production in general. Thornton (1996: 81) reports that the method of elicited production usually works well with children who are at least 3;00, and that certain children as young as 2;06 can perform the task.

Elicited production has several advantages over naturalistic observation. First, the investigator can obtain considerable amounts of data concerning sentence-types that occur only rarely, if at all, in the child's spontaneous speech. Second, the investigator can collect information at the time of his or her choosing. Naturalistic observation requires greater patience. Third, the investigator has a fair amount of control over the meaning of the child's utterance. In contrast, it is often difficult to know the child's intended meaning in spontaneous speech.

For parametric research on child language, however, the crucial question is the following: If a child produces a given grammatical form in elicited production, is she necessarily committed to a grammar that allows that form? There is good reason to think the answer is no.

To justify this statement I will present a single, concrete example and examine it in some detail. The example concerns left-branch extractions in children's English. Adult English speakers obey the Left Branch Constraint in (2).

(2)   Movement of an element in the left-branch position is possible only by pied-piping the entire phrase. (Ross 1986: 127)

For example, the *wh*-expression *how many* in (3) can be extracted only by pied-piping, as in (3b).

(3a)   ***How many** did John read [__ books]?

(3b)   [How many books] did John read?

In contrast to English, most of the Slavic languages allow left-branch extractions, as shown for Russian in (4).

(4)   **Skol'ko**   prochita-l Ivan [__ knig-Ø]?
       how.many read-PST John   book-GEN.PL
       "How many books did John read?"

Several researchers, myself among them, have examined whether preschool children acquiring English know that their target language obeys the Left Branch Constraint. Interestingly the answer seems to vary, depending on the methodology.[1]

Thornton and Gavruseva (1996, summarized in Gavruseva 1998) conducted an elicited-production study, and reported that most of the monolingual English-learning pre-schoolers in their sample (11 out of 12, aged 4;05 to 6;00) allowed extraction of *wh*-possessors out of NP. Examples are provided in (5) (Gavruseva 1998: 236, ex.5).

---

[1] Additionally, there is reason to think that the answer varies depending on the language being acquired. See Snyder et al. (1999), and references therein, for discussion of left-branch extractions in children acquiring Dutch. The present discussion, however, will focus on English.

(5a)   *Who* do you think *'s cat* came up on the building?
        (Whose cat do you think came up on the building?)

(5b)   *Who* do you think *'s food* the baboon tried?
        (Whose food do you think the baboon tried?)

Inspired by this result, several students and I asked whether the children who produce forms like (5a) and (5b) actually have a grammar that allows left-branch extraction, along the lines of the adult grammar for Russian. Here I will discuss the findings of Chen, Yamane, and Snyder (1998), although additional results, supporting the same conclusions, can be found in Yamane, Chen, Pichler, and Snyder (1999) and Snyder, Chen, Yamane, Conway, and Hiramatsu (1999).

To address the question, we constructed materials based closely on those used by Thornton and Gavruseva (1996), but with the addition of items for *how many*. Some examples are provided below (cf. Chen et al. 1998: 96).

(6)   LONG-DISTANCE WHOSE QUESTION
       Puppet: Dino the baby dinosaur.
       Props: A toy dog, some dolls.
       Experimenter: Look at that dog! He looks sad. He's a missing dog! He must be somebody's dog, but we don't know whose. Ask Dino whose he thinks.
       Child (target response): Whose dog do you think that is?
       Dino [Pointing to one of the dolls]: I think it's *her* dog.

(7)   LONG-DISTANCE HOW-MANY QUESTION
       Puppet: Dino the baby dinosaur.
       Props: Some marbles in a jar.
       Experimenter: Do you know what's in this jar? Marbles! It seems like there are a lot in there, but we don't know how many. Ask Dino how many he thinks.
       Child (target response): How many marbles do you think are in there?
       Dino: I think there are ten marbles in there.

The subjects in our study were eleven children at the University of Connecticut Child Development Laboratories, aged 4;03 to 5;11 (mean 5;01). Each child was prompted for two long-distance *whose* questions (cf. 6), and two long-distance *how-many* questions (cf. 7), as well as five short-distance *whose* questions and two short-distance *how-many* questions.

Note that the prompts in (6) and (7) all but force the child to use a left-branch extraction if she can. The reason is that children in an elicited-production study are strongly inclined to model their response on the experimenter's lead-in phrase. For example in (6), the lead-in *Ask Dino whose he thinks* biases the child to begin her response with the words *Whose do you think*. Even if the child's grammar permits both left-branch extractions *and* pied-piping (like adult Russian), the form of the prompt makes it awkward to use pied-piping, since the pattern of the lead-in would be interrupted by the noun (*Whose, X, do you think*). Hence, if a child's grammar permitted left-branch extractions, then we expected her to produce them consistently in our task.

Instead, what we found was that children produced left-branch extractions only sporadically. Only one of the eleven children produced more than a single left-branch extraction on the two long-distance *whose* items, and none of the eleven children produced more than a single left-branch extraction on the two long-distance *how-many* items. On the short-distance items, no child ever produced a left-branch extraction.

Moreover, we were extremely liberal in what we counted as a left-branch extraction. The following are complete lists of the left-branch extractions produced with *whose* (8) and *how many* (9) (Chen et al. 1998: 93–4). (The symbol "#" indicates a pause.)

(8a)   Who do you think whose dog this is? (Subject 4, 4;08)

(8b)   Who do you think this bottle's is? (S6, 4;03)

(8c)   Whose is thinks this is his # whose bottle? (S7, 4;08)

(8d)   Whose you thinks # that # that's bottle belongs to? (S9, 4;04)

(8e)   Who do you think this dog is # wh whose dog is this? (S10, 4;08)

(8f)   Who do you think this bottle is? (S10, 4;08)

(9a)   How many do you think marbles are in there? (S1, 4;09)

(9b)   How many do you think # pencils are in there? (S2, 4;01)

(9c)   How many # do you think how many # marbles are there in there? (S6, 4;03)

(9d)   How many # do you think marb # how much marbles is in there? (S7, 4;08)

(9e)   How many do you think pe # how much pencils are in there? (S9, 4;04)

The lists in (8) and (9) include utterances resembling those reported by Thornton and Gavruseva. For example, (8b) and (8d) both contain a possessive marker *'s* that remains stranded somewhere in the embedded clause, separated from the *wh*-word *who(se)* that appears in the matrix clause. Moreover, utterances (9a) and (9b) correspond fairly closely to forms that would be possible in adult English if it lacked the Left Branch Constraint.

Yet, this is the exception rather than the rule. Indeed, almost all of the utterances in (8) and (9) contain clear dysfluencies, indicating that the child has simply "painted herself into a corner" by following the experimenter's lead-in too closely. If her grammar actually allowed left-branch extractions, there would be no difficulty, and no dysfluency.

Another useful perspective on the examples in (9) comes from a comparison with spontaneous-production data. Part of the motivation for an elicited-production study is usually that relevant utterances are too rare in children's spontaneous speech to be informative, but in the case of *whose* and *how many* questions, we will see that this is not entirely true. My study here will be based on three of the principal longitudinal corpora for English in CHILDES, the ones that include data from the same age range (4;03 to 6;00) that was studied in Thornton and Gavruseva (1996) and Chen et al. (1998): the Adam and Sarah corpora from Brown (1973), and the Naomi corpus from Sachs (1983).

To identify all relevant utterances, I will search the 08-May-05 version of these corpora using the following CLAN commands:

```
combo +t*CHI +show^*^many -w2 *.cha > how_many.txt
combo +t*CHI +swho* -w2 *.cha > whose.txt
```

The first command identifies all utterances containing at least one occurrence of *how*, followed (eventually) by a use of *many*. The second command identifies all utterances containing at least one occurrence of a word beginning with the string *who*, such as *who*, *whose*, or *who's*. I will then hand-search the output files for potentially relevant utterances. The commands above provide two lines of preceding context for each utterance, but where more context is needed I will examine the original transcripts.

The results for the children's possessive questions appear in Table 6.1. (I exclude echo questions, as well as questions consisting of the *wh*-phrase alone, because these do not allow us to distinguish between

TABLE 6.1 Possessive questions

Child	Age	Utterance
Adam	2;07,14	who glove dat?
	2;08,16	who sug(ar) [?] dat?
	3;00,11	who pen dat?
	3;00,11	who comb dat?
	3;08,26	whose house is dat?
	3;11,01	whose cat is dat?
	4;03,13	whose seeds are dose?
	4;06,24	whose bottle is dis?
	4;06,24	know who's dis name?
Naomi	2;08,14	whose his grave?
	3;03,26	whose seed was it?
Sarah	2;08,25	who milk is dat?
	4;08,20	whose voice is that (a)n(d) this?

pied-piping and a left-branch extraction.) Of the thirteen utterances in the table, only two, Adam's question *Know who's dis name?* and Naomi's question *Whose his grave?*, could possibly be left-branch extractions.

Moreover, examination of the context for these two utterances makes it implausible to interpret them as left-branch extraction. In the case of Adam, the utterance occurs at a point in the transcript when he is playing with a number of toy animals. He has just explained to his mother that the toy dinosaur's name is "Callie". In context, the intended meaning of his question is fairly clearly "Do you know what this one's name is?", because in his next utterance he supplies a newly invented name (*John Pee_pee*). To be a left-branch extraction, the question would need to mean something like "Do you know whose name this is?", which does not fit the context.

In the case of Naomi, her father begins by saying, "It's George Washington's birthday!" and Naomi asks "Who's George Washington?" Her father replies, "Well, if he were alive today, Nomi, he'd turn over in his grave." Naomi's question, transcribed as *whose his grave?*, is understood by her father as "Where's his grave?" Even setting aside the possibility of a transcription error, however, for her utterance to be a left-branch extraction it would have to mean something like "Whose grave is his?", which makes no sense in the context.

A complete list of the children's quantity questions appears in Table 6.2. Only Sarah produces any, but hers all clearly involve pied-piping.

TABLE 6.2 Quantity questions

Child	Age	Utterance
Adam		(None)
Naomi		(None)
Sarah	4;04,01	how many pieces <&n> [//] left?
	4;04,01	how many pieces we got left?
	4;04,11	what [//] how many toes I have?
	5;00,16	how many days is that?

Notice that Adam's question *Know who's dis name?* may well be a genuine syntactic comission error, which is unusual in spontaneous-production data (as we saw in Chapter 4). Nonetheless, the sorts of left-branch extractions that are frequent in the two elicited-production studies discussed above (and indeed, that are attested in the data of eleven out of twelve children in the age range of 4;05 to 6;00, according to Thornton and Gavruseva) are quite simply absent from the spontaneous-production data. This is the result expected from the child's grammatical conservatism in spontaneous production. In contrast, the presence of relatively frequent syntactic comission errors in the elicited-production data is a clear indication that elicited production lacks the property of grammatical conservatism: elicitation can yield utterance types that are ungrammatical even for the child who produces them.

The fact that we cannot rely on children to exhibit grammatical conservatism in the elicited-production task does not, however, mean that elicitation is without value for parametric research on child language. On the contrary, it simply means that we need to use caution when interpreting the findings. The following one-way implication is still plausible: if a given form is in fact grammatically available to the child, then it can be elicited in a well-designed elicited-production study.

In other words, the discussion above focused on the error patterns (namely left-branch extractions) that can be obtained using elicited production, but that was precisely the wrong approach. Instead, we should focus on designing materials that will provide a fair test of whether the child has acquired the grammatical knowledge needed to construct a form that is actually possible in the adult language. If the child has not yet acquired this knowledge, then we expect circumlocutions and errors (as well as occasional successes) in a properly designed elicitation study. Crucially, though, the presence in elicited-production data of something that is an error, from the perspective of the adult language, does not necessarily mean that the error is grammatical for the child.

6.1.2 Truth-value judgement

A good review of the truth-value judgement task is provided by Gordon (1996). The technique normally involves acting out a scenario using toys, although some researchers prefer to explain the scenario using a picture. Afterwards, a puppet utters a declarative sentence. The child's task is to reward the puppet (usually by giving it a food that it likes) if its utterance is true of the scenario, and to "punish" the puppet (typically by giving it a food that it dislikes, or perhaps a food that will make it smarter) if its utterance is false. In my experience, truth-value judgement works best with children in the age range of three to six years.

Truth-value judgement, like elicited production, has a number of advantages over naturalistic observation. First, the investigator can obtain considerable amounts of data concerning sentence-types that occur only rarely, if at all, in the child's spontaneous speech. Second, the investigator can collect information at the time of his or her choosing. With naturalistic observation, the researcher has to be more patient. Third, and most importantly, with truth-value judgement the investigator has complete control over sentence meaning. In naturalistic observation, the investigator is often uncertain what meaning the child is trying to express.

For many years now, and quite famously, Stephen Crain has been using evidence from the truth-value judgement task to argue that pre-school children obey the same grammatical constraints that are obeyed (universally) in adults' languages (e.g. Crain and McKee 1985, on Condition C for R-expressions; Crain and Thornton 1998, ch. 30, on Strong Crossover). Truth-value judgement can also be used, however, to assess whether the pre-schooler has acquired a given point of grammar that is specific to her target language. This latter use is more directly relevant to parametric research.

A good example is provided by Sugisaki and Isobe's (2000) work on children's acquisition of the Japanese resultative construction. As shown in (10a), Japanese (like English) permits resultatives.

(10a) Koji-ga   ie-o   aka-ku   nut-ta.
Koji-NOM house-ACC red-NONFINITE paint-PST
"Koji painted the house red."

(10b) (*) Paul a   peint   la maison rouge. [*on resultative reading]
Paul has painted the house   red
"Paul painted the house red."

French, however, is an example of a language that disallows this type of resultative, as illustrated in (10b). Hence, the child acquiring Japanese or French has to decide whether the target language allows the construction.[2]

Sugisaki and Isobe used truth-value judgement to assess whether a given child acquiring Japanese knew that the resultative was grammatically possible. The relative freedom of word order in Japanese permitted the creation of minimal pairs, as in (11) (based on Sugisaki and Isobe 2000: 501, exs. 15–17):

(11a) Pikachu-wa   aka-**ku**   isu-o
Pikachu-TOP red-**NONFINITE** chair-ACC
nutte-imasu.
paint-POLITE.NONPAST
"Pikachu is painting a chair red."

(11b) Pikachu-wa   aka-i   isu-o
Pikachu-TOP red-**NONPAST** chair-ACC
nutte-imasu.
paint-POLITE.NONPAST
"Pikachu is painting a red chair."

Japanese attributive adjectives (as in 11b) are inflected for past/non-past tense, but the adjective in a resultative construction (11a) bears a nonfinite ending.

In a trial corresponding to the item in (11a), the child was presented with the following scenario (based on Sugisaki and Isobe 2000: 501, ex. 17), in Japanese translation:

---

[2] In Snyder (1995, 2001) I proposed that the resultative, like the English-style verb–particle construction, depends on the positive setting of TCP. Sugisaki and Isobe's study tested this hypothesis and found a significant contingency between a child's success or failure on the Japanese resultative (in a truth-value judgement task), and her success or failure on novel endocentric compounding (in an elicited-production task).

Pikachu is playing in Ash's room, where there are two chairs: a blue chair that belongs to Ash, and a red chair that belongs to Pikachu. Pikachu decides that he wants the two chairs to be the same color. He thinks about painting Ash's chair with red paint, but he realizes that Ash will get angry if he does so without permission. Then he gets a good idea: He paints his own chair with blue paint.

Note that the scenario was presented without any use of the resultative construction: a circumlocution like "paint it with red paint" was used in place of "paint it red". Next, the puppet said that it knew what was happening, and uttered the sentence in (11a). The child was then required to judge the truth of the puppet's sentence.[3]

In this example the resultative reading made the puppet's sentence false. Note that the scenario satisfied Crain and Thornton's (1998: 225–6) criterion of "plausible dissent", because the outcome expressed by (11a) was only one of the possible outcomes under discussion: Pikachu first considered painting a chair red, but then thought better of it. Accordingly, the child's task of judging the truth of the puppet's sentence was pragmatically felicitous. If her grammar permitted a resultative reading, she should have used it.

If the child lacked the grammatical basis for a resultative reading, however, a likely outcome was that she would give the sentence an attributive interpretation (cf. 11b), and judge it true. (This would have required her to ignore the anomalous morphology on the adjective.) Alternatively, she might have felt unsure what the sentence meant, and simply guessed. Across the experiment, resultative sentences like (11a) were paired with both "true" and "false" scenarios, as were attributive sentences like (11b). Hence, a child who was guessing randomly, or always saying "true", had an expected score of about 50 percent correct.

When using truth-value judgement to assess the child's knowledge of a given point of grammar, we need to decide (in advance) what to count as a passing score. For example, truth-value judgement imposes non-trivial processing demands on the child. Hence, if we insist on 100 percent correct performance, we are likely to classify some children as non-adult-like when they actually know the relevant point of grammar.

---

[3] A methodological innovation in the Sugisaki–Isobe study was the use of computer animation, on a laptop computer, to present the scenario. In place of an actual puppet, the animated character Meowce appeared on the screen when the animation was over, and the computer played a sound file containing the stimulus sentence. The child then pointed at one of two cards that Meowce was holding: the card with a circle, if Meowce's description was correct; or the card with an "X", if the description was incorrect. Note that this method provided highly consistent presentation of the materials, and was quite successful at holding the children's interest.

On the other hand, if we set the criterion for passing too low, some of the children who are simply guessing will probably pass. For any choice of criterion, the data obtained with truth-value judgement will contain some noise. Fortunately, the proper use of statistical methods (discussed below, in Section 6.2) permits a researcher to isolate the signal from the background noise.

Now, for parametric research on child language, a crucial question is the following: In truth-value judgement, does the child ever have access to an interpretation that is inconsistent with her current grammar? My assessment of the current literature is that the answer has to be yes.

Consider Principle B of the Binding Theory (e.g. Chomsky 1986*b*). Chien and Wexler (1990) reported that children acquiring English still have difficulties with Principle B well into the pre-school years. McKee (1992) evaluated this claim with a truth-value judgement task, illustrated below:

(12)   *Toys*: A cabbage-patch baby, a princess, a tub of water, and a towel.
        Scenario: The princess falls in the tub of water. The cabbage-patch baby says, "You're wet," and goes away. The princess dries herself off with the towel.
        Sentence: The princess dried her.

McKee tested thirty American children, ranging in age from 2;06 to 5;03 (mean 3;11), and presented each child with four items like (12) (in the context of a larger study on Principles A and B of the binding theory). Overall, the children incorrectly accepted sentences like the one in (12), on the interpretation "The princess dried herself", 82 percent of the time (98/120 examples).

Does this mean that pre-school children acquiring English have a grammar that lacks the relevant constraints? Probably not. One especially striking piece of evidence comes from Bloom, Barss, Nichol, and Conway's (1994) investigation of spontaneous-production data. These authors examined the longitudinal CHILDES corpora for Abe (Kuczaj 1976), Adam, and Sarah (Brown 1973), which together provided a sample of 39,426 child utterances. The age ranges examined were 2;04,24 to 4;11,27 for Abe, 2;03,04 to 5;02,12 for Adam, and 2;03,05 to 5;01,06 for Sarah. The authors identified all utterances containing a first-person singular objective pronoun, *me* or *myself*, used as a direct object. The sample included 2,834 (relevant) tokens of *me*, and 75 tokens of *myself*.

TABLE 6.3 Principal findings of Bloom et al. (1994)

	me	myself
John hit ___.	2,830	8
I hit ___.	4	67

Crucially, errors of the type found in McKee's truth-value judgement study were exceedingly rare. Collapsing across the three children, the results were as in Table 6.3, where "John hit __" refers to any sentence with a non-first person subject, and "I hit __" refers to any sentence with a first-person subject.

Thus, where McKee found that her subjects interpreted English pronominals as reflexives approximately 82 percent of the time in a truth-value judgement task, Bloom et al. (1994) found that their subjects made the corresponding error only 0.14 percent of the time (4/2,834) in spontaneous speech.

Children's Principle-B errors in comprehension tasks are a topic of on-going research. An especially interesting proposal, developed in Grodzinsky and Reinhart (1993) and more recently in Reinhart (2004), is that the errors occur because the child lacks the computational resources needed to judge whether "coreference", rather than binding, is a permissible relation between the pronoun and its antecedent: in a comprehension task, many children simply give up and guess. In the child's own production, however, there is no need to make this type of judgement.

Whatever the explanation, the discrepancy between truth-value judgement and spontaneous production means that we need to proceed cautiously. Which method (if either) should we trust? As argued by Bloom et al., the findings from spontaneous production are quite difficult to explain except by granting that the child knows the relevant grammatical principles. In contrast, failure to obey these principles, as seen in truth-value judgement, can be accounted for by performance factors. Hence, I am led to conclude (once again) that children exhibit grammatical conservatism in their spontaneous speech. In contrast, the child sometimes gives responses in truth-value judgement that violate her own grammar.

Much as in the case of elicited production, the lack of grammatical conservatism does not mean that truth-value judgement is without value for parametric research. Rather, it means that we need to use particular caution in interpreting the findings. Once again, a one-way implication is plausible: if a given <sentence, meaning> pair is in fact grammatically available to the child, then the child will accept that <sentence, meaning> pair in a well-designed truth-value judgement study.

The discussion above focused on an error pattern (namely Principle-B violations) that can be obtained using truth-value judgement, but (once again) that was probably the wrong approach, at least for purposes of parametric research. The very fact of grammatical conservatism in children's spontaneous speech means that the child probably never makes a real commitment to a grammar that is substantially different from the adults'. (This point will be elaborated in Chapter 8, Sections 8.2 and 8.5.) Instead, we need to focus on designing materials that will tell us when the child has acquired a given grammatical property that is in fact present in the target language. Truth-value judgement is an especially valuable technique when this grammatical knowledge has a direct effect on the <sentence, meaning> pairs that are permitted in the language.

6.2 Statistical hypothesis testing

In Chapter 2 (Section 2.1.3), I introduced two main types of prediction that can be derived from a parametric hypothesis. The first of these was a prediction of concurrent acquisition, as in (13):

(13) If the grammatical knowledge (including parameter settings and lexical information) required for construction A, in a given language, is identical to the knowledge required for construction B, then any child learning the language is predicted to acquire A and B at the same time.

The next question is how to test this type of prediction using the "cross-sectional" data that we obtain from elicited production or truth-value judgement: data from many different children, each of whom is evaluated at a single point in time.

First, note that for any given child in an elicitation or truth-value judgement study, and for each condition of the experiment, we obtain information that can be summarized by three numbers: the number of correct responses, the number of incorrect responses, and the number of irrelevant or uninterpretable responses. In the category of "irrelevant" responses I would include circumlocutions that allow the child (in an elicited-production study) to avoid the point of grammar being tested. Such responses are not literally irrelevant, of course, because they represent missed opportunities for the child to use the grammatical form of interest, and are one of the likely response types from a child who lacks the requisite grammatical knowledge.

The number of correct responses should serve as a good indication of whether the child has already acquired the grammatical knowledge of interest. If the experiment is designed well, a strategy of simply guessing, for example, or of always responding "true" (in truth-value judgement), will be expected to result in a correct response no more than half the time. In elicited production it is sometimes difficult to gauge the exact likelihood of a correct response from a child who lacks the grammatical knowledge being tested, but in most cases it will clearly be far less than 50 percent.

If certain children receive fewer opportunities than others to give a correct response, we need to use the percentage correct (instead of the raw number correct) as our dependent variable. This might be appropriate, for example, when one or two of the children in a study complete most of the experimental protocol, but become tired and have to stop before they reach the very end. Whether we use raw numbers or percentages, the prediction is that a child will perform well on construction A if, and only if, she performs well on construction B.

Two general types of statistical test are relevant here: tests of correlation and tests of contingency. If we keep the data in quantitative form, that is, each child's number/percentage correct on construction A and construction B, then we predict a positive correlation between the two numbers. The Pearson correlation test is an appropriate choice, provided we have data from at least ten children (see Chapter 5, Section 5.1, for further details).

If we convert each child's scores on A and B into a categorial classification, either "pass" or "fail", then we can apply a statistical test of contingency: χ^2 or Fisher Exact Test. The data should first be placed in a contingency table, as shown in Figure 6.1. Crucially, each child must be counted only once in the table. Thus, for the table shown in Figure 6.1, the number of subjects in the study was necessarily twenty-eight.

The question of interest is how likely it was that we would obtain so many children in the "concordant" cells (pass–pass, fail–fail) and so few children in the "discordant" cells (pass–fail, fail–pass) simply

Construction A

		Pass	Fail
	Pass	11	3
Construction B			
	Fail	2	12

$\overline{|\ 28}$

FIGURE 6.1 Contingency table, in a case of concurrent acquisition

by chance, if passing on Construction A and passing on Construction B were entirely independent of one another. This probability can be calculated exactly, with the Fisher exact test; or it can be approximated, with the χ^2 ("chi square") test . In the case of the data in Figure 6.1, we obtain the following: Fisher exact two-tailed p = .00184; $\chi^2(1)$ = 9.19 (with Yates correction), p = .00243.

At one time χ^2 was strongly favored over the Fisher exact test, because χ^2 was much simpler to calculate. Nowadays, however, computers can readily calculate Fisher exact test for a contingency table with as many as several hundred subjects. Also, the approximation provided by the χ^2 test is rather poor whenever the "expected frequency" in a given cell of the two-by-two contingency table is lower than five. (Details can be found in almost any statistics textbook.) For these reasons, I recommend using the Fisher exact test instead of χ^2.[4]

Like the χ^2 test, however, the Fisher exact test is subject to the following requirement: in the contingency table for subjects in a cross-sectional study, each subject must be counted exactly once. In other words, the sum of the numbers in the four cells must equal the number of subjects in the study. Computer programs that calculate the Fisher exact test (or χ^2, for that matter) usually have no mechanism for detecting violations of this requirement, and will simply provide the unsuspecting user with a p-value that is completely meaningless. The responsibility for checking is left to the researcher.

When using a contingency test, it is necessary to select a minimum score for "passing". As noted earlier (in Section 6.1.2), if we set the requirement too high, we are likely to misclassify some of the adult-like

---

[4] I should note that there is one important advantage of the χ^2 test over the Fisher exact test: χ^2 is readily generalizable to tables larger than two-by-two, and the Fisher exact test is not. Yet, larger tables seldom arise in parametric studies on child language. Moreover, computer programs for the most common cases (2 × 3, 2 × 4, 3 × 3) are now widely available.

children as lacking the adult grammar. This is because both elicited production and truth-value judgement impose task demands on the child that go beyond mere grammatical knowledge. On the other hand, if we set the requirement too low, then (in a truth-value judgement task, at least) many of the children who are simply guessing will appear to be adult-like.

As a rule of thumb, I suggest setting the criterion for passing somewhere around 80 percent correct. I also recommend checking the distribution of scores, after the experiment has been completed, by creating histograms of the scores for Construction A and for Construction B. (Programs such as Microsoft Excel® make this fairly easy to do. If the information is in the form of percentages, scores in the same decile should be grouped together.) The ideal outcome is a bimodal distribution, with one group of children who are clearly adult-like, another group who are clearly non-adult-like, and very few children in the middle. If the distribution is not bimodal, the best option is probably to test for a correlation instead of a contingency.

Finally note that in truth-value judgement studies, children's limited patience normally precludes having more than five to ten test items for each of the two constructions, especially if filler items are used to create a balance between "true" and "false" trials. Twenty items, including practice items and filler items, is usually an upper limit for a single testing session with a child (although the exact limit varies, depending on factors such as the child's age, the complexity of the scenarios, and the theatrical skills of the investigator). Moreover, the use of multiple testing sessions is risky: for reasons that are not entirely clear, the child's performance on a given truth-value judgement or elicited-production task sometimes varies quite a bit from one day to the next. If we choose not to take this risk, for fear of getting extra noise in the data, then a single testing session, with five to ten test items, will be all we have.

As a consequence, whenever we categorize children as passers and failers on a truth-value judgement task, the small number of test items means that "exception" children, those who fall into the discordant cells of the contingency table, are almost certain to turn up. This is true even when the hypothesis of concurrent acquisition is correct. Hence, I would caution researchers: the presence of such children does not necessarily call for a linguistic explanation.

Consider the sample data in Figure 6.1. Note that two children passed on B but failed on A, and three children passed on A but failed on B. Now suppose that our study included exactly five truth-value judgement items for each of A and B, and that our criterion for passing was to answer at least four out of five items (80 percent) correctly. In this case, a child who was simply guessing randomly had the following likelihood of passing:

$$p = (1 + 5)(1/2)^5 = 6/32 = .1875$$

The above calculation is based on the Binomial Theorem. Each particular sequence of five guesses (e.g. CCICI, where "C" is a correct guess and "I" is an incorrect guess) had a likelihood of $(1/2)^5 = 1/32$. There was one such sequence ("CCCCC") in which all five guesses were correct, and there were five such sequences (e.g. "CICCC") in which exactly one of the guesses was incorrect, for a total of six sequences that resulted in a passing score. The resulting probability is $(6)(1/32)$, or .1875.

Now, in Figure 6.1, some fifteen children failed on Construction A. Our hypothesis of concurrent acquisition predicts that each of these children lacks the grammatical basis for Construction B as well. Suppose that this prediction is correct, and they guessed randomly on each of the test items for Construction B. In that case, we should expect about $(15)(.1875) = 2.81$ children to pass on Construction B just by luck. The observed number, three such children, agrees quite well with this value. Hence, it would be foolhardy to revise our theory on account of these exceptions.

Let us turn now to the second main type of prediction that can be derived from a parametric hypothesis, a prediction of ordered acquisition, as in (14).

(14)   If the grammatical knowledge (including parameter settings and lexical information) required for construction A, in a given language, is a proper subset of the knowledge required for construction B, then the age of acquisition for A should always be less than or equal to the age of acquisition for B. (No child should acquire B significantly earlier than A.)

Once again, the question is how to test this type of prediction with cross-sectional data.

As with a prediction of concurrent acquisition, we have two main approaches available. We can keep the data in the form of a raw number (or percentage) correct on A and B, or we can convert each score into a pass/fail classification. In the former case, a good option for statistical hypothesis testing is the paired t-test (also known as the t-test on correlated samples, the repeated-measures t-test, or the within-subjects

Construction A

		Pass	Fail
	Pass	9	1
Construction B			
	Fail	8	10

$\overline{}$
$|28$

FIGURE 6.2 Contingency table, in a case of ordered acquisition

t-test). If the hypothesis is correct, and each child who knows the grammatical basis for B also knows the grammatical basis for A, then we expect (at most) three types of children to occur in our sample: children who score well on both A and B, children who score well on A but not B, and children who score poorly on both A and B. We do not expect children who score poorly on A, but well on B. If our prediction is correct, we should see a significant contrast between the scores for A and B in a paired *t*-test.[5]

If we convert the children's data to a categorial (pass/fail) classification, and construct a contingency table (as in Figure 6.2), then we can use the Fisher exact test for statistical hypothesis testing. Our hypothesis predicts (at most) three types of children in any given sample: children who succeed on both A and B, children who succeed on A but not B, and children who succeed on neither A nor B. The hypothesis does not predict children who fail on A but succeed on B.

Unfortunately, the Fisher exact test is less sensitive to ordering effects than it is to concurrent acquisition: concurrent acquisition yields a table like the one in Figure 6.1, where the subjects are concentrated on a single diagonal of the table (i.e. the upper left and lower right cells). In contrast, an ordering effect typically yields a table like the one in Figure 6.2, where the subjects are distributed more evenly over three of the four cells (all but the upper right cell). This has the effect of making it harder to reach significance by Fisher exact test (or for related reasons, by χ^2 test). Nonetheless, in the case of the table in Figure 6.2, for example,

---

[5] When running the statistics, one should double-check that the statistics software is performing a paired *t*-test rather than a (much less sensitive) unpaired *t*-test. In certain software packages, the input format is the same for the two tests. To confirm that the computer is actually running a paired test, check the degrees of freedom: in a paired *t*-test, the degrees of freedom will be N–1, or one less than the number of subjects in the study.

we do have a significant effect (at the .05 level): Fisher exact two-tailed $p = .0407$.

6.3 Example: scrambling and case-marking in Korean

Let us turn now to a real life example, namely Kang's (2005) work on the acquisition of scrambling and case-marking in Korean, which was already discussed briefly in Chapter 2 (Section 2.2.5). Recall that Bošković (2004) provides a Minimalist treatment of two generalizations: first, languages with Japanese-style scrambling lack true articles, and second, languages with this type of scrambling always have a system of overt case-marking. Kang focuses on the second generalization, and observes that it predicts an acquisitional ordering effect: if a child is acquiring a language with Japanese-style scrambling, then overt case-marking will be acquired prior to, or concurrently with, but never significantly later than, this type of scrambling.

To test this prediction, Kang conducted a cross-sectional comprehension study on two-year-olds and (young) three-year-olds acquiring Korean, a language with Japanese-style scrambling. The fact that she was working primarily with two-year-olds led her to choose an alternative to truth-value judgement, namely picture selection, that works well with children of that age (Gerken and Shady 1996: 142). The picture-selection task requires the child to listen to a sentence and choose one of two pictures that matches. The correct choice appears on either side (left or right) exactly half the time.

Kang's experiment began with a training period, in which she made sure that the child knew the names of the animals she would use. She then presented practice items involving a single animal. For example, she showed the child a picture of a turtle swimming, and another picture of the same turtle sleeping on a rock. She then said the following (in Korean): "A turtle is sleeping on the rock! Which picture is it?" Any child who failed on a practice item was excluded from further study.

Each of the remaining children was then tested on materials like those in (15–18) (cf. Kang 2005: 136–7, exs. 14–17).

(15)   kongwon-e ttokki-ga   issess nunte, kubuki-ga   Ø
       park-in   rabbit-NOM was   then   turtle-NOM *pro*
       milesseyo.
       pushed
       "There was a rabbit in the park, and then a turtle pushed him."

(16)   kongwon-e koyangi-ga issess nunte, Ø ttoki-ul   milesseyo.
        park-in   cat-NOM   was   then *pro* rabbit-ACC pushed
        "There was a cat in the park, and then he pushed a rabbit."

(17)   supsok-e taramci-ga   issess nunte, ku daramchi-ga
        forest-in squirrel-NOM was   then   that squirrel-NOM
        kangaci-lul coagasseyo.
        dog-ACC   chased
        "There was a squirrel in the forest, and then that squirrel chased
        a dog."

(18)   supsok-e horangi-ga issess nunte, ku   horangi-ul
        forest-in tiger-NOM was   then   that tiger-ACC
        wonsungi-ga   chottagaeyo.
        monkey-NOM chased
        "There was a tiger in the forest, and then a monkey chased that
        tiger."

Each child heard exactly five items of each type, for a total of twenty
test items. The verb in the second clause was always "push", "chase",
or "bite". For any given item, the two pictures depicted the same two
animals, and contrasted only in which of the two was the agent/patient
of the action.

The items in (15) and (16) test the child's knowledge of the Korean
nominative and accusative case-markers. In each such item the verb
is transitive, and one of its arguments is a phonetically null pronoun
(which is a grammatical option in Korean). The overt NP is equally
plausible as subject or object, and the listener has to use the case-
marker to decide. The items in (17) and (18) test the child's knowledge
of JSS in Korean. In (17), the second clause uses the canonical word
order of subject–object–verb (SOV), while in (18) the clause exhibits
a scrambled order, object–subject–verb (OSV). Again, the NPs are
equally plausible as subject or object.

Any child who answered incorrectly on more than one of the five
nominative-case items like (15), or more than one of the five canonical-
order items like (17), was excluded from further analysis. All of the
children tested succeeded on the nominative-case items, but only half
succeeded on the canonical-order items. This left twenty-five subjects
for analysis.

Crucially, for a child who knows the Korean nominative-marker,
mastery of the accusative-marker is not logically necessary for success
on a scrambling item like (18). The verb (*chottagaeyo* "chased") requires

a subject and an object, and the subject (*wonsungi-ga* "monkey-NOM") bears the subject-marker (i.e. nominative case, *-ga*). By a process of elimination, *horangi-ul* "monkey-ACC" must be the object, even if the child does not yet recognize *-ul* as the object-marker (i.e. as accusative case). What is needed for success on an item like (18), beyond knowledge of the nominative-marker, is the recognition that scrambled word order is grammatically possible in Korean.

Bošković's work predicts that the child will have a grammatical basis for Korean scrambling (i.e. Japanese-style scrambling) only if she actually knows the overt marker for accusative case in Korean. Being able to distinguish the object from the subject by some other means, such as a process of elimination, is not sufficient. Hence, the prediction that Kang derived from Bošković's work was an acquisitional ordering effect: Japanese-style scrambling cannot be acquired earlier than the accusative case-marker. In terms of her cross-sectional study, the prediction took the following form: a child will succeed on scrambling items like (18) only if she succeeds on accusative items like (16).

Kang then categorized each child as passing or failing on the two conditions. Her criterion for passing was to get at least four of the five test items correct. As discussed in Section 6.2 above, the child's chance of passing simply by guessing was therefore $p = .1875$. The twenty-five children who were included in the analysis were then arranged in a contingency table, as shown in Figure 6.3. Analysis by Fisher exact test indicated that a contingency of the observed strength was highly unlikely to have resulted by chance: two-tailed $p < .001$.

Note that the data in Figure 6.3 are similar to what we would expect from concurrent acquisition. There is only one instance of a child who passed on the object-marker items and failed on the scrambling items, even though such children are fully compatible with the prediction of ordered acquisition. Indeed, if the ten children who failed

		Object-marker	
		Pass	*Fail*
JSS	*Pass*	15	0
	Fail	1	9

|25

FIGURE 6.3 Contingency table of results from Kang (2005)

on Japanese-style scrambling had all lacked knowledge of the object-marker, we would still have expected to see one or two children passing the object-marker test simply by guessing: expected frequency = $(10)(.1875) = 1.875$ children. Hence, despite the presence of one child in the lower-left cell of Figure 6.3, it is tempting to think that having an overt object-marker is not only necessary, but also sufficient, for Japanese-style scrambling.

Yet, the cross-linguistic evidence speaks against this. Languages like Icelandic, for example, have distinctive, overt accusative case-marking, but disallow Japanese-style scrambling. Hence, a better interpretation of Kang's data is that the other requirements for Japanese-style scrambling, beyond having an overt object-marker, tend to be acquired earlier than the object-marker.

In summary, Kang's work provides a good example of parametric research using a cross-sectional approach. Contemporary work in comparative syntax, namely Bošković (2004), proposed a generalization about cross-linguistic variation. Kang converted this generalization into a testable hypothesis about children's acquisition of Korean. She derived a prediction of an ordering effect, which she then tested by administering a comprehension task to two-year-old and young three-year-old children who were acquiring Korean as their first language. She classified the children as passing or failing on each of the two constructions of interest, and then demonstrated a significant contingency, using the statistical method of the Fisher exact test. Her findings provide strong acquisitional support for Bošković's proposal.

7

Case Studies in the Parametric Approach

In this chapter I present three case studies in the parametric approach to child language. The first is a study of children's acquisition of syllable structure in Dutch, which I conducted in collaboration with Ning Pan. The second example concerns a type of empty-category phenomenon in Spanish that I term "noun-drop", and was conducted in collaboration with Ann Senghas and Kelly Inman. The final example is a study of children's acquisition of prepositional questions in English, and was conducted with Koji Sugisaki.

7.1 Syllable structure in Dutch

In Chapter 3, Section 3.2, I presented an overview of Government Phonology (GP), a Principles-and-Parameters approach to phonology that is modeled on P&P syntax. Recall that GP includes a highly restrictive account of syllabification. Specifically, GP recognizes only three basic constituents: onsets, rhymes, and nuclei. What might be treated as a word-final coda in other frameworks is analyzed as an onset. According to GP, any onset must be followed by a rhyme, and the rhyme must contain at least a nucleus. Hence a word-final consonant is necessarily followed, in GP, by a rhyme with a phonetically empty nucleus.

Actual codas (or "postnuclear rhymal positions", in the vocabulary of GP) are permitted only in word-medial positions, because they require government by a following, phonetically overt onset. Furthermore such government is possible only between certain combinations of consonants. Specifically, the postnuclear rhymal position must be filled by a sibilant, nasal, liquid, or glide. The following onset is typically a non-sibilant obstruent, although exceptions exist (due to the possibility of "government licensing", as discussed in Kaye (1992)).

Thus, the s-initial consonant cluster in the English word *wasp* receives the analysis in (1).

(1)

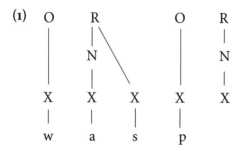

The /s/ occupies a postnuclear rhymal position, and is governed by a non-sibilant obstruent (/p/) in the following onset. The fact that this onset is phonetically word-final means that it must be followed by a rhyme whose nucleus is empty.[1]

S-initial consonant clusters in word-initial position have a special status in GP. For an English word such as *spy*, the principles of the system lead to the analysis in (2). (The reasons are presented in detail in Kaye (1992).)

(2)

Here the word-initial /s/ is analyzed as occupying the postnuclear position of a rhyme with a phonetically empty nucleus.[2]

[1]   In much of the GP literature the practice is to simplify the representation of a rhyme dominating only a nucleus, by omitting the R node from the structure. In the interest of clarity, however, I include both the R node and the N node in all cases.

[2]   Note that the structure here includes not only an empty nucleus but also an empty onset at the beginning of the word. Kaye's (1992) assumption seems to be that empty onsets are freely available in all languages. As noted in Chapter 3, Section 3.2, the principles of GP might well permit an empty onset when the following nucleus is phonetically overt, because overt segments are usually taken as potential governors for empty segments. Yet, the immediately following nucleus in the present structure is itself empty. Moreover, the general availability of empty onsets appears to be a point of cross-linguistic variation,

The special status of s+C sequences in word-initial position is not unique to GP. Indeed, such sequences require special treatment in any framework, because of their distinctive characteristics. For example in English, /s/ is the only word-initial consonant that can be followed by a homorganic consonant (e.g. /st-/, /sl-/), by either a nasal or a stop (e.g. /sm-/, /sn-/, /sp-/), and by a two-element consonant cluster (e.g. /spr-/, /spl-/, /str/). In many cases, word-initial s+C sequences violate the Sonority Sequencing Generalization (e.g. Selkirk 1984: 118).

Yet, while the special status of word-initial /s/ is nothing new, and the approach in (2) is all but forced by the principles of GP, this approach remains problematic: the word-initial empty nucleus in this structure is not licensed by any of the usual GP mechanisms for licensing empty categories. Kaye (1992) concludes that a new licensing mechanism must be added to the framework, which he terms "magic licensing". Specifically, Kaye proposes (1992: 306) that s+C sequences can potentially license an immediately preceding empty nucleus, subject to parametric variation.

In Pan and Snyder (2004) we dubbed this point of cross-linguistic variation the "Magic Empty Nucleus (MEN) Parameter". Hence, the structure in (2) is available in precisely those languages that take the positive settings for two parameters: the Branching Rhyme Parameter (Kaye 1989; Harris 1994) and the MEN Parameter, as formulated in (3) and (4).

(3) BRANCHING RHYME PARAMETER:
     Rhymes may branch [No/Yes]

(4) MEN PARAMETER:
     Empty nuclei are licensed before an s+C sequence [No/Yes]

The postnuclear rhymal position is available only in a language with branching rhymes, and the nucleus preceding this position can be empty only if the language has magic licensing.

and Pan and Snyder (2005a, 2005b) have therefore proposed the Empty Onset Parameter: Empty onsets are allowed [No, Yes].

If the structure shown here depends on the positive setting of this parameter (as seems likely), the prediction is that s-initial clusters at the beginning of a word will be found only in languages (or child grammars) that take the positive setting of the Empty Onset Parameter (and that therefore allow onset-less words more generally). The evidence reported for Dutch children's onset-less syllables (in Pan and Snyder 2005b) and word-initial s+C clusters (in Pan and Snyder 2004) is consistent with this prediction: the four children (Jarmo, Noortje, Tom, Elke) for whom both pieces of information are reported all acquired onset-less syllables prior to word-initial s+C sequences.

In a language with the negative setting of the Branching Rhyme Parameter, the positive setting of the MEN Parameter has no effect. On the other hand, in a language with the negative setting of the MEN Parameter, the positive setting of the Branching Rhyme Parameter does have an effect: It makes it possible to have postnuclear rhymal consonants following an overt nucleus, as in the English word *wasp*.

Spanish is an example of an adult language with the negative setting of the MEN Parameter and the positive setting of the Branching Rhyme Parameter. In Spanish one never finds s+C clusters in word-initial position. Hence, when English words like *spray* and *sphere* were borrowed into Spanish, an epenthetic vowel was added: *esprey* "spray", *esfera* "sphere". In GP terms, the /s/ could only occur in a postnuclear rhymal position (since it was followed immediately by a non-sibilant obstruent), but the unavailability of magic licensing meant that a phonetically realized V was required in the preceding nucleus.

The fact that words like *esprey* and *esfera* are possible in Spanish, once the initial V is added, indicates that Spanish must allow branching rhymes. Otherwise there would be no position available for the /s/. Precisely as predicted, Spanish permits branching rhymes in word-medial positions, for example in the words *pintar* "to paint" and *costar* "to cost". Just as Spanish exhibits branching rhymes but no magic licensing, the child acquiring a language like English could temporarily have a grammar with this combination of properties.

More generally, Kaye's approach to word-initial s+C sequences predicts an acquisitional ordering effect: in a language like English, any given child will acquire the possibility of branching rhymes (as in *wasp*) prior to, or at the same time as, but never significantly later than, the possibility of s+C clusters in word-initial position. In other words, a child might temporarily lack branching rhymes and s+C clusters altogether, or she might have a Spanish-type grammar with branching rhymes but no s+C clusters, but if she has s+C clusters then she should necessarily have word-medial branching rhymes as well.

As noted in Chapter 4, the Fikkert–Levelt corpora for child Dutch (which were formerly available through CHILDES) provide an especially rich source of phonological data. Moreover, adult Dutch is like English in allowing word-initial s+C clusters. As predicted by Kaye's account, Dutch also permits branching rhymes following an overt nucleus. Hence, Dutch is an excellent place to check for the predicted acquisitional ordering effect.

Ning Pan and I, in a 2004 paper, did precisely this. We searched each child's corpus for the first several examples of a word containing a branching rhyme following an overt nucleus, and the first several examples of a word containing a word-initial s+C sequence. We then checked whether any child appeared to acquire the word-initial s+C sequences prior to word-medial branching rhymes.

As noted in Chapter 4, the Fikkert–Levelt corpora contain longitudinal, spontaneous-production data from twelve children acquiring Dutch as their first language. Each child was tape-recorded regularly for a period of approximately one year, beginning when the child was between 1;00 and 1;11. Each transcript takes the form of an alphabetical list of the words the child produced in the given recording. Each word is presented in the standard Dutch spelling, followed by information including a phonetic rendition of the child's pronunciation (in IPA symbols, using the IPA roman font, on the "%pho" tier); and a schematic representation of the child's utterance, in terms of Cs and Vs (on the "%sch" tier). The version of the corpora used here is available from my website:[3] http://web.uconn.edu/snyder/parametric.

The CLAN software makes the necessary searches relatively straightforward. A given child's uses of word-initial s+C sequences can be obtained as follows. (Here I illustrate the procedure for the child Noortje.) First, we obtain a list of all the child's sinitial words:

```
combo +t*CHI +ss* +o% +d noortje.cha > noortje_s.cha
```

The instruction "+ss*" tells the program to return each utterance containing a word beginning with the letter "s". The instruction "+o%" tells the program to include the dependent tiers (such as %pho and %sch) in the output for each matching word, and the instruction "+d" tells the program to give the output in legal CHAT format, so that we can run a second search on the output file.

The next step is to search the file noorte_s.cha for child utterances that begin with a CC sequence:

```
combo +t%sch +scc* +o% noortje_s.cha > noortje_sC.cha
```

---

[3] When working with the Fikkert–Levelt corpora, in the form available from my website, one should be aware of one problem: most of the vowel-initial utterances have had a (spurious) glottal stop inserted at the beginning. This error should be corrected in the next version of the corpora that is released through CHILDES. Also, the age information available in the present version of the corpora is incomplete. The missing information can be found in Levelt (1994: 9).

Here the instruction "+t%sch" tells the program to examine the tier containing the CV structure of the child's utterance, and the instruction "+scc*" tells the program to look for utterances whose CV structure begins with a sequence of two consonants. The final step is to search the file noortje_sC.cha by hand, to identify the actual child utterances beginning with an s+C sequence. (The file also includes a number of irrelevant phrases, in which one word begins with an [s], and another word begins with a CC sequence.)

When looking for Noortje's first utterances with a branching rhyme (following an overt nucleus), we should first recall that GP treats a (phonetically) word-final "VC" sequence as the result of a word-final empty nucleus, rather than a branching rhyme. In GP, a true branching rhyme occurs only when it is followed by a C in onset position. Thus, to find the relevant examples we can search on the %sch tier for child utterances whose CV representation includes the sequence "vcc":

combo +t%sch +s*vcc* +0% noortje.cha > noortje_vcc.cha

The results, for both word-medial branching rhymes and word-initial s+C sequences, are shown in Table 7.1. The ages provided there are for the second clear use, followed soon afterwards by regular use. More precisely, we chose as our measure of acquisition the second relevant word-type (not word-token) that the child produced, out of a concern that repeated use of the first word-type might be possible even without mastery of the relevant point of the adult grammar.

TABLE 7.1 Ages of second clear use for branching rhymes and word-initial s+C sequences

Child	Branching rhymes	Word-initial s+C sequences
Catootje	1;11	2;04
David	1;11	1;11
Elke	2;03	2;04
Leon	1;10	1;11
Noortje	2;05	2;08
Robin	1;06	2;02
Tirza	1;10	2;07
Tom	1;06	1;10
Eva	1;08	(Not found)
Enzo	1;11	(Not found)
Leonie	1;11	(Not found)
Jarmo	(Not found)	(Not found)

As can be seen in Table 7.1, the data were entirely consistent with the prediction of Kaye's account: eight of the children acquired both branching rhymes and word-initial s+C sequences before the end of their corpora. Of these children, seven acquired branching rhymes prior to word-initial s+C clusters, and one acquired branching rhymes and s+C clusters in the same transcript. Crucially, none of these children acquired word-initial s+C sequences prior to (other) branching rhymes.

Moreover, the findings for the remaining four children were also fully consistent with the prediction. Three of these children acquired branching rhymes during the time period covered by their corpora, but failed to acquire word-initial s+C sequences. These children clearly acquired branching rhymes prior to word-initial s+C sequences, as predicted. The remaining child, Jarmo, failed to acquire either branching rhymes or word-initial s+C sequences by the end of his corpus.

Importantly, none of the children gave so much as the impression of acquiring s+C sequences prior to branching rhymes, but if they had, the next step would have been to assess whether the gap was statistically significant. This step would have involved the use of the Binomial Test, discussed in Chapter 5. For informational purposes, let me indicate how this would have worked.

Binomial testing is actually somewhat difficult because the Fikkert–Levelt transcripts take the form of alphabetical word lists, in which any given word (or more precisely, any given pronunciation of the word) is listed only once. Hence, for any particular utterance, there is no information available about how many actual utterances preceded or followed it within the same recording, let alone which particular words were uttered on those occasions. Nonetheless, if the two utterances of interest occurred in different transcripts, then a binomial test can be applied.

Two main approaches are available. One is to use the relative frequency of word-medial branching rhymes and word-initial s+C sequences, obtained from a sample of the child's speech that was collected shortly after both word-types came into use. The second is to use the absolute frequency of word-medial branching rhymes in a sample of the child's speech that was collected shortly after those began to appear. In either case the frequency is calculated in terms of "distinct utterances" (i.e. utterances that were listed in the Fikkert–Levelt transcripts), rather than utterances *per se*.

For example, the relative frequency (f_R) is the number of distinct utterances containing a word-initial s+C sequence, divided by the total number of distinct utterances containing either a word-initial s+C sequence or a word-medial branching rhyme. We then determine the number of distinct utterances (x) containing a word-initial s+C sequence in the transcripts prior to the one where word-medial branching rhymes appeared for the second time. (Recall that our measure of acquisition here is the second clear use, followed soon after by repeated use.) The following gives the probability of sampling at least x examples of a word-initial s+C sequence, just by chance, prior to the second use of a word-medial branching rhyme, under the null hypothesis that word-medial branching rhymes were available as early as word-initial s+C sequences: the formula is simply $p = f_R \char`^ x$, where "$\char`^ x$" means "raised to the x power".

The second option, using the absolute frequency, requires that the transcripts containing the two utterances of interest were separated by at least one intervening transcript. Suppose, for example, that the child produced her second distinct use of a word-initial s+C cluster in Transcript 7, and did not produce her second distinct use of a branching rhyme until Transcript 10. We would need to determine three pieces of information: How many distinct utterances (x) occurred in Transcript 10? How many of these utterances (y) contained a branching rhyme (other than an s+C sequence)? And how many distinct utterances (z) occurred in Transcripts 8 and 9? The following formula gives the probability of *not* sampling more than a single branching-rhyme utterance (other than a word-initial s+C sequence) until Transcript 10, just by chance, under the null hypothesis that such branching-rhyme utterances were grammatically possible for the child as early as Transcript 7: $p = [(x–y)/x] \char`^ (z–1)$.

In other words, under the null hypothesis, each time the child produced a distinct utterance in Transcripts 8 and 9, the likelihood that the utterance would *not* contain a branching rhyme was the same as the frequency of such utterances observed in Transcript 10: $(x–y)/x$. The likelihood of observing a "run" of z utterances or more, in which at most one example of a branching rhyme occurred, is obtained by raising this frequency to the power of $(z–1)$.

In the present case the data in Table 7.1 are exceptionally clear-cut. No child gave even the appearance of acquiring word-medial branching rhymes prior to word-initial s+C sequences. Therefore, neither type of binomial testing described above is actually required in this case. Nonetheless, we might ask the following question: given the observed variability in children's ages of acquisition for both word-medial branching rhymes and word-initial s+C sequences, how likely was it that the observed ordering effect would have occurred simply by chance?

To address this question a reasonable approach is to run a paired *t*-test, as discussed in Chapter 5. The one complication is that several children failed to acquire one or both of the word-types of interest by the end of their corpora. In the case of Jarmo, the one child who acquired neither word-type by the end of his corpus, the appropriate course of action is simply to exclude him from the analysis.

For the three children (Eva, Enzo, and Leonie) who acquired word-medial branching rhymes but not word-initial s+C sequences by the end of their corpora, an appropriately conservative approach is to assume that the word-initial s+C sequences would have appeared immediately after the recordings ended. The estimated ages of acquisition for word-initial s+C sequences are then 1;11 for Eva, 2;06 for Enzo, and 2;00 for Leonie. The results of the paired *t*-test are now as follows: the ordering effect is clearly significant ($t(10) = 4.09$, two-tailed $p = .0022$).

Finally, recall that the strongest support for parametric proposals is provided by converging evidence from multiple sources of data. Therefore, in addition to examining evidence from child language acquisition, Pan and I checked the available typological evidence: Do the languages of the world that permit word-initial s+C sequences consistently permit (other types of) branching rhymes? Indeed, in our search of the literature we were unable to find a counterexample. The relevant languages that we found are characterized in (5–14) (Pan and Snyder 2004: 441–3, exs. 11–20). (Note that the listings of /s/-initial clusters are not necessarily exhaustive.)

(5) DUTCH
     Language family: Indo-Eurpean (Germanic)
     Data source: Trommelen (1984)
     /s/-initial clusters: sp, st, sk, sf, sx, sl
     Branching rhymes: *slurf* "trunk", *darm* "bowel", *molm* "mold"

(6) ENGLISH
     Language family: Indo-European (Germanic)
     Data source: Harris (1994)

/s/-initial clusters: st, sp, sk, sl, sw, sm, sn, str, spr, spl, skr
Branching rhymes: *chapter, mist, winter*

(7) ISTHMUS ZAPOTEC
Language family: Zapotec/Amerindian
Data source: Marlett and Pickett (1987)
/s/-initial clusters: st, sk
Branching rhymes: *randa* "able", *yanda* "cold"

(8) ITALIAN
Language family: Indo-European (Romance)
Data source: Davis (1990)
/s/-initial clusters: sp, st, sk, sf, sl, sn, sm
Branching rhymes: *scampo* "rescue", *smalto* "pavement"

(9) MISANTLA TOTONAC
Language family: Language isolate
Data source: MacKay (1994)
s/-initial clusters: st, sk, sp, sq, sm, sn, sl, sw, sy
Branching rhymes: *čıškú?* "man", *čukúNku̱* "cold"

(10) SERBO-CROATIAN
Language family: Indo-European (Slavic)
Data source: Hodge (1946)
s/-initial clusters: sp, st, sk, sf, sv, sh, sr, sl, sl', sm, sn, sn', sj,
spr, str, skr, svr, smr, svj, smj, stv, skv, spl, skl, svl
Branching rhymes: *jèsti* "to eat", *nòkta* "fingernail", *krùmpiir*
"potatoes"

(11) SERI
Language family: Hokan
Data source: Marlett (1988)
s/-initial clusters: st, sk, sp, sł, sn
Branching rhymes: *kApkA* "rain", *?Ast* "stone", *?onk* "duck"

(12) WICHITA
Language family: Caddoan
Data source: Rood (1975)
s/-initial clusters: sk
Branching rhymes: *iskʷA* "go!", *ksA:r?A* "bed"

(13) YATEE ZAPOTEC
Language family: Zapotecan
Data source: Jaeger and Van Valin (1982)

s/-initial clusters: st, sč, sw
Branching rhymes: *gasx* "black", *zápx* "chayote vine"

(14) YUCHI
Language family: Language isolate
Data source: Wolff (1948), Crawford (1973)
s/-initial clusters: st, sp, sʔ, sy, stʔ, skw, sʔy
Branching rhymes: *dompa* "hand", *ʔispi* "black", *bʔaxte* "horse"

Thus, child language acquisition and cross-linguistic variation provide converging evidence in support of Kaye's (1992) proposal.

7.2 Noun-drop in Spanish

Next I turn from phonology to syntax, and examine a point of cross-linguistic variation in syntactic empty categories. This study was conducted in collaboration with Ann Senghas and Kelly Inman, and the report in this subsection is a revised version of Snyder, Senghas, and Inman (2001).

Spanish, and to a lesser degree Italian, French, and Dutch, all exhibit a DP-internal phenomenon ("noun-drop" or "N-drop") that is reminiscent of the well-known null-subject ("pro-drop") phenomenon of Italian and Spanish. Where English employs the nearly vacuous noun *one* in the DP *the blue one*, for example, a language of the Spanish type employs a DP of the form *el azul* "the blue", which lacks an (overt) noun altogether. Many of the issues raised by the literature on the syntax and acquisition of null subjects arise in much the same form in the domain of N-drop. In particular, alongside hypotheses relating the availability of null subjects in certain languages to the "richness" of subject agreement morphology on the verb, a widespread hypothesis (e.g. Muysken 1983; Barbiers 1991; Kester 1994) relates the grammatical possibility of N-drop to the richness of overt agreement morphology within the DP. As in the null-subject literature, however, a fully successful, cross-linguistic characterization of "rich morphology" has not yet been achieved.

7.2.1 Theoretical issues

The present case study approaches the broad question of how syntax and morphology interact during language acquisition by investigating the specific case of N-drop. N-drop permits a test of several influential proposals concerning the nature and acquisition of syntactic knowledge. Chomsky (1993: 3–4) has proposed that the syntactic component of the human language faculty is essentially invariant across languages, and that language-particular syntactic properties follow from the morphosyntactic properties of individual words (including, in particular, functional heads). According to this view, however, the relevant morphosyntactic properties typically take the form of abstract features, which do not necessarily have any overt phonological expression. A related hypothesis, proposed by Borer (1984), connects language-particular properties of syntax to inflectional morphology that is phonologically overt.

Borer's proposal suggests that children's acquisition of syntax could, in at least some cases, take the form of learning language-particular characteristics of the morphology. This idea can be interpreted in two distinct ways, both of which have important acquisitional implications. The first interpretation is procedural. The child's procedure for learning language-particular properties of syntax could take the form of analyzing overt morphology, provided that the morphology is a reliable indicator of syntactic characteristics. The second interpretation is representational. The child's (and adult's) mental representation of language-particular aspects of syntax could take the form of knowledge about overt morphology if, as Chomsky has proposed, points of syntactic variation are determined by information outside the computational component of syntax, in conjunction with a richly deductive set of universal principles.

A number of researchers investigating the acquisition of null-subject phenomena (notably Hyams 1987; Lillo-Martin 1991) have been influenced by the idea that children's acquisition of at least certain aspects of syntax could take the form of learning the overt morphology of a language. While null subjects are unlikely to represent a unitary phenomenon across languages (see Jaeggli and Safir 1989; Lillo-Martin 1991), in languages such as Italian and Hebrew, there has nevertheless been a strong and persistent intuition that the availability of null subjects is closely related to the richness of overt subject-agreement morphology on the inflected verb.

A striking piece of evidence in support of this intuition comes from Borer's (1984) discussion of null subjects in Hebrew, where only certain verb forms exhibit overt subject agreement morphology, and the distribution of null subjects corresponds rather closely to the environments with agreement. Thus in (15a) Borer (1984: 208), where the first-person-singular past-tense verb is overtly inflected for person, number, and gender, the subject pronoun need not be overt.

(15a)   ('Ani) 'axalti 'et   ha-banana.
         (I)   ate   ACC the-banana
         "I ate the banana."

(15b)   *('Ani) 'oxelet 'et   ha-banana.
         (I)   eat   ACC the-banana
         "I am eating the banana."

In (15b), however, where the first-person-singular present-tense verb carries gender and number marking, but no overt person marking, a phonetically overt subject pronoun must appear. Thus, the mixed pro-drop/non-pro-drop pattern of Hebrew provides impressive evidence for a link between null subjects and agreement morphology.

Yet, attempts to reduce the cross-linguistic variation in availability of null subjects entirely to variation in agreement paradigms have been problematic. For example, McCloskey and Hale (1984) note that Irish has two agreement paradigms, the richer of which licenses null subjects. Even this richer agreement paradigm, however, makes fewer person/number distinctions than the agreement paradigm of German, and German disallows null subjects.

The difficulty in pinning down the relationship between null subjects of the Italian type and paradigms of verbal agreement morphology could in principle be due to an emphasis on cross-linguistic comparison. Given that languages vary from one another in many respects, it is effectively impossible to find "minimal pairs" of languages that differ only in the richness of verbal agreement. Furthermore, if null subjects have multiple grammatical sources, as seems likely, there is little reason to expect that a single measure of "richness of agreement" will emerge from cross-linguistic comparisons.[4]

An alternative approach is to investigate the issue acquisitionally. If we adopt the strong hypothesis that knowledge of the null-subject properties of a language such as Italian is mentally represented directly as knowledge of the overt distinctions in the verbal agreement paradigm, then we predict that any given child learning Italian will begin producing null subjects at approximately the same point that the agreement paradigm is mastered. Unfortunately, two problems have plagued attempts to test this prediction. First, verbal agreement morphology in

---

[4] Thus, the proper interpretation of McCloskey & Hale's observation about Irish and German depends on whether Irish subject-drop is in fact the same type of phenomenon as subject-drop in Romance languages. Interestingly, Breton has a form of subject-drop similar to that found in Irish, and Anderson (1982) argues that in contrast to any of the Romance languages, Breton subject-drop involves incorporation of a subject pronoun into the verb.

richly inflected languages tends to be predominantly correct as early as children begin talking (e.g. Hyams 1986 for Italian). Thus, determination of the age of acquisition is extremely difficult. Second, children learning English, a non-null-subject language, omit subjects with considerable frequency (see Hyams 1986, and much subsequent literature).[5] Thus, the fact that a child is omitting subjects in spontaneous speech is not a reliable indicator that the null-subject properties of the target language have been acquired.

N-drop provides a new domain in which to examine children's acquisition of syntax in relation to their acquisition of overt agreement morphology. As in the case of null subjects, there is a strong intuition that N-drop is related to richness of overt agreement morphology. Furthermore, as will be seen below, children learning English, which does not allow N-drop, seldom produce determiner-adjective sequences without a noun. Hence, an abrupt onset of high-frequency N-drop in spontaneous child Spanish plausibly indicates a change in the child's grammar, and can be evaluated in relation to the child's use of agreement morphology.

7.2.2 N-drop in Spanish

Spanish normally employs DP's that lack an overt noun, as illustrated in (16), whenever the content of the noun is recoverable from context. In this respect Spanish resembles, to varying degrees, Italian, French, Dutch, German, and Swedish (see among others Muysken 1983; Barbiers 1991; Bernstein 1993a, 1993b; Sleeman 1993, 1996; Kester 1994, 1995, 1996). In contrast to (16), the direct English translation in (17) is ungrammatical without insertion of the pro-form *one*. Spanish in fact prohibits the English construction, as illustrated in (18).

(16)   L-a   camis-a   que quier-o   comprar es l-a
       the-F.SG shirt-F.SG that want-1SG to.buy   is the-F.SG
       roj-a.
       red-F.SG
       "The shirt that I want to buy is the red (one)."

(17)   *The shirt that I want to buy is the red.

---

[5] Whether omission of subjects by children acquiring English is due to a non-adult grammar or to performance factors is a topic of debate. See Hyams and Wexler (1993) and Bloom (1993) for contrasting views. Note, however, that my claim of grammatical conservatism in children's spontaneous speech strongly commits me to the view that English-learning children never employ the Italian-type grammatical basis for null subjects.

(18)   *l-a   roj-a   un-a   / *l-a   un-a   roj-a
       the-F.SG red-FSg one-FSg / the-FSg one-FSg red-FSg
       "the red one"

Note that the Spanish DP in (19a), unlike its English counterpart (19b), contains overt (feminine singular) gender- and number-marking on the determiner and the adjective.

(19a)   l-a   camis-a   roj-a
        the-F.SG shirt-F.SG red-F.SG

(19b)   the red shirt

Following the work of Muysken (1983), some recent analyses of N-drop (e.g. Barbiers 1991; Kester 1994, 1995, 1996) ascribe a central role to the distinctions of number, gender, and case that are overtly expressed by the morphological agreement paradigms for determiners and adjectives. Kester, for example, proposes that in N-drop the non-lexical head of NP, which she refers to as *pro*, has default features of [+human], [+generic], and [+plural]; thus even in English it is possible to find expressions such as *the rich* or *the homeless*, where the non-lexical head is human, generic, and plural. Any other features of *pro* must be "licensed by strong grammatical gender features, which is not possible in a language with weak inflectional morphology like English" (1994: 13). Dutch, in contrast, permits cases of N-drop where the non-lexical head is abstract (e.g. *het besprokene* "the (thing) discussed", with a neuter singular determiner) or human and specific (e.g. *de besprokene* "the (person) discussed", with a non-neuter singular determiner).[6]

Yet, the idea that availability of N-drop follows from properties of overt agreement morphology (such as overt gender distinctions in the form of the determiner and adjective) is controversial. Bernstein (1993a, 1993b), for example, proposes that Spanish N-drop with the indefinite article (e.g. *uno rojo* "a red (one)") depends on a syntactically independent "word marker" which incorporates into the D and surfaces as a terminal vowel (-*o* or -*a*). The word marker head governs, and thereby licenses, a null NP projection. On Bernstein's account, the word marker may exhibit gender agreement, but richness of overt agreement is not taken to play any role in the availability of N-drop. Thus, French N-drop in indefinite DPs (e.g. *un rouge* "a red (one)") lacks the overt word

---

[6] The view that N-drop is closely related to overt paradigms of agreement morphology can also be found in the diachronic literature on English. For example, Hewson (1972: 52) asserts that the use of the pro-form *one*, in place of N-drop, arose in Late Middle English as a result of the loss of declensional morphology on the English attributive adjective.

marker (i.e. there is no extra vowel affixed to the indefinite article), and Bernstein treats this case as involving an "abstract" word marker that is phonetically null.[7] Hence, even though the availability of N-drop is perhaps one of the points of syntactic variation likeliest to have a direct connection to variation in overt morphology, there is by no means a consensus among syntacticians that such an analysis is correct.

The question addressed in this case study is whether the availability of N-drop in Spanish, as opposed to English, follows directly from the morphological agreement paradigms for Spanish determiners and/or adjectives. If N-drop follows directly (i.e. if the rich agreement in Spanish is both necessary and sufficient for N-drop), then any child who has fully mastered the Spanish agreement system should also permit N-drop. If richness of agreement morphology is not a sufficient condition for N-drop, however, and N-drop in Spanish depends on independent properties of the language (e.g. an independent syntactic parameter, or an abstract syntactic feature of Spanish determiners), then we predict that at least some children will acquire N-drop significantly later than the agreement system. The hypothesis that agreement is sufficient would be disconfirmed, in other words, if any child passed through a stage in which she demonstrated full mastery of the agreement system within DP, and nonetheless insisted on pronouncing an overt N in every DP.

As discussed in Chapter 5, longitudinal corpora of spontaneous production permit a test of these predictions. The age at which a given child's grammar first includes N-drop will be identified by the age of first clear use of a determiner–adjective sequence, provided that this is followed soon afterward by repeated use. In other words, the measure of acquisition will be the FRU, or "first of repeated uses". This is an appropriate measure because N-drop is strongly preferred, in the Spanish of adults and older children, whenever it is permitted, and because (as will be seen below) erroneous use of N-drop in a non-N-drop language such as English is relatively infrequent. Moreover, nouns, determiners, and (with lower frequency) adjectives are well-represented in spontaneous production data, and the presence of correct agreement morphology is readily checked.

The next subsection presents the findings for two children acquiring Spanish. One child (María) begins to use N-drop approximately as early as overt gender- and number-marking on determiners and adjectives.

---

[7] For full details of the proposal, see Bernstein (1993a, ch. 3).

The other child (Koki), however, uses the full Spanish system of DP-internal agreement morphology significantly earlier than N-drop.

7.2.3 Method

A number of longitudinal corpora of monolingual Spanish acquisition data are publicly available through the CHILDES database. The Linaza corpus (for the child Juan) was analyzed in Snyder (1995), but the results were difficult to interpret.[8] Here, two of the more recent corpora are analyzed. The first corpus comes from the child María (López-Ornat, Fernandez, Gallo, and Mariscal 1994), recorded in Madrid by her mother, with transcripts at approximately monthly intervals between the ages of 1;07 and 3;00 (6,619 lines of child speech), and with intermittent transcripts from 3;00 to 4;00 (1,333 additional lines of child speech). The second corpus comes from a child named Koki (Montes 1987, 1992), recorded in Mexico by her mother, with transcripts at approximately two-month intervals from 1;07 to 2;02, and at approximately one-month intervals from 2;02 through 2;11 (for a total of 4,332 lines of child speech).[9]

Koki's and María's data were hand-coded by fluent Spanish speakers. Beginning with the earliest transcripts, each use of a potentially attributive (DP-internal) adjective was identified and classified according to whether the DP contained (a) an overt D and (b) an overt N. This procedure was continued through a point at which N-drop was well attested in the child's speech. Following the procedures discussed in Chapters 4 and 5, the FRU of N-drop was determined for each child. The child's use of correct and incorrect agreement morphology with

---

[8] Juan began producing clear examples of N-drop at the age of 2;08, when he was in the late stages of mastering the Spanish determiner system. In this respect his data are similar to María's (discussed below). A difficulty in interpreting Juan's data, however, is that even as late as 2;08 he exhibited a fairly high rate of determiner omission. Hence, it is possible that N-drop was part of his grammar somewhat earlier, and was obscured in his production by the absence of a determiner. Similarly, his real command of the determiner system, prior to 2;08, is difficult to assess. For further details and discussion, see Snyder (1995).

[9] Koki is the daughter of two linguists. The mother speaks Spanish natively, while the father speaks it as a second language. The parents sometimes speak to one another in English, but consistently address Koki in Spanish. Koki lived in Poland from birth to age 0;06, Argentina from 0;06 to 1;00, the United States from 1;01 to 1;03, and Mexico from 1;04 onward. A check of Koki's lexicon revealed that out of 1,350 word-types, and 12,674 word tokens, only ten types (32 tokens) were of English origin, all were nouns, and eight of these were proper names (e.g. *Bert*, *Ernie*). In 4,332 lines of transcribed speech, Koki never produced a sentence of English. Thus, Koki appears to have been engaged in the monolingual acquisition of Spanish.

determiners and adjectives was then assessed for the period up to the first use of N-drop.

In addition, the longitudinal corpus of spontaneous speech from an English-learning child, Eve (Brown 1973; ages 1;06 to 2;03, with 9,282 lines of child speech), was analyzed for frequency of (erroneous) N-omission and D-omission in DPs containing an attributive adjective. This analysis provides a baseline measure of N-omission where it is ungrammatical in the target language.

7.2.4 Results

7.2.4.1 María   María exhibited early mastery, by age 2;01, of agreement-marking for gender and number on both determiners and adjectives. Moreover, her first clear examples of N-drop occur at approximately the same age as her first clear uses of attributive adjectives. N-drop was well attested in María's speech by the age of 2;03, and the utterance taken as the first clear use occurred at 2;01. The early uses of N-drop and overt nouns in DPs with attributive adjectives were as follows:[10]

[2;01: N-drop (FRU)]
> co(e) [= con el] malo, [. . .]
> "with the bad (one)"
> [possibly referring to a dog that had escaped and frightened her]

[2;01: determiner noun adjective]
> [. . .] co(n) el pepe malo, sabes
> "with the bad Joe, you know"
> co(n) el pepe malo que s'ascapao [= se ha escapado], [. . .]
> "with the bad Joe that got loose"

---

[10] Spanish allows N-drop not only with adjectives, but also with PPs headed by *de* "of", and with relative clauses introduced by *que* "that". A check of María's corpus revealed that these forms of N-drop entered her speech only slightly later than adjectival N-drop. The first clear uses (soon followed by regular use) were *la de Pulgacito* "the (one) about Pulgacito" at age 2;03, and *lo que no quieres* "the (thing) that you do not want" at 2;04.

At least two of the utterances produced by María merit special comment. First, the word *uno* in *uno más pequeño* (at age 2;03) is a special form of the indefinite masculine singular article that is required (instead of *un*) when N-drop has occurred. Thus, María correctly substitutes *uno* for *un* in this example. Second, the word *otro* is ambiguous in Spanish between (at least) adjectival ("other") and determiner ("another") uses. In the example *ot(r)o neg(r)o y ot(r)o neg(r)o, los dos* ("another black (one) and another black (one), the two", at age 2;03), María presumably intends *otro* as a determiner.

[2;02: No relevant utterances]

[2;03: N-drop]
    un bicho, voy a bu(s)ca(r) los gigantes
      "a bug, I'm going to look for the giant (ones)"
      [looking at picture book]
    ot(r)o neg(r)o y ot(r)o neg(r)o, los dos
      "another black (one) and another black (one), the two"
    ahora viene ot(r)a chiquitita
      "now comes another tiny (one)"
    uno más pequeño
      "a smaller (one)"
    mira, a unos pequeños
      "look, some small (ones)"

[2;03: determiner noun adjective]
    [...] en el coche grande
      "in the big car"
    [...] los patitos bonitos
      "the pretty ducks"
    [...] que he tomado un trago g(r)ande
      "since I've drunk a big gulp"

In the period from 2;01 to 2;03, excluding unclear utterances and closed-class modifiers (specifically, the possessive pronouns and uses of *otro* "(an)other" as a determiner), María produces seven masculine-singular attributive adjectives (*malo* [three uses], *neg(r)o*, *pequeño*, and *grande* [two uses]), one feminine-singular attributive adjective (*chiquitita*), and three masculine-plural attributive adjectives (*gigantes*, *pequeños*, and *bonitos*). In all eleven cases, the gender-number marking is consistent with the determiner and the (overt or understood) noun.

Examination of María's speech at age 2;01 already provides clear evidence for knowledge of the gender- and number-marking on Spanish determiners. At 2;01 María's masculine-singular determiners (29 uses) include *el* "the", *un* "a", and *ese* "that", as well as three non-adult forms with overextension of the regular masculine-singular ending *-o*: *uno* (for the adult form = *un*) "a", *eso* (for the adult form = *ese*) "that", and *e(s)to* (for the adult form = *este*) "this". Her feminine-singular determiners (37 uses) include *la* "the", *una* "a", *e(s)ta* "this", and *mucha* "much". Masculine-plural determiners (four uses) are *unos* "some" and

TABLE 7.2 Number-marking on María's determiners at age 2;01

| | | Required: | |
		Singular	Plural
Produced:	Singular	50	2
	Plural	0	11

Fisher Exact Test (two-tailed): $p < .001$

los "the"; and the sole feminine-plural determiner (seven uses) is *las* "the".

Of the seventy-seven determiner uses at 2;01, the correct adult form can be determined in all but fourteen cases (eight unclear cases involving a masculine-singular determiner, and six unclear cases involving a feminine-singular determiner). Of the sixty-three clear cases, 100 percent are correct in gender agreement, and all but two (96.8 percent) are correct in number agreement. As shown in Tables 7.2 and 7.3, the contingencies between the required gender/number-marking and the gender/number-marking actually produced are both robust and statistically significant. Hence, by the age of 2;01, when open-class attributive adjectives first appeared in María's speech, María already controlled the masculine/feminine distinction and the singular/plural distinction in the Spanish determiner system. The early attributive adjectives found from 2;01 to 2;03 were correctly marked for gender and number, and were almost evenly divided between overt-noun environments (five cases) and N-drop environments (six cases).

TABLE 7.3 Gender-marking on María's determiners, at 2;01

| | | Required: | |
		Masculine	Feminine
Produced:	Masculine	25	0
	Feminine	0	38

Fisher Exact Test (two-tailed): $p < .001$

7.2.4.2 Eve   A possible concern about the data from María is that her (apparent) early uses of N-drop could result from performance-related omission of nouns, rather than knowledge of the grammatical option of N-drop in adult Spanish. To evaluate the possible role of performance-related omission of nouns, independent of grammatical N-drop, in María's data, we examined the longitudinal corpus for the English-learning child Eve, whose speech was sampled at approximately two-week intervals between the ages of 1;06 and 2;03. Given that N-drop is ungrammatical in adult English, any N-omission observed in child English presumably reflects either performance-based word omission, or the use of a non-target grammar.

To measure the frequency of N-omission in the Eve corpus, color terms were chosen as representative of the child's early adjectives. All child utterances containing one of the adjectives *red, orange, yellow, green, blue, purple, black, white, gray/grey, pink,* or *brown* were extracted using the CLAN program COMBO. The resulting utterances were then hand-searched for attributive (DP-internal) uses of the adjectives, which in practice involved a pre-adjectival determiner or a post-adjectival noun (or both). For such utterances the transcript context was then checked, and imitations, routines, repetitions, and otherwise unclear utterances were excluded. The results are presented in Table 7.4, where uses of the adult-English pro-form *one* are indicated separately, in the two rightmost columns.

For present purposes the most important finding is that N-omission was considerably less frequent than either the use of a full "D A N" sequence or the use of a D-less DP ("_ A N" sequence). Thus, the functional element (D) appears to be more susceptible to omission than the content word (N), in Eve's early DPs. The ratio of N-less DPs ("D A _" sequences) to full "D A N" DPs was 10:37. The frequency of N-omission from DPs containing at least a D and an attributive A was therefore only 21.3 percent. In María's corpus, during the period from 2;01 to 2;03, when open-class attributive adjectives were first entering her speech, the ratio of (apparent) N-drop ("D _ A" sequences) to full "D N A" DPs was already 6:5 (N-drop frequency of 54.5 percent). The probability of obtaining six or more cases of apparent N-drop (out of eleven relevant DPs) simply by chance, under the null hypothesis that María's early omission of Ns had the same source and frequency as Eve's, is less than .05: p ($x \geq 6$ | p(omission) = .213, N = 11) = .016 by binomial test. Hence, María's early use of N-drop is significantly

TABLE 7.4 N-omission and D-omission in the Eve corpus

Age	DAN	_AN	DA_	"DA one"	"_ A one"
1;06a	0	0	0	0	0
1;06b	0	0	0	0	0
1;07a	0	0	0	0	0
1;07b	0	0	0	0	0
1;08	0	2	0	0	0
1;09a	1	4	0	1	4
1;09b	0	1	0	0	0
1;09c	0	2	0	0	0
1;10a	0	0	0	0	0
1;10b	2	2	0	0	0
1;11a	2	2	1	1	2
1;11b	0	0	0	0	0
1;12	4	5	0	4	2
2;00	10	3	3	9	3
2;01a	7	1	0	3	1
2;01b	1	0	0	0	0
2;02a	3	1	0	0	1
2;02b	2	3	3	2	1
2;03a	1	1	1	1	1
2;03b	4	1	2	2	0
Total	37	28	10	23	15

greater than would be expected by chance, when we take Eve's rate of N-omission as the baseline.

7.2.4.3 Koki The main finding from the Koki corpus is that Koki mastered agreement-marking for gender and number on determiners and adjectives well before she began using N-drop. Clear uses of open-class, attributive adjectives entered Koki's speech at age 2;02. By this age Koki had already demonstrated productive use of the determiners *el, un, otro, ese, este, mucho* (masculine singular, forty-one uses in the transcripts from 1;07 to 2;02); *la, una, otra, esa, esta* (feminine singular, forty-two uses); *los, muchos, otros* (masculine plural, nine uses); and *las* (feminine plural, three uses). Of these ninety-five determiners, ninety-two (97 percent) agreed with the noun in both gender and number. As shown in Tables 7.5 and 7.6, the contingencies between the required gender/number-marking and the gender/number-marking actually produced are both robust and statistically significant. Also by the age of 2;02, Koki was making correct use of the (masculine and

TABLE 7.5 Number-marking on Koki's determiners between ages 1;07 and 2;02

| | | Required: | |
		Singular	Plural
Produced:	Singular	81	2
	Plural	1	11

Fisher Exact Test (two-tailed): $p < .001$

TABLE 7.6 Gender-marking on Koki's determiners between ages 1;07 and 2;02

| | | Required: | |
		Masculine	Feminine
Produced:	Masculine	50	0
	Feminine	0	45

Fisher Exact Test (two-tailed): $p < .001$

feminine) singular and (masculine and feminine) plural agreement-morphology on adjectives, as well as the plural marker (-s) for nouns.

Yet, Koki's first use of N-drop did not occur until the age of 2;06, and followed some seven uses of full "determiner noun adjective" (or "determiner adjective noun") DPs in the transcripts for the period from 2;02 to 2;05:[11]

[2;01,29]
    e pob(r)e camita
        "the poor (little) bed"
    (l)as medias coloradas
        "the red stockings"

---

[11] Note that in *e pob(r)e camita* (age 2;01,29), Koki substitutes the form *e* for *la*. She appears to use *e* as a gender-neutral "proto-determiner" in some of her earliest speech (cf. among others López-Ornat 1997). Also, notice that in one of her first N-drop examples, *un azul* "a blue (one)" (at age 2;06,10), Koki substitutes *un* for adult-Spanish *uno*.

[2;04,18]
    (l)as medias [='meyas] <amarillos [*>]
      "the yellow stockings"
      [gender mismatch]

[2;05,24]
    el oso chiquitito
      "the little bear"
    el oso # grande
      "the big bear"
    a (e)l osito chiquit(o)
      "(to) the little bear"
    el pelito [/] ve(r)de
      "the green hair"

Among these early attributive uses of adjectives, only one clear error was noted in gender-number agreement between the adjective and the head noun: the gender mismatch in *(l)as medias [='meyas] <amarillos [*]>* "the yellow stockings", at 2;04.

On the other hand, in the transcript where N-drop first appears (transcript 09), N-drop predominates over full determiner–noun–adjective DPs by a ratio of at least 11:1. In fact, the ratio may be as high as 13:1, but we chose to exclude two possible cases of N-drop that were judged to be ambiguous. Uses of N-drop and overt nouns were as follows:[12]

---

[12] Again, it is of interest to check when Koki began using "non-adjectival" N-drop with PPs headed by *de* "of", and with relative clauses headed by *que* "that". The relative-clause construction entered Koki's speech at the same age (2;06,10) as adjectival N-drop. The first clear use was *esto que estaba pegado ahí* "this (thing) that was stuck there". (The form *esto* appears to correspond to the adult-Spanish masculine-singular form *éste*.) The onset of N-drop with *de*-phrases is slightly more difficult to determine. If we adopt the measure of FRU, then the age of acquisition is 2;06,10, and the key utterance is *ése de éste* "that (one) of/about this (one)". Yet, Koki produced one isolated use of this construction much earlier, at age 2;02,27: *ot(r)o del papá* "another (one) of/about the father". Koki was singing when she produced this utterance, which suggests that it could have been part of a memorized song. Following this occurrence there were no clear uses in her transcripts for over three months. After the next use, *ése de éste*, the construction occurred at least once in every transcript. If we discount the isolated occurrence at 2;02, then the evidence from both Koki and María supports analyses in which adjectival and non-adjectival forms of Spanish N-drop have a common grammatical source, possibly related to characteristics of the Spanish determiner, but independent of any property of the Spanish adjective.

[2;06,10: N-drop]

    el pequeño "the small (one)" [2 distinct uses]
    la pequeña "the small (one)" [4 distinct uses]
    esos bonitos "those pretty (ones)"
    un azul "a blue (one)"
    ot(r)o azul "another blue (one)"
    el ot(r)o pegado "the other stuck-on (one)" [2 distinct uses]

Not counted:

    (ver) los # sacaditos "the taken-out (ones)" [? *los* may be clitic or Det]
    la pequeño "the small (one)" [? gender mismatch]

[2;06,10: determiner adjective noun]
      esas bonitas cortinas "those pretty curtains"

Thus, in absolute terms, Koki's first clear use of N-drop occurred approximately four months later than the age at which she began producing clear DPs with overt determiners and attributive adjectives, and also at least four months after she had mastered the system of gender-number agreement on the Spanish determiner. To test whether this temporal gap could have been the result simply of sampling an infrequent construction, we performed a binomial test using the 11:1 ratio observed at age 2;06 between N-drop and overt "determiner–noun–adjective" sequences. We thereby determined the probability of sampling seven full "determiner–noun–adjective" DPs before the first instance of N-drop simply by chance, under the null hypothesis that both constructions were grammatically possible by age 2;02 and had the same relative probability of production observed at age 2;06 (when both were clearly attested in Koki's speech). The resulting probability was substantially less than one in a thousand: $p(x = 7 \mid p$ (overt noun) $= .083, N = 7) < .001$.

7.2.5 Discussion

The findings of this case study have clear implications for the psychological representation of grammatical knowledge: most importantly, the availability of N-drop in Spanish cannot be represented purely as knowledge of a morphological agreement paradigm. Koki clearly mastered all potentially relevant morphological aspects of Spanish significantly earlier than she acquired N-drop.

The findings likewise speak against any account in which overt morphology is the learner's principal source of evidence concerning N-drop. Moreover, the fact that Koki actually added words (i.e. overt nouns), where the adult language would normally omit them, speaks strongly against a performance account of her non-adult utterances, and indicates instead that Koki was obeying the requirements of a grammar different from that of adult Spanish.

Nonetheless, our findings are compatible with certain weaker relationships between N-drop and overt morphology. For example, Kester (1995, 1996) distinguishes between "licensing" and "identification" of the *pro* in N-drop (following Rizzi (1986) on licensing versus identification of null pronominals in Italian). Adopting Kester's distinction between licensing and identification (but diverging considerably in the details), one could consider an analysis for Spanish N-drop in which the non-lexical noun can be identified by overt agreement morphology, but in which the licensing of this empty category depends on separate, more abstract properties.[13]

By distinguishing between licensing and identification we might also account for a discrepancy between our findings and the results of Lillo-Martin (1991) for American Sign Language (ASL). Children learning ASL have been observed to acquire certain types of null arguments in tandem with the spatial agreement system of the language, in contrast to what we have seen for Koki. Yet, both the agreement system and the null arguments in question are acquired considerably later in ASL than is N-drop in Spanish. Thus, if children learning ASL master the language-particular requirements for licensing of null arguments relatively early, perhaps at approximately the age when Koki mastered N-drop, a delay in acquisition of the mechanisms for identification of null arguments would make identification the limiting factor. Null arguments would in this case be expected to appear in tandem with the agreement system, even though the

---

[13] Kester (1995, 1996), however, relates both the identification and the licensing of the empty category in Dutch N-drop to (different) aspects of overt agreement morphology. She proposes that the Dutch adjectival suffix -*e* serves to license *pro*, which in turn can be identified by a lexical antecedent, by the ending -*n* [+human, +plural] or -*s* [+mass] on the adjective, or by grammatical gender features (neuter versus non-neuter) on the determiner. This move, if carried over to Spanish, would be problematic in light of the acquisitional evidence reported here for Koki. To make sense of Koki's pattern of acquisition, the licensing mechanism for Spanish N-drop would at least need to be logically independent of the DP-internal system of agreement morphology.

agreement morphology is not by itself a sufficient condition for null arguments.

A prediction for Spanish N-drop, on this approach, is that only two of the three logically possible acquisitional orderings of agreement morphology and N-drop will in fact be attested: in particular, we should never encounter a child who entirely lacks the DP-internal agreement system of Spanish, and yet employs the adult Spanish option of N-drop. On the other hand, the patterns exhibited by María and Koki are both expected. First, a child may acquire the abstract licensing component of N-drop either prior to, or concurrently with, the morphological agreement system (the identification component). In this case we expect to see N-drop as soon as the child starts producing both DP-internal agreement marking and attributive adjectives; María's data are consistent with this scenario. Alternatively, the child can acquire the morphological agreement system strictly prior to the abstract licensing component of N-drop. If the child starts producing both DP-internal agreement marking and attributive adjectives early enough (before the licensing component is acquired), a clear stage will be evident in which the child produces DPs with overt Ns, and systematically refrains from N-drop. Koki's data are consistent with this second scenario.

A question for future longitudinal studies of Spanish acquisition is whether these two scenarios indeed turn out to be the only ones attested. In addition to analyzing further corpora of spontaneous speech, experimental studies could be useful. While techniques such as grammaticality judgement are generally too demanding for children in the relevant age range of two to three years (McDaniel and Cairns 1996: 248), an elicited-production study might be feasible. The main prediction would be that some of the children exhibiting mastery of the morphological marking for gender and number would nonetheless refrain from producing N-drop, and would instead supply an overt N, in their elicited speech. These would be children who mastered the overt morphology before they acquired the abstract licensing component of N-drop. On the speculation that overt morphological agreement is a necessary (although not sufficient) condition for N-drop, a further prediction would be that children failing to make appropriate morphological distinctions for gender and number would necessarily refrain from using N-drop.

7.2.6 Conclusion

N-drop was among the likeliest candidates for a point of syntactic variation that could be tied directly to a morphological paradigm. Yet, the results of this case study are compatible with only a more limited connection to overt morphology. The results therefore favor a model of the human language faculty in which points of syntactic variation are not fully reducible to the overt inflectional and declensional morphology.

7.3 Preposition-stranding in English

Next let us turn to a case study of children's acquisition of prepositional *wh*-questions. This study was conducted in collaboration with Koji Sugisaki, and the report in this subsection is a revised version of Sugisaki and Snyder (2003). The chief question that we address is whether children begin the language-acquisition process with "default" values for all the points of syntactic variation.

Chomsky (2001*a*) has suggested that prior to linguistic experience, each parameter of UG has a default setting:

(20)   DEFAULT SETTINGS, HYPOTHESIS I (Chomsky 2001*a*:1):
       At S_0 [initial state], all parameters are set with unmarked values.

This is not the only possible situation, however. It might be the case that some parameters have a default specification while others do not, as stated in (21).

(21)   DEFAULT SETTINGS, HYPOTHESIS II:
       Not every parameter has a default setting.

Fodor (1998: 26) points this out explicitly: "There are several possibilities. One is that some or all parameters are in a specific 'unset' state prior to unambiguous triggering."[14] Given this competing view, an important question arises as to whether the stronger position adopted by Chomsky can be maintained, and this awaits an empirical answer.

In this case study we evaluate the views in (20) and (21) with data from child language acquisition. We argue that the acquisition of preposition stranding (P-stranding) in English and of pied-piping in Spanish provides an empirical argument that not every parameter has a default specification, contrary to Chomsky's suggestion.

---

[14] Similarly, Clark's (1992) approach to parameter-setting in terms of natural selection does not postulate default settings.

7.3.1 Default values of parameters: evidence from acquisition

In this subsection we briefly review two pieces of evidence provided in the acquisition literature for the existence of default parameter-settings. The first piece of evidence comes from the seminal study of early null subjects by Hyams (1986). It has been reported at least since the 1970s that child English (around the age of two) permits both overt and null subjects (Bloom, Lightbown, and Hood 1975). In addition, overt expletives are reportedly absent during this stage. These characteristics are shared by adult Italian and Spanish, as illustrated in (23).

(22) CHILD ENGLISH:

(22a)   _want more apples. / I want doggie.

(22b)   Yes, _is toys in there.   "Yes there are toys in there."

(23) ITALIAN (Hyams 1986: 30–1, 70)

(23a)   Mangia una mela.   "Eats an apple."
        Gianni mangia una mela.   "Gianni eats an apple."

(23b)   Piove oggi.   "Rains today."

Hyams explained this observation in the following way. UG is equipped with a parameter that divides languages into two major types, null-subject languages like Italian/Spanish, and non-null-subject languages like English, and the value that corresponds to the former is specified as the default. As a consequence, child English exhibits the properties of adult Italian/Spanish.[15]

The second argument for default settings is presented in the study of children's wh-questions by McDaniel, Chiu, and Maxfield (1995). Their study is based on the observation, originally reported in de Villiers, Roeper, and Vainikka (1990) and Thornton (1990), that English-learning children (around the age of three to five years) sometimes produce wh-questions as in (24) in experimental situations. According to McDaniel et al., such "wh-copying" constructions are also used by adult speakers of Romani (as illustrated in 25) and in certain dialects of German.

(24) CHILD ENGLISH (Thornton 1990: 87):
      <u>What</u> do you think <u>what</u> Cookie Monster eats?

---

[15] For arguments against the account of Hyams (1986), see Bloom (1990) and Valian (1991), among others.

(25)   ROMANI (McDaniel *et al.* 1995: 712):

    Kas   mislin-e   kas   o
    who-ACC think-2SG.PRS who-ACC the-NOM.M.SG
    Demìr-i   dikh-ol?
    Demir-NOM see-3SG.PRS
    "Who do you think that Demir sees?"

Given the similarity between (24) and (25), McDaniel *et al.* (1995) proposed that there is a parameter determining availability of the *wh*-copying construction, and that the value that permits this construction is specified as the default setting. Hence, children learning English produce *wh*-questions as in (24) in the course of acquisition.

The two pieces of evidence reviewed above suggest that default values have the effects summarized in (26).

(26)   EFFECTS OF DEFAULT SETTINGS:

(26a)   For a certain period of development, the child produces forms that are not observed in the target grammar.

(26b)   The relevant forms are permitted in other adult grammars.

If the strong hypothesis in (20) is correct, then all parameters should exhibit the effects stated in (26), provided that (i) the child is acquiring a language in which the parameter takes its marked value; (ii) the default value permits grammatical constructions that are disallowed under the marked value; and (iii) the child is already producing relevant utterances in her spontaneous speech before the parameter is set to its marked value.[16] In light of the discussion in Chapters 5 and 6, however, we should set higher standards than did Hyams (1986) or McDaniel *et al.* (1995) when evaluating these predictions. First, we should focus on errors of comission, which are far less likely to result from simple processing difficulty than the omission errors considered by Hyams.

Second, we should examine spontaneous speech, which is far less likely to contain substantive violations of the child's own grammar than is evidence from the experimental tasks employed by McDaniel and colleagues.

Note that if children are in fact grammatically conservative in their spontaneous speech, then we do not expect default settings to play a very large part in the language-acquisition process. The only default

---

[16] In other words, the predictions do not hold for parameters that are set "very early" (by the beginning of multi-word combinations, around 1;6). See Wexler (1998: 29) for a proposed list of such early-set parameters.

settings that would be compatible with grammatical conservatism are those that result in a proper subset of the phenomena associated with the marked setting. In other words, if the default setting makes it possible for the child to use grammatical constructions that are unavailable under the marked setting, then generally we would expect to see substantive errors (i.e. errors of comission) in the spontaneous speech of children acquiring languages with the marked setting.

In the present case study we will test this prediction directly, by investigating the acquisition of P-stranding in English, and of pied-piping in Spanish. First, though, we will summarize several accounts of cross-linguistics variation in the availability of P-stranding. Our focus will be on the characteristics that are shared by these different accounts.

7.3.2 Parameters of preposition-stranding: a brief history

It is well known that languages differ with respect to the movement possibilities for prepositional complements. For example, in English, the *wh*-movement of a prepositional complement can strand the preposition, while in Romance languages like Spanish, prepositions must be pied-piped along with the *wh*-word.

(27)   ENGLISH: Which subject did they talk <u>about</u> *t* ?

(28)   SPANISH:

(28a)   *[Cuál asunto] habl-aba-n   [<u>sobre</u> *t*] ?
         which subject speak-IPFV-3PL about

(28b)   [<u>Sobre</u> cuál   asunto] hablaban   *t* ?
         about which subject speak-IPFV-3PL

A number of attempts have been made to formulate a parameter of P-stranding, and several of these are summarized below.[17]

One of the earliest works on P-stranding, van Riemsdijk (1978: 275), suggested that the possibility of P-stranding (with *wh*-movement) in English results from the availability of the "COMP" position in PPs (which would correspond to [Spec, PP] in current terms): PPs constitute an island in every language, but in English they can project a COMP position, and as a consequence, *wh*-movement of the prepositional complement can use that position as an "escape hatch", making P-stranding possible. In those languages that do not have this COMP

---

[17] There are many syntactic studies of P-stranding that are not discussed here. See Abels (2003), Ayano (2001), and Stowell (1981), for example.

position, the entire PP is moved in order to avoid an island violation. The relevant parameter is stated in (29).

(29)   PARAMETER (van Riemsdijk 1978: 275):
        A language {has, does not have} COMP position within PP.

An alternative account was proposed by Hornstein and Weinberg (1981: 63), who claimed that cross-linguistic variation in P-stranding stems from the availability of a certain syntactic operation, rather than a certain syntactic position. Specifically, they proposed a syntactic rule of *Reanalysis*, which creates a complex verb from a verb and any set of contiguous elements to its right in the domain of VP. For example, this operation creates the structure in (30b) from the one in (30a).[18] The availability of this operation is parameterized, as shown in (31).

(30a)   John [$_{VP}$ [$_V$ talked] [$_{PP}$ about Fred]].

(30b)   John [$_{VP}$ [$_V$ talked about] Fred].

(31)   PARAMETER:
        A language {has, does not have} the Reanalysis operation.

According to Hornstein and Weinberg, UG provides a universal filter that rules out traces marked with oblique Case, the Case that is assigned by prepositions. Given this filter, *wh*-movement of prepositional complements is excluded under ordinary circumstances. Yet, in languages like English that have the Reanalysis rule, a verb and a preposition may undergo this operation, and as a result, the NP in the complement of a preposition can be assigned objective Case by the complex verb. Thus, P-stranding does not induce a violation of the relevant UG filter in English. In contrast, languages like Spanish do not have the Reanalysis operation, and thus *wh*-movement of prepositional complements must pied-pipe the preposition in order to avoid violating the UG filter.

The previous two analyses have been quite influential, but they share one conceptual disadvantage: the proposed parameters are narrow in scope, in the sense that they are relevant only to the phenomenon of P-stranding. As discussed in Chapter 2, Section 2.1.1, considerations of learnability favor having smaller numbers of parameters, each with consequences for a greater range of surface phenomena: the result is that the child has fewer opportunities for error, and has more types of evidence available to guide her decisions. Hence, a parameter for P-stranding becomes conceptually more attractive when it has additional consequences for the surface grammar.

---

[18] See Baltin and Postal (1996) for empirical challenges faced by the Reanalysis proposal.

Kayne (1981) proposes a parameter of this type.[19] He argues that the possibility of P-stranding is associated with the availability of what we will call the prepositional complementizer (PC) construction, namely an infinitival clause with an overt subject headed by a (possibly null) prepositional complementizer.

(32a)   English: John wants [$_{CP}$ (for)   [$_{IP}$ Mary to leave]].

(32b)   Spanish: *Juan quiere [$_{CP}$ (para) [$_{IP}$ María salir]].

Kayne claims that English prepositions are structural governors, and their government domain extends to the nearest barrier. Prepositions in Romance languages, however, govern only in the sense of subcategorization, and their government domain is restricted to their sister. Given this difference, case-assignment by the prepositional complementizer to the subject of an infinitival clause is possible in English but not in Spanish, leading to the contrast illustrated in (32). Furthermore, under Kayne's system, even though Reanalysis is available in every language, UG dictates that this rule can apply only when prepositions and verbs govern in the same way. English satisfies this condition, since both prepositions and verbs structurally govern NP. On the other hand, Romance prepositions never meet this condition, because they differ from verbs in that their governing domain extends only to their sister. This way, the contrast between English and Spanish regarding P-stranding also follows from the difference in the government properties of prepositions. The parameter that Kayne proposed is formulated in (33).

(33)   PARAMETER:

(33a)   P structurally governs NP

(33b)   P governs NP only in the sense of subcategorization.

Kayne's (1981) parametric system is quite attractive, in that it covers not only cross-linguistic variation in P-stranding but also variation in the PC construction, but it cannot be maintained in the current Minimalist framework.[20] Kayne's parameter crucially relies on the notion of *government*, which is abandoned in the present

---

[19]   Kayne (1981) attempts to explain the contrast between English and French, but we use examples from Spanish for ease of exposition. This will not affect the main point of Kayne's proposal.

[20]   Nonetheless, there is evidence from acquisition which suggests that Kayne's basic idea might be on the right track. See Sugisaki, Snyder, and Yaffee (2000) and Sugisaki (2003) for details.

framework due to its lack of conceptual necessity (Chomsky 1995: 176). In light of this theoretical development, a Minimalist parameter of P-stranding has been proposed by Law (1998), which is given in (34).[21]

(34)   PARAMETER:
A language {has, does not have} D-to-P incorporation.

If the positive value of the parameter in (34) is taken, as in Spanish, the head of the DP in the complement of P always incorporates into P. This syntactic incorporation is sometimes reflected in morphology as P+D suppletive forms.

(35)   P+D SUPPLETIVE FORM IN SPANISH:
Juan habló <u>d-el</u>   asunto más difícil.
Juan talked about-the subject most difficult
"Juan talked about the most difficult subject."

Under the assumption that *wh*-words belong to the category D, they always incorporate into the preposition, and hence *wh*-movement to the specifier of CP necessarily results in pied-piping of the preposition. On the other hand, a language like English, which takes the negative setting of the parameter, has no D-to-P incorporation, and as a consequence, the language has neither a P+D suppletive form nor obligatory pied-piping.

(36a)   Languages with the positive setting:
[$_{CP}$ [$_{IP}$ ...   [$_{VP}$ ...   [$_{PP}$ P+D   [$_{DP}$ t$_D$ NP]]]]]
                                              about   which   subject

(36b)   Languages with the negative setting:
[$_{CP}$ [$_{IP}$ ...   [$_{VP}$ ...   [$_{PP}$ P   [$_{DP}$ D   NP]]]]]
                                              about   which subject

At this point we have seen four proposals that vary considerably but have an important point in common: namely, there exists a parameter of P-stranding that comprises two values, one leading to the availability of P-stranding and the other leading to obligatory pied-piping.[22] This

---

[21] A similar idea is independently developed in Salles (1997). See Isobe and Sugisaki (2002) for an acquisitional evaluation of Law's (1998) parametric system.

[22] An alternative approach would be to posit two independent parameters, one for P-stranding and one for pied-piping, but none of the proposals reviewed above actually takes this approach. Accordingly, we will defer further discussion of this possibility until Chapter 8.

basic property, combined with the hypothesis in (20), means that one of the two predictions in (37) should hold:

(37a)   *Prediction A*:
If the P-stranding value is the default, then children learning either English *or* Spanish should use P-stranding when they first begin to apply *wh*-movement to prepositional objects.

(37b)   *Prediction B*:
If the pied-piping value is the default, then children learning English should pass through a pied-piping stage before they begin to use P-stranding.

7.3.3 Evaluating the predictions: transcript analyses

In order to evaluate the predictions in (37), we examined sponta-neous speech data from children acquiring English or Spanish as their first language. For English, we selected ten longitudinal corpora from CHILDES, yielding a total sample of more than 124,000 lines of child speech. For each child, we located the first clear uses of (a) a direct-object *wh*-question, and (b) a *wh*-question or null-operator construc-tion involving the complement to a preposition. The English corpora we analyzed are summarized in Table 7.7.

For Spanish, we analyzed four longitudinal corpora, to obtain a total sample of 22,130 lines of child speech. Three corpora are from CHILDES, and one corpus was recorded and transcribed in our lab-oratory at the University of Connecticut, as part of the CLESS project (Child Language Early Syntax Study). The Spanish corpora we exam-ined are described in Table 7.8.

TABLE 7.7 English corpora analyzed

Child	Collected by	Age	# of utterances
Abe	Kuczaj (1976)	2;04,24–2;08,18	3,110
Adam	Brown (1973)	2;03,04–2;07,00	9,254
Allison	Bloom (1973)	1;04,21–2;10,00	2,192
April	Higginson (1985)	1;10,00–2;11,00	2,321
Eve	Brown (1973)	1;06,00–2;03,00	12,473
Naomi	Sachs (1983)	1;02,29–4;09,03	16,634
Nina	Suppes (1973)	1;11,16–3;00,03	23,586
Peter	Bloom (1970)	1;09,08–3;01,20	26,898
Sarah	Brown (1973)	2;03,05–3;05,13	17,881
Shem	Clark (1978)	2;02,16–2;08,29	10,311

TABLE 7.8 Spanish corpora analyzed

Child	Collected by	Age	# of utterances
Juan	Jose Linaza	1;7–4;11	2,577
Koki	Rosa Montes	1;7–2;11	4,548
Maria	Susana Lopez-Ornat	1;7–3;11	8,433
Inés	UConn CLESS Project	1;2–2;5	6,572

The CLAN program COMBO was used, together with complete files of prepositions and *wh*-words in English and Spanish, to identify potentially relevant child utterances. These were then searched by hand and checked against the original transcripts to exclude imitations, repetitions, and formulaic routines. The age of acquisition for a given construction was taken as the FRU (First of Repeated Uses, as described in Chapter 5). The ages of acquisition for Spanish are shown in Table 7.9, and the actual utterances are presented in an appendix at the end of this chapter.

Among the four children, Koki and María acquired both direct-object *wh*-question and pied-piping by the end of their corpora. For these children, the ages of acquisition for these two properties were quite close to each other. For the remaining two children, the first clear use of a direct-object *wh*-question appeared late in their corpora, and there was no clear use of pied-piping. Crucially, no Spanish-learning child showed any use of P-stranding. This result is consistent with the view that the default for the P-stranding Parameter is the setting that leads to pied-piping, but also with the view that neither setting is a default.

Let us now turn to English. Of the ten children, nine acquired both direct-object *wh*-questions and P-stranding by the end of their corpora.

TABLE 7.9 Ages of acquisition (Spanish)

Child	Direct object *wh*-question	Pied-piping
Juan	3;09	—
Koki	2;03,21	2;04,18
María	2;00	2;01
Inés	2;05,11	—

TABLE 7.10 Ages of acquisition (English)

Child	Direct object *wh*-question	P-stranding
Abe	2;05,00	2;07,07
Adam	2;05,00	2;05,00
Allison	2;10,00	—
April	2;01,00	2;09,00
Eve	1;08,00	2;02,00
Naomi	1;11,30	2;08,30
Nina	2;01,12	2;09,13
Peter	2;01,18	2;05,03
Sarah	2;10,11	3;03,07
Shem	2;02,16	2;06,06
Average	2;03	2;07

The ages of acquisition are summarized in Table 7.10, and the actual utterances are presented in the Appendix.[23]

In order to evaluate the statistical significance of observed age differences between the acquisition of direct-object *wh*-questions and the acquisition of P-stranding, we counted the number of clear uses of the earlier construction before the first clear use of the later construction. We next calculated the relative frequency of the two constructions in the child's own speech, starting with the transcript after the first use of the later construction, and continuing for the next ten transcripts or through the end of the corpus (whichever came first). We then used the binomial test to obtain the probability of the child's producing at least the observed number of examples of the first construction, before starting to use the second construction, simply by chance. The null hypothesis for the test is that the second construction was grammatically available at least as early as the first construction, and had the same relative frequency observed in later transcripts.

The results are summarized in Table 7.11. Of the nine children who acquired both properties, four (Abe, Eve, Naomi, and Shem) acquired direct-object *wh*-questions significantly earlier than P-

[23] Note that our findings for P-stranding are consistent with the elicited-production results of McDaniel, McKee, and Bernstein (1998), who successfully elicited P-stranding relative clauses (e.g. *the one that the girl is jumping over*) from their youngest group of subjects (3;05 to 5;11).

TABLE 7.11 Results of binomial tests

| Child | Relative frequency | | p-value |
	Direct object *wh*-question	P-stranding	
Abe	.583	.417	$(.583)^{11} < .01$
Adam	—	—	—
Allison	—	—	—
April	.842	.158	$(.842)^{1} > .10$
Eve	.818	.182	$(.818)^{48} < .001$
Naomi	.833	.166	$(.833)^{42} < .001$
Nina	.826	.174	$(.826)^{12} > .10$
Peter	.904	.096	$(.904)^{26} = .073$
Sarah	.786	.214	$(.786)^{10} = .090$
Shem	.714	.286	$(.714)^{18} < .01$

stranding ($p < .01$). For two others (Peter, Sarah) the difference was marginally significant ($p < .10$). Moreover, every child showed productive use of PPs before the first clear use of a direct-object *wh*-question. Therefore, the acquisition of PP is not responsible for the delayed acquisition of P-stranding. Since these children did not use P-stranding as soon as they acquired *wh*-movement, Prediction A in (37) is falsified: the value that leads to P-stranding cannot be the default.

Furthermore, in the utterances of these six children, we found no example of pied-piping before the acquisition of P-stranding. Since these English-learning children did not pass through a pied-piping stage, Prediction B in (37) is also false: the value that leads to pied-piping cannot be the default, either.

7.3.4 Conclusions

In sum, the acquisitional evidence from English and Spanish clearly indicates the following: If there is indeed a binary parameter for prepositional questions, with pied-piping and P-stranding as the two options, then neither setting of this parameter is a default: neither pied-piping nor P-stranding is employed until the child determines the correct choice for her target grammar. The broader implications of this result will be considered in Chapter 8, Section 8.5.

Appendix: FRUs from Section 7.3

English: [(a) = direct-object question, (b) = P-stranding]

Abe:
(a)	*ABE: what you doing?	(Transcript 002, Line 119)
(b)	*ABE: Mom # what's that for?	(Tr. 21, L. 274)

Adam:
(a)	*ADA: what shell doing?	(Tr. 05, L. 24)
(b)	*ADA: where dat come from?	(Tr. 05, L. 9)

Allison:
(a)	*ALI: what does the pig say.	(Tr. 6, L. 411)

April:
(a)	*APR: what goat say?	(Tr. 02, L. 854)
(b)	*APR: owl to play with.	(Tr. 04, L. 419)

Eve:
(a)	*EVE: what doing # Mommy?	(Tr. 05, L. 69)
(b)	*EVE: it's a bathtub for a boy get in.	(Tr. 18, L. 1980)

Naomi:
(a)	*NAO: what-'is Mommy doing?	(Tr. 34, L. 78)
(b)	*NAO: what-'is this go in?	(Tr. 70, L. 105)

Nina:
(a)	*NIN: what is daddy holding?	(Tr. 14, L. 1119)
(b)	*NIN: who's that you talking to #. Momma	(Tr. 32, L. 1429)

Peter:
(a)	*PET: Mommy # what you doing.	(Tr. 08, L. 528)
(b)	*PET: what this come from?	(Tr. 13, L. 2043)

Sarah:
(a)	*SAR: what my doing?	(Tr. 033, L. 522)
(b)	*SAR: whe(r)e you at.	(Tr. 052, L. 332)

Shem:
(a)	*SHE: what is mommy doing?	(Tr. 01, L. 539)
(b)	*SHE: i(t)'s step for sitting on.	(Tr. 15, L. 801)

Spanish: [(a) = direct-object question, (b) = pied-piping]

Juan:
(a)	*NIN: zapatillas de deporte no # no cuál zapatillas de deporte me pongo cuál me pongo.	(Tr. J39, L. 76)

"tennis shoes no # no which tennis shoes am-I-putting-on
which am-I-putting-on?"

Koki:

(a)   *KOK: qué tiene?   (Tr. 06Mar81, L. 152)
       "what does-he-have?"

(b)   *KOK: &pa [/] para qué la comp(r)ó?   (Tr. 07Apr81, L. 400)
       "for what it bought?" (i.e. "what did he buy it for?")

María:

(a)   *CHI: qué tomas?
       "what are-you-eating?"   (Tr. 200, L. 313)

(b)   *CHI: [% señalando a la cámara]   (Tr. 201, L. 321)
       xxx de quién es?
       [pointing to the camera]
       "xxx of whom is?" (i.e. "to whom does it belong?")

Inés:

(a)   *INE: qué lo hacía más?   (Tr. 126, L. 1421)
       "what did-he-do it else" (i.e. "what else did he do?")

8

Conclusions: Grammatical Conservatism and Cross-Linguistic Variation

In the preceding chapters I first surveyed the leading theories of exactly what the child must acquire, in order to know the syntax and phonology of her native language. I then turned to the ways in which acquisitional data can be used to evaluate such theories. In several of the chapters I presented evidence that children make remarkably few of the logically possible errors as they acquire the grammar of their target language. In particular, in children's spontaneous speech, syntactic errors of comission are strikingly rare. When such errors do occur they belong to one of a few consistent types.

In this chapter I will briefly review the main points of the earlier chapters, and then I will explore the implications of this special property, grammatical conservatism, for the nature of grammatical knowledge. How is it possible for the child to avoid errors of comission? How can she keep track of what she does not yet know? How can her language faculty even function, without temporarily adopting provisional, and potentially incorrect, grammatical options?

Indeed, the very fact of grammatical conservatism has important implications for explanatory adequacy. To achieve explanatory adequacy, a theory of grammar must now be able to solve a somewhat stronger version of the Logical Problem of Language Acquisition: How, in principle, could a *grammatically conservative* learner identify the correct grammar from among the permitted options, given only the types of information that are in fact required by children? I will argue that this version of the Logical Problem provides new insights into the nature of the human language faculty.

8.1 What must the child acquire?

Chapter 2 surveyed current proposals about the syntactic information that a child must acquire. The two leading frameworks are
Principles-and-Parameters (P&P) and the Minimalist Program (MP).
With respect to the information that the child must acquire, the fundamental difference is that MP calls for all the points of syntactic
variation to be located outside syntax proper, preferably in the lexicon,
while P&P does not impose this restriction. As we saw in Sections 2.2.3
through 2.2.5, actual MP accounts of syntactic variation differ in the
degree to which they actually obey this restriction, or perhaps simply
in their interpretation of what the restriction means. Here I would like
to explore some of the possible interpretations.

In Section 2.2.2 I provided what I take to be a standard interpretation,
namely that *lexicon* refers to the listed idiosyncrasies of particular, individual words. On this interpretation, the conceptual appeal of reducing
syntactic variation to lexical variation lies in the fact that the lexicon is
independently required as a repository of learned information, namely
the actual words of the language. If we grant that the lexicon includes
entries for functional heads, as well as open-class words, then the child
must acquire the particular syntactic features that are included in her
language's lexical entries for each of these functional heads. (On this
interpretation, the actual inventory of functional heads is constant
across languages.)

We saw in Section 2.2.3 that Longobardi's Referentiality Parameter
conforms to this version of lexical variation, while in Sections 2.2.4
and 2.2.5 we saw that the same could not be said for Bobaljik and
Thráinsson's (1998) Split IP Parameter or Bošković's (2004) DP Parameter. The latter two proposals fall squarely within MP in most respects, but postulate points of syntactic variation that cannot be reduced
to differences in the lexical entry for any single, universally attested
functional head. Rather, they take the form of cross-linguistic differences in the inventory of functional heads that the language employs.

This amounts to an alternative interpretation of the term *lexicon*.
In addition to listed information about specific vocabulary items, the
lexicon might be taken to include information about which of the
possible functional heads the language actually employs. To a first
approximation, this resembles the simple presence or absence of a
particular word in the vocabulary of a given language, and therefore
seems unobjectionable.

Yet, this first approximation is misleading. Take Boškovič's DP Parameter, for example. In a language that normally requires the presence of a DP layer above NP, simply omitting the determiner in a particular sentence does not suddenly make Japanese-style scrambling grammatical (even if all the other requirements for this type of scrambling happen to be present in the language). The positive setting of the DP Parameter requires the presence of a DP layer, and regardless of the particular lexical items that are included in the numeration, failure to satisfy this requirement results in ungrammaticality, not new possibilities for scrambling.

In contrast, when a language has a given open-class word available in its lexicon, the use of that word in any particular sentence remains optional. The properties encoded in its lexical entry have no effect on a sentence whose numeration does not contain it. When a language takes the positive setting of the DP Parameter, however, not only does the lexicon provide one or more lexical items with the D feature, but indeed the use of those lexical items becomes obligatory.

Perhaps we could say that the setting of the DP Parameter is lexically encoded, by the presence or absence of words in the lexicon that have a D feature. If, and only if, a language has at least one such word in its lexicon, then it must include a DP layer above every NP. I think this is a reasonable way of construing the DP Parameter as a point of lexical variation, but it requires the syntactic component to have exceptionally broad access to the lexicon: C_{HL} will need to examine the entire lexicon, not simply the lexical items that are selected for a particular numeration, in order to decide whether a DP layer is required above a given NP.

Bobaljik (1995) suggests (or at least hints at) still another way of interpreting the term *lexicon* for purposes of MP treatments of cross-linguistic variation. His suggestion has been referred to as *bundling* by researchers working within the Distributed Morphology framework (e.g. Marantz 2001). The leading idea is that the inflectional features for a given sentence need to be "bundled together" into discrete lexical items before they can be inserted into the numeration. Languages then might vary parametrically in the types of features that go together in the same bundle. The [+SIP] languages keep AGRs, T, and AGRo features in separate bundles, while [−SIP] languages place the three types of features together in a single bundle.

Note that once again, the point of parametric variation is not encoded in terms of the listed properties of any single lexical item.

Moreover, Bobaljik's suggestion is to use an abstract parameter, one that might be difficult to reduce to the presence or absence of particular types of words in the lexicon (in the way I suggested above for the DP Parameter). The parameter is outside C_{HL}, however, in the sense that it concerns the material inserted into the numeration, before the syntactic derivation begins. The parameter can also be construed as lexical, at least in the sense that it concerns the contents of word-level constituents (i.e. syntactic heads).

The next question is whether Bobaljik's approach is really distinct from the P&P approach to syntactic variation. The best answer may be that it simply represents a more restricted version of the standard P&P approach. The point of parametric variation expressed by the SIP, at least on the "bundling" view, does lie outside C_{HL} proper. The SIP has effects, but only indirect ones, on the actual syntactic derivation.

The claim that the SIP is a point of "lexical" variation may be more contentious, but at least from the perspective of Distributed Morphology (Halle and Marantz 1993) it makes good sense. In Distributed Morphology the lexicon is reconceived in a fairly radical way. The heads that are inserted in the syntactic numeration contain only syntactic and semantic features, not phonological material. The phonological material is not inserted until after the point of spell-out. Hence, the MP directive to keep information about syntactic variation "in the lexicon" requires some special work. If the actual vocabulary items are chosen only post-syntactically, too late to affect the course of the syntactic derivation, then the packaging of the features for the numeration is perhaps the only sort of "lexical" information that could have an effect on the syntax.

In sum, at least three interpretations of *lexical* are available. First, setting aside the special assumptions of Distributed Morphology, the term *lexical* might refer to listed information about individual lexical items, including functional heads, that are available for inclusion in the numeration. This interpretation is attractive because it makes the acquisition of syntactic knowledge conceptually quite similar to the acquisition of open-class words.

Second, the term *lexical* might refer to parameters whose value can be encoded through the presence or absence of a particular type of item in the lexicon. As we saw above for the DP Parameter, this approach may require C_{HL} to survey the entire lexicon, rather than just the particular lexical items chosen for a single numeration. Nonetheless, the information that varies across languages is indeed stored in the form of listed information about the vocabulary of the language.

Finally, the term *lexical* might refer to parametric variation in the bundling of features, at the point of insertion into the syntactic numeration. This interpretation is the farthest from the traditional idea that the lexicon is simply a repository of listed, idiosyncratic information about particular words. Nonetheless, as we have seen for the SIP, it permits cross-linguistic variation to be factored out of C_{HL} proper, the actual engine of the syntactic derivation. Moreover, it constitutes an intriguing point of contact between Minimalist Syntax and Distributed Morphology.

In Chapter 3 I turned to the corresponding question for phonology: What is the nature of the information that the child must acquire, according to the theories that are currently the most influential in phonology? There I chose to focus on two frameworks, OT Phonology (Optimality Theory) and Government Phonology (GP). In GP the answer was that the child must set switch-like parameters, directly analogous to the parameters of P&P syntax. In OT, however, the answer was that the child must deduce the correct ranking of a universal set of constraints (CON). Each language's grammar takes the form of a specific ranking.

In Chapter 3 I devoted considerable attention to the question of whether acquisitional data can help us decide between these two approaches. The answer was far less clear than I would have liked. The trouble is that OT is not so much a theory as a technique: a way of modeling constraint interaction. The constraints themselves are up for grabs, and indeed, GP phonologists are nowadays experimenting with the implementation of GP proposals within an OT framework. Hence, the question of deciding between GP and OT was ill-posed.

The broader question of deciding between constraint-ranking and switch-like parameters is only slightly better. As observed by Tesar and Smolensky (2000), an OT grammar is equivalent to a collection of binary "dominance parameters": each constraint either dominates, or is dominated by, each of the other constraints in CON.

The most distinctive characteristic of the OT system is that changing one dominance relation tends to have collateral effects on other dominance relations. Suppose that CON includes three constraints C_1 through C_3, and the learner's initial hypothesis is that they are unranked: $\{C_1, C_2, C_3\}$. If the learner demotes C_2 below C_1, the new grammar will be $\{C_1, C_3\} >> C_2$. This has the desired effect of moving C_2 below C_1, but it also has the collateral effect of ranking C_2 below C_3.

In principle this situation could lead to a distinctive acquisitional prediction: in the course of acquiring the correct constraint ranking, the child will necessarily adopt relative rankings that are unmotivated by the data. Such rankings could easily lead to substantive errors of comission that would be detectable in children's spontaneous speech.

My attempt to illustrate this type of prediction in Section 3.1.3 was only partially successful, however. There I chose the much discussed Basic CV Syllable Theory of (Prince and Smolensky 2004) as a test domain, and had considerable difficulty in constructing a situation in which the learner would be expected to make errors of comission. The reason was that the constraints in this theory interact with one another only minimally: the constraints affecting onsets (ONSET, FILL^{Ons}, PARSE) and the constraints affecting codas (NoCODA, FILL^{Nuc}, PARSE) have only one point of overlap (PARSE), and can therefore be ranked completely independently of one another. The fact that PARSE affects both onsets and codas means that its demotion to handle a fact about onsets can (temporarily) have undesired effects on the treatment of codas, and vice versa. Yet, the effect of ranking PARSE too low is an error of omission, not comission.

Thus, the most distinctive characteristic of constraint-ranking, namely the prospect of comission errors during the acquisition process, did not in fact arise in the Basic CV Syllable Theory. This situation leads to two questions, which remain open: first, do other influential accounts of cross-linguistic variation in OT involve enough constraint-interaction to predict errors of comission during acquisition, or is the case of the Basic CV Syllable Theory typical? And second, do errors of comission actually occur in the domain of phonology, any more than they do in the domain of syntax? I will leave the first question open, but I will take up the second question in the next section.

8.2 Is the child grammatically conservative?

At this point I would like to review the evidence for children's grammatical conservatism, and address the following questions: What types of errors are found during child language acquisition? How do these errors differ as a function of research methodology (naturalistic observation, elicited production, comprehension)? And how do these errors differ as a function of grammatical domain (syntax, morphology, phonology)?

In Chapter 4 I provided fine-grained information about the error-patterns in children's syntax, when this area of grammar is examined by naturalistic observation. Specifically, I designed and conducted a near-exhaustive search for errors with the English verb–particle construction in the longitudinal corpus for Sarah. This corpus includes over 37,000 child utterances, covers an age span from 2;03 to 5;01, and has a mean gap of only 7.4 days between recordings. Moreover, the first-of-repeated uses (FRUs) for transitive and intransitive verb–particle constructions both occur at age 2;06,20, well after the beginning of the corpus.

The findings for Sarah were typical of spontaneous-speech studies of children's syntax: errors almost always took the form of omission, rather than comission. For example, from the beginning of her corpus through the age of 2;10 (transcript 35), Sarah produced only 32 errors with verb–particle constructions (for an error rate ranging from 0.6 to 6.6 errors per 1,000 utterances), and 29 of these (90.6 percent) were errors of omission. Of the three examples that were coded as comission errors, only one was unambiguously an error: *I [...] go downed* (which appeared in Transcript 34, line 569, of the version of Sarah's corpus used in Chapter 4). Thus, Sarah made a rapid transition from never using the construction to using it in an adult-like fashion, with remarkably few errors and with very nearly zero errors of comission.

This general pattern was replicated in the study of prepositional questions that I reported in Chapter 7, Section 7.3. There Koji Sugisaki and I (2003) examined ten longitudinal corpora for children acquiring English, and four longitudinal corpora for children acquiring Spanish. The question of interest was whether there exists any "default option" for the formation of prepositional questions: Do children acquiring English initially use the pied-piping option that is required in Spanish? Do children acquiring Spanish initially use the P-stranding option that is required in colloquial English?

The findings were that neither error-pattern ever occurred: no child acquiring Spanish ever used P-stranding, and no child acquiring English ever used pied-piping (which would have been an error from the perspective of conversational English). Hence, there was nothing to support the idea that either of these question types was a default option.

Moreover, four of the children acquiring English (Abe, Eve, Naomi, and Shem) passed through a stage in which they were clearly avoiding prepositional questions. Each of these children had a substantial gap between the point at which they were clearly using both PPs and direct-object *wh*-questions, on the one hand, and the point at which they began to use prepositional questions. The gap was statistically significant by binomial test, based on the relative frequency of direct-object questions and prepositional questions in slightly later transcripts.

This finding provides a striking piece of evidence about the nature of grammatical conservatism: when children do not yet know how to construct a given sentence-type correctly, it appears that they actually refrain from producing the sentence-type, rather than risking an error of comission. This is true even though they very probably need the sentence-type for purposes of communication. During this stage the children we examined had no way to express prepositional questions, a type of question that they used reasonably frequently at slightly later ages. This constitutes an especially strong form of conservatism.

At this point, however, I would like to consider the limits of children's grammatical conservatism. The two studies above were both based on naturalistic observation: when children were speaking spontaneously, they successfully avoided syntactic comission errors. I should note, however, that there do exist a few well-known exceptions to grammatical conservatism even in the syntax of children's spontaneous speech.

Some of the most widely discussed examples concern the auxiliary-verb system of English. For example, as observed by Klima and Bellugi (1966), children acquiring English sometimes produce non-inversion errors of the type in (1).

(1)   What I will read? (Adam, age 3;03)

Here the presence of a sentence-initial *wh*-word should trigger subject–auxiliary inversion, but children sometimes produce such questions with the auxiliary left *in situ*.

To assess the frequency of these and other potential errors during children's acquisition of the English auxiliary system, Stromswold (1990) performed an extremely fine-grained analysis of more than 200,000 spontaneous utterances from children acquiring American English, drawn from fourteen longitudinal corpora in CHILDES. The principal findings were as follows. First, the children made astonishingly few of the logically possible comission errors. Second, the comission errors that did occur almost all involved subject–auxiliary inversion: either the failure to invert in a matrix question, or the use of inversion in an embedded question.

According to Stromswold (1990: 71), an average of 7 percent of the children's matrix questions that contained an auxiliary were uninverted, and an average of 10 percent of the children's embedded questions that contained an auxiliary were inverted. Yet, as Stromswold emphasizes, the children's successes were also considerable. For example (1990: 14), children practically never inverted a verb that was not invertible in adult English, and no child consistently failed to invert any given verb that should invert.

Moreover, the situation for inversion was very much the exception rather than the rule. Other potential comission errors, such as the double-tensing error in (2), were extremely rare.

(2)   You didn't caught me. (Sarah, age 3;05,20)

According to Stromswold, double tensing occurred in less than 0.02 percent (31/160,000) of the children's declarative statements (1990: 61), and in only 0.48 percent (195/40,600) of the children's questions (1990: 220–2). More than half of the double-tensing errors involved irregular verbs (1990: 60), where the child may simply have had difficulty retrieving the verb stem from memory.

In sum, the error types in (1) and (2) are both conspicuous when they occur, and it is therefore unsurprising that they have attracted the attention of acquisitionists. Yet, the error type in (2) and most of the other errors of comission that could occur in principle are actually vanishingly rare when one searches for them systematically in transcripts of children's spontaneous speech. English subject–auxiliary inversion is therefore an important exception to children's grammatical conservatism, and it is precisely this exceptional status that acquisitionists should try to explain.

In Chapter 6 we saw that the picture changes considerably when we move from naturalistic observation to elicited production or tests of comprehension. For example, Thornton and Gavruseva (1996) sometimes obtained utterances like (3) from children in the age range of 4;05 to 6;00, using an elicited production task:

(3)   *Who* do you think *'s food* the baboon tried? (Gavruseva 1998: 236, ex.5)

This sentence contains a left-branch extraction, which is a violation of the grammar of adult English and a clear-cut error of comission.

Does this mean that the children in Thornton and Gavruseva's study had actually hypothesized an incorrect grammar, one that would be more appropriate for a language like Russian that permits left-branch extraction? The evidence reviewed in Chapter 5 suggested that they had not. Specifically, when Chen et al. (1998) conducted an elicited-production study modeled on Thornton and Gavruseva's, we found

that children in this age range did produce a number of examples that
could be analyzed as involving left-branch extraction, but that most of
these involved clear dysfluencies, as illustrated in (4) (see Chapter 6,
Section 6.1.1, for a full list).

(4a)   Whose is thinks this is his # whose bottle? (Subject #7, age 4;08)

(4b)   Whose you thinks # that # that's bottle belongs to? (Subject #9,
        age 4;04)

The utterances in (4) clearly conform neither to the grammar of adult
English nor the grammar of adult Russian. Instead, the child appears to
have been "painted into a corner" by the experimenter's lead-in, "Ask
Dino whose he thinks."

An important implication is that grammatical conservatism is not
a feature of elicited production, at least not in the same way that it is
for spontaneous speech. Under the task demands of elicited production, children sometimes produce utterances like those in (4). These
utterances presumably violate the requirements of any UG-compatible
grammar. This is not to say that the technique of elicited production
is without value. Quite on the contrary, the technique can provide
extremely valuable tests of hypotheses about the child's grammatical
knowledge, as discussed at some length in Chapter 6, provided that the
results are interpreted with appropriate caution. The present point is
simply that grammatical conservatism is not a reliable feature of elicited
production.

Much the same is true of children's sentence comprehension, as
discussed in Chapter 6, Section 6.1.2. There I reviewed McKee's (1992)
investigation of English-learning children's knowledge of binding theory's Principle B. McKee's main finding was that pre-school children
routinely indicated that a sentence like *The princess dried her* was
true in a situation where the princess dried only herself. Yet, Bloom
et al.'s (1994) study provided compelling evidence that children in the
same age range reliably respected Principle B in their own spontaneous speech. In tests of comprehension it seems, children sometimes
endorse sentence interpretations that their own grammar does not in
fact license.

Again, this is not to impugn the value of the Truth Value Judgement
Task when testing hypotheses about children's grammatical knowledge.
Rather, the studies using this technique simply need to be constructed
with the task's limitations in mind. For present purposes, the point is
that grammatical conservatism is not a reliable feature of children's

performance on comprehension tasks. As in the case of elicited production, the child sometimes provides responses that are incompatible
with her own grammar. Clearly, then, the child's performance is not
limited to the grammatical options that she is confident are available in
the target language.

Turning from the choice of methodology to the domain of grammar
examined, we again see some variation in the degree to which children are grammatically conservative. Most strikingly, in the domain
of inflectional morphology, children spontaneously produce over-
regularization errors like the ones in (5).

(5a)   *comed* [for "came"]

(5b)   *foots* [for "feet"]

These errors are conspicuous when they occur, and have long attracted
the notice of child language researchers. Yet, given the attention that
they receive, their actual frequency of occurrence is much lower than
one might expect.

Marcus, Pinker, Ullman, Hollander, Rosen, and Xu (1992) examined
a sample of 11,521 utterances containing an irregular past-tense verb,
collected from a total of eighty-three children acquiring American
English. The data were drawn from longitudinal and cross-sectional
corpora in the CHILDES database. Most of the corpora contained transcripts of spontaneous speech. A notable exception was the corpus for
Abe, whose data were collected by Stan Kuczaj (1976) using a mixture of
naturalistic observation and elicited production (including elicitation
of past-tense verb forms).

Focusing on the ten children (including Abe) with longitudinal corpora and some fifteen additional children with extensive individual
data, Marcus *et al.* found that the children had a median frequency
of 2.5 percent over-regularization errors in utterances containing an
irregular verb. The frequency ranged from 0.0 percent to 24 percent.
The maximum frequency was Abe's. The next highest frequency was
13 percent (for April), and the remaining twenty-three children all
had frequencies well below 10 percent. In the longitudinal corpora
for Adam and Sarah, each of which covers an age span of more than
2.5 years, the greatest frequency of over-regularization errors in any
single transcript was 6.8 percent for Adam, and 15.8 percent for Sarah.
For both children this maximum frequency occurred around the age
of 4;06.

Marcus et al. observe that over-regularization errors continue to occur even in the spontaneous speech of adults, although with a substantially lower frequency. Moreover, both children and adults produce far greater rates of over-regularization in elicited-production tasks than they do in spontaneous speech. Marcus and his colleagues conclude that children are using the same grammatical architecture for inflectional morphology as adults, and that the difference lies in the fact that adults are faster than children at retrieving irregular forms from memory. When an irregular form cannot be retrieved quickly enough, the child or the adult invokes a morphological rule and produces the regular form instead.

Hence, for present purposes two points are crucial. First, errors of comission are more frequent in the domain of inflectional morphology than they are in the domain of syntax (But see Michael Maratsos, 1998, in *Handbook of Child Psychology*, on the scarcity of comission errors in children acquiring richly inflected languages.). Second, the morphological errors are nonetheless compatible with my claim of grammatical conservatism in children's spontaneous speech: There is nothing to suggest that the child has adopted an actual grammatical option that is unavailable in the adult language.

A somewhat different conclusion seems warranted for optional infinitives, which are the other main type of error reported in observational studies of children's inflectional morphology. A number of languages are associated with a fairly protracted acquisitional stage in which the child (sometimes) substitutes an infinitive for the finite verb of a matrix clause. Such languages reportedly include Dutch (Weverink 1989), French (Pierce 1992), German (Poeppel and Wexler 1993), Icelandic (Sigurjónsdóttir 1999), and Russian (Bar-Shalom and Snyder 1997), among others.

Interestingly, the choice of an optional infinitive has consequences for the syntax of the clause in which it occurs. For example, Poeppel and Wexler (1993) provide a detailed case study of one German-learning child, Andreas, who leaves his optional infinitives down in clause-final position, where infinitives occur in the adult language, rather than raising them into verb-second position, the normal location for the finite verb of a matrix clause. As argued by Poeppel and Wexler, this result indicates that the child knows quite a bit about the syntax of adult German.

Yet, the optional infinitive itself is a clear departure from adult grammar. To my mind, the explanation for the phenomenon must lie partly in biological maturation: for a certain period of development, probably ending around the third birthday, the child has a grammar that differs qualitatively from any adult grammar. The consequences of this qualitative difference are quite restricted, however, and also vary depending on the characteristics of the target language. In particular, the actual production of non-adult infinitives appears to end quite early, if it occurs at all, in children acquiring Italian (Guasti 1994), Spanish (Torrens 1995), and Polish (Bar-Shalom and Snyder 1998), for example.

Is the existence of an optional-infinitive stage compatible with my claim of grammatical conservatism in children's spontaneous speech? I believe that it is. This is because optional infinitives do not, strictly speaking, result from an acquisitional error. To the extent that the child in the optional-infinitive stage has made commitments concerning the morphology and syntax of the adult language, those commitments appear to be correct. For example, during this stage the child acquiring German clearly knows that the target language has head-final order in the verb phrase, has verb-second order in the matrix clause, and restricts verb-second position to morpho-syntactically finite verbs. Whatever the difference is, exactly, between the child's grammar and the adult's, the consistency of timing for the optional-infinitive stage (in children acquiring an optional-infinitive language) indicates that the explanation cannot lie wholly in the particulars of the individual child's linguistic experience. Rather, the grammatical information that the child has acquired from the input is overwhelmingly correct, and the optional-infinitive stage will end of its own accord, following a maturational schedule. For these reasons, the existence of an optional-infinitive stage is fully compatible with my claims about grammatical conservatism.

Finally, let us consider the error types that occur in children's phonology. Focusing again on spontaneous speech, where children show a high degree of grammatical conservatism in their syntax, can the same be said of phonology? The question is vexed somewhat by the issue of how to interpret the idea of an "error of comission" in the domain of phonology. For example, consider the case of phonotactics (which was the principal area of phonology examined in Chapters 3 and 7). What would a comission error look like there?[1]

---

[1] One type of phonetic/phonological error that is ubiquitous in children's spontaneous speech is the simple substitution of one segment for another. Yet, it remains unclear whether this error type qualifies as a genuinely grammatical error of comission, or is better construed as a lower-level failure of articulation. I will tentatively assume the latter, and look for less ambiguous cases.

The best candidate may be a non-adult use of epenthesis. Here the child will indeed be adding material that an adult would not employ. Moreover, if the child makes the same error in a variety of words, it can reasonably be attributed to a systematic grammatical operation, rather than a sporadic error of performance.

In fact, epenthesis errors do occur in children's spontaneous speech. A good example is provided in Fikkert's (1994) discussion of Catootje, one of the same Dutch children examined in Chapter 7, Section 7.1. Fikkert observes, on the basis of spontaneous-speech data, that Catootje passed through a stage in which she often inserted a vowel before /s/-initial clusters, as shown in (4), but not before other clusters.

(4)   *schapen* /ˈsXaːpə[n]/ → [əsˈhaːpə] (2;05,08)
       schoen /sXuːn/   → [əsˈhuːn] (2;05,08)
       staart /staːrt/   → [əstaːt] (2;05,08)
       stoel   /stuːl/   → [əstuː]   (2;05,22)

(cf. Fikkert 1994: 112)

In terms of the GP analysis proposed in Chapter 7, Catootje's errors conform perfectly to what we would expect if her grammar during this stage was [+BR, -MEN]. In other words, she could produce branching rhymes, as evidenced by the fact that she syllabified the initial /s/ in a rhymal-complement position. Yet, her use of vowel epenthesis before the initial /s/ indicates that her grammar did not yet allow magic empty nuclei.

Hence, this is quite plausibly a genuine phonological comission error, and one that was produced systematically, for a period of time, in the child's spontaneous speech. If so, this suggests that children might be considerably less conservative in their phonology than in their syntax.

Yet, we should not be too hasty. Note that the error pattern was (arguably) the result of the child disallowing a grammatical option, namely magic empty licensing, that is available in adult Dutch, but unavailable in many other languages. We should therefore consider the possibility that the child was indeed being grammatically conservative in her phonology, but that this can have slightly different surface consequences in phonotactics than it does in syntax.

Suppose that Catootje wanted to avoid any use of magic licensing for an empty nucleus, because she was uncertain that this mechanism was in fact available in adult Dutch. In principle, then, she might have had two options: omit the word-initial /s/ altogether, or perform epenthesis. Would the second option have been any better than doing magic licensing? Perhaps. If it turns out that epenthesis is generally available, as a kind of "last resort" operation, in all languages, then the use of epenthesis would not have required a commitment to a potentially incorrect choice. On this view, Catootje could have satisfied her conservative tendencies either by omitting the /s/ or by doing non-adult epenthesis.

The above speculation hinges on the idea that epenthesis could really be a universal option. I am uncertain whether this is plausible. What of languages that simply disallow /s/-initial clusters altogether, without even the possibility of epenthesis? The existence of such languages could still be compatible with the present idea, as long as there is something else to block the use of epenthesis. For example, if the language is [–BR], and /s/-initial clusters necessarily involve syllabifying the /s/ in a rhymal-complement position, then the use of epenthesis in this context will be independently excluded: there will be no position available for the epenthetic vowel.

I will leave it to others to evaluate the plausibility of this speculation. The larger question is whether we will find *bona fide* phonological comission errors in children's speech, errors that clearly require the child to have made a (temporary) commitment to an incorrect grammatical option. For the present I will also leave this question open.[2]

8.3 How can we translate hypotheses about grammatical variation into testable, acquisitional predictions?

The preceding chapters focused on two main types of acquisitional predictions, repeated here as (5) and (6).

(5) If the grammatical knowledge (including parameter settings and lexical information) required for construction A, in a given language, is identical to the knowledge required for construction B, then any child learning the language is predicted to acquire A and B at the same time.

---

[2] Note that the child's non-adult use of epenthesis therefore bears on a broader issue, namely the issue of whether grammatical conservatism is better construed in "extensional" or "intensional" terms. By this I mean the question of whether the child is avoiding the actual production of comission errors, or avoiding (at a more abstract level) any unmotivated decision on a point of grammatical variation. Examination of other cases like epenthesis, when they are identified, should help to illuminate this issue.

(6)   If the grammatical knowledge (including parameter settings and
       lexical information) required for construction A, in a given lan-
       guage, is a proper subset of the knowledge required for construc-
       tion B, then the age of acquisition for A should always be less than
       or equal to the age of acquisition for B. (No child should acquire
       B significantly earlier than A.)

At this point I would like to make brief mention of a third type of
prediction, one that has been delineated and tested in some recent work
of Miwa Isobe (2005).

This third type of parametric prediction is a prediction of earliness.
It requires four steps, as indicated in (7):

(7a)   Child-directed speech contains insufficient evidence for the child
       to learn, directly, that construction A is grammatically possible in
       the target language.

(7b)   Yet, every language that permits construction B also permits
       construction A.

(7c)   Moreover, evidence for construction B is robustly present in
       child-directed speech.

(7d)   Hence, if UG actually links construction A and construction
       B, we should find that children know about the possibility of
       construction A just as early as they know about construction B.

The reasoning in (7) is a form of "argument from the poverty of the
stimulus". Such reasoning can be found in the literature on second-
language acquisition by adults, and in the literature on children's first-
language knowledge of language universals, but it is less commonly
encountered in the literature on children's acquisition of parameter
settings. Nonetheless, a good example can be found in Isobe (2005).

Isobe's work concerned children's acquisition of the Japanese Head-
Internal Relative Clause (HIRC), illustrated in (9) (cf. Isobe 2005: 73,
ex. 3):

(9)   John-wa [[Mary-ga   teeburu-no ue-ni   ringo-o
       John-TOP   Mary-NOM table-GEN top-on apple-ACC
       oitekure-ta]no]-o   tabeta.
       put-PST   COMP-ACC ate
       "John ate the apple that Mary put on the table."

The Japanese construction in (9) is translated into English using a head-
external relative clause (because English disallows HIRCs), but a more

literal translation would be something like "John ate (the one) that Mary put the apple on the table". The head, *ringo* "apple", is actually located inside the relative clause.

Isobe determined that HIRCs are extremely rare in adults' child-directed speech. In a sample of more than 124,000 lines of adult Japanese, drawn from two children's longitudinal corpora, Isobe found only two potential examples of an HIRC (2005: 88). Therefore HIRCs should be acquired quite late, probably during the school-age years, if Japanese children have to learn them directly from the examples provided by adults.

Yet, Cole (1987) has argued that the availability of HIRCs in a given language is closely linked to two other characteristics of the language: object–verb word order, and the availability of null pronouns. The acquisition literature for Japanese reports that both object–verb word order (i.e. the setting of the Head Parameter) and the availability of null subject and object pronouns are early acquisitions, and are reliably mastered by the third birthday. Hence, Isobe derived a parametric prediction of earliness: by the age of three years, any normal child acquiring Japanese should correctly comprehend HIRCs.

To test this prediction, Isobe used a truth-value judgement task with sixteen three- and four-year-old children (mean age 3;11). Stories were presented in the form of animated films on a laptop computer. At the end of each story a character appeared on the screen and said a sentence about the story.

Crucially, the materials included sentences that were structurally ambiguous between head-internal and head-external structures, with different truth values depending on which structure was chosen. More-over, the materials were designed to favor an HIRC interpretation if it was available to the child. The materials also included certain sentences that required a head-external interpretation (at least for adult speakers), due to the use of a scrambled word order.

Overall, the children in Isobe's study provided the HIRC interpreta-tion about 97 percent of the time when it was permitted by the adult grammar. Yet, they chose a head-external interpretation about 88 per-cent of the time when the HIRC reading was ungrammatical for adults. The findings from language acquisition therefore support an analysis of the HIRC in terms of abstract points of parametric variation. The child does not need to wait for direct evidence of this particular construction, but rather can infer its availability from superficially unrelated charac-teristics of Japanese grammar.

8.4 What are the relative merits of child language acquisition versus other domains in which to test parametric hypotheses?

The evidence reviewed in Section 8.3 indicates that children are grammatically quite conservative in their spontaneous speech, although the details are slightly different depending on whether one examines syntax, morphology, or phonology. Nonetheless, in all these areas of grammar, children make numerous errors of omission yet seldom make errors of comission. When they do make a comission error, as in the case of non-adult uses of phonological epenthesis, it is plausibly the result of avoiding a more serious violation of grammatical conservatism: the use of a grammatical option (in this case, Magic Empty Licensing) that is available in certain languages, but not yet clearly available in the particular language she is acquiring.

As discussed extensively in Chapter 5, the property of grammatical conservatism means that children's spontaneous speech provides an excellent testing ground for parametric predictions. These include predictions of concurrent acquisition and ordered acquisition, as well as the predictions of "early" acquisition that were described in Section 8.3. Children's elicited speech and language comprehension do not share the property of grammatical conservatism, but are also valuable testing grounds for parametric predictions, as explained in Chapter 6.

Nonetheless, the strongest support for parametric hypotheses will always take the form of converging evidence from multiple sources. For example, it was important in Snyder (2001), reviewed in Chapter 5, to present converging evidence from child language acquisition, on the one hand, and comparative syntax, on the other. This is because each source of evidence has its own characteristic strengths and weaknesses.

A major weakness of acquisitional evidence is that our information about the child's grammar is fairly indirect. Most of the "action" in first-language acquisition happens before the child is three years old. At such early ages, our best source of information is the child's spontaneous speech. An intrinsic limitation of spontaneous-speech studies, however, is that low-frequency constructions are not reliably sampled, even when they are grammatically possible for the child.

Typological studies of the world's languages have strengths and weaknesses that are complementary to the strengths and weaknesses of acquisitional studies. A major weakness of typological surveys is that superficial diagnostics for a given grammatical characteristic are seldom fully reliable. For example, if one is interested in the English double-object construction, and would like to identify other languages that have the same construction, the problem is that many languages can be described as having "double-object constructions", yet there are good reasons to think that the abstract grammatical basis for these constructions varies widely.

To put the problem differently, if one asks the question whether language X has a double-object construction, one may get conflicting answers depending on which of the following diagnostics one applies: (i) identical morphological case on the indirect object and the direct object; (ii) promotion of the indirect object to subject position when the verb is passivized; (iii) rigid scope relations between quantifiers in the (unscrambled) indirect- and direct-object positions; or (iv) the possibility of *wh*-extraction from the direct-object position. Japanese is an example of a language with a double-object construction for which diagnostics (ii) and (iii) seem to be satisfied, diagnostic (i) is clearly not satisfied (but perhaps for irrelevant reasons, given that Japanese has a more general prohibition on clauses with two accusative-marked arguments), and diagnostic (iv) cannot be applied (because Japanese is a *wh-in-situ* language).

Thus, if one wants to know whether Japanese has a particular, abstract grammatical characteristic that is relevant to the English double-object construction, one needs to conduct in-depth syntactic analysis of Japanese. Superficial diagnostics, by themselves, will not answer the question. In contrast, when a child acquiring English begins to create double-object constructions, the property of grammatical conservatism gives us considerable reason to believe that they have the same abstract, grammatical basis as double-object constructions in adult English. Hence, this particular weakness of typological surveys can be offset by a corresponding strength in acquisition studies.

The reverse is also true: weaknesses of an acquisition study can be offset when it is combined with a comparative, cross-linguistic survey. An obvious example is the weakness mentioned above: information about the young child's grammar is largely restricted to what we can infer from spontaneous speech, and low-frequency constructions are not reliably sampled. In contrast, the adult consultants in a typological survey can be asked for quite subtle judgements of grammaticality, even about low-frequency grammatical constructions. Also, for at least some of the languages in a typological survey there may exist detailed linguistic analyses, and linguistic specialists who can be consulted.

Two additional sources of evidence deserve mention here: historical linguistics and second-language acquisition. Before I proceed, I should caution the reader that I am not a specialist in either of these areas. The remarks that follow are the impressions of a relative outsider, and might well meet with vehement disagreement from the experts. Nonetheless, here are my impressions, for whatever they might be worth.

In principle, historical change in a language can offer a wealth of information concerning parametric variation. When an abstract grammatical characteristic of the language undergoes a change, we expect to see consequences in multiple, superficially independent areas of the grammar. Of course, historical evidence has its own particular combination of strengths and weaknesses.

Weaknesses include the following: when examining the grammar of an extinct language, the evidence is largely restricted to what can be inferred from written records. In some cases (for example, the case of ancient Sanskrit) there exist sophisticated grammars that were composed when some version of the language was still spoken. In many cases, though, we have only a collection of texts written in the language, from which experts try to infer the internal grammar(s) of the authors.

Of course, written language often diverges quite markedly from spoken language, for example in the more frequent use of artificial stylistic devices. Furthermore, the writers may imitate the language of earlier authors, and include grammatical constructions in their writing that are no longer possible in their own spoken language. Also, to the extent that grammatical innovations are accepted into the written language much more gradually than in the spoken language, a written text might contain a curious mixture of features, including grammatical characteristics that never actually co-occurred in the native language of any single human being. The same may be true of the grammar books that were composed when the language was still spoken, because those grammars were usually intended as prescriptions for acceptable written language, rather than descriptions of normal spoken language.

Diachronic evidence has its own special strengths, as well. For example, if two surface characteristics in a modern language are proposed to share a common grammatical basis, then the prediction (all else being equal) is that the constructions instantiating those characteristics will have appeared around the same point in the history of the language. This prediction is a counterpart to the prediction of concurrent acquisition by children learning the modern language. Similarly, a prediction of ordered acquisition in children might correspond to a prediction of ordered appearance in the historical record for the language. The stipulation of "all else being equal" is crucial, of course, but converging evidence from child language acquisition and language history, when this occurs, is quite compelling.

Finally, second-language acquisition by adults (arguably) constitutes still another source of evidence about the possibilities permitted by universal grammar. Of course, this interpretation is sill controversial. Researchers studying second-language acquisition are by no means in complete agreement that a second-language grammar is necessarily a possible first-language grammar. Relevant literature, with divergent views, includes Bley-Vroman (1990), Schwartz and Sprouse (1996), Hawkins and Chan (1997), White (2003), and Hawkins and Hattori (2006).

Yet, if one accepts that second-language grammars do in fact obey the constraints of UG, then second-language acquisition is a potentially rich source evidence about those constraints. In particular, the predictions of "early" acquisition by children, as described in Section 8.3, have a direct counterpart in second-language acquisition: learners should know certain characteristics of the target language even when those characteristics are absent from their native language, and even when there is no direct evidence for those characteristics in their input. This situation obtains whenever the characteristics in question follow from a combination of UG constraints, on the one hand, and points of grammar that are clear from the second-language learner's input.

Furthermore, predictions of concurrent acquisition and ordered acquisition in first-language acquisition have direct translations for second-language acquisition. The time course of second-language acquisition is seldom investigated longitudinally, but cross-sectional methods are readily available: when concurrent acquisition is predicted, each second-language learner in the sample should exhibit knowledge of both points of grammar, or neither point of grammar. In the case of ordered acquisition (A before B), each learner who exhibits knowledge of B should also exhibit knowledge of A.

Of course, weaknesses of second-language studies also need to be borne in mind. Prominent among these is the fact that second-language learners are adults, and probably have greater powers of analytical reasoning than the young child. Hence, success on an individual point of grammar in the second language could perhaps result from conscious analysis of the data, even without strong guidance from UG.

This difficulty is compounded by the fact that adults can perfectly well solicit guidance from native speakers, including grammaticality judgements and intuitive explanations, on the points of grammar that puzzle them. If the learner works out a rule permitting native-like performance on an individual point of grammar, without discovering the abstract point of grammar that actually guides the native speaker, then there is a distinct possibility that points of grammar that are linked together in UG will diverge in the second-language learner. All the same, if one does obtain converging evidence from second-language acquisition and domains such as first-language acquisition or typological variation, then the combined evidence permits powerful conclusions about the structure of UG.

8.5 What are the implications of grammatical conservatism for linguistic theory?

In this section I turn to the question of what children's grammatical conservatism means for linguistic theory. What needs to be true of the grammar, in order for grammatical conservatism even to be possible? How can the child ever compose and produce an utterance, without risking an error of comission? How can the child possibly keep track of what she does not yet know?

To approach these questions, let me begin by sketching a model of grammar that would be able to provide answers. This model may sound overly simplistic, and it probably is, but please bear with me. Suppose that the human language faculty takes the form of a principles-and-parameters system, with a number of binary, switchbox-style parameters: points of variation with two discrete options. Suppose further that for each parameter, one of the settings is specified as the initial choice, the "unmarked" option. Now, crucially, suppose that the marked setting of any given parameter has the effect of adding a new way to compose linguistic units into well-formed expressions.

In other words, choosing a marked parameter-setting will never take away an option that existed with the unmarked setting. In this hypothetical scenario, the parameters satisfy both the Subset Condition and the Independence Principle of Wexler and Manzini (1987): for every parameter, the marked setting gives rise to a proper superset of the sentence-types that were possible with the unmarked setting, and this remains true regardless of how the other parameters are set.

In the scenario that I just sketched, grammatical conservatism can be achieved, at least in principle. The child begins with the unmarked parameter-settings, which allow only a very restricted set of sentence-types, all of which are guaranteed to be well-formed in the adult language. To achieve grammatical conservatism, we still need to ensure that the child refrains from adopting any marked parameter-setting until she has compelling evidence that it is correct for the target language. In other words, in the terms of Gibson and Wexler (1994), the child might have to wait until she encounters a "global trigger" for the marked parameter-setting: a sentence-type in the input that is grammatically possible if, and only if, the parameter takes the marked value. By definition, a global trigger has this property regardless of how the other parameters are set.[3]

Continuing with this hypothetical scenario, the child initially lacks the grammatical means to express most of her thoughts clearly. Instead she relies on the grammatical devices that are available to her, and the result is that she routinely omits material that would be required in the adult language. Indeed, we might attribute the holophrastic speech of the one-year-old to a grammar in which there is simply no means available for combining two words into a phrase.

Instead of a Head Parameter that provides two options, head-initial or head-final, our hypothetical language faculty would provide two parameters, one of which allows head-initial phrases on its marked setting, and the other of which allows head-final phrases on its marked setting. When the child has the unmarked settings for both of these parameters, it will be impossible for her to combine a head with a complement. Instead she will omit either the head or the complement from her utterance. When she finally sets one of these parameters to its marked value, two-word utterances containing both a head and a complement will begin to appear, and they will exhibit appropriate head-complement order, as we in fact observe when a child enters the telegraphic stage.

Finally, we might speculate that the child will suspend her grammatical conservatism in certain contexts. Most importantly, the child will need to consider marked parametric options when analyzing the adult input, even before she is ready to commit herself to those options. Otherwise she will never be able to exploit the triggers in her input

---

[3] An alternative to global triggers might be "unambiguous triggers", in the sense of Fodor (1998), which will be discussed below.

when they present themselves. This might also account for the common perception that "comprehension precedes production": in comprehension, the child allows herself to exploit grammatical options that may or may not actually be available in the target language.

Similarly, we might speculate that the demands of elicited production can pressure the child into assembling linguistic units in ways that her grammar does not in fact allow. This could account for the child's use of grammatical options that are UG-compatible but incorrect for her target language, as well as the UG-incompatible utterances that we sometimes encounter in elicited-production tasks (cf. Chapter 6, Section 6.1.1).

At this point I think I have sketched a fairly appealing picture of the human language faculty, one that neatly accommodates the child's grammatical conservatism in her spontaneous speech. Unfortunately it runs counter to a great deal of research in contemporary linguistics. Most importantly, some of the most influential parametric proposals do not have a subset-superset character of the type required in this scenario.

A case in point is the Head Parameter. Contrary to the scenario presented above, the version of the parameter that is actually discussed in the literature offers head-complement and complement-head as the only two options. A language chooses one or the other. Theoretical linguists might, perhaps, be willing to consider the merits of alternative formulations, but (to my knowledge) the alternatives that would be more conducive to children's grammatical conservatism are not yet under discussion.

In other cases the picture is less clear-cut. Consider the case of prepositional questions, discussed at some length in Chapter 7, Section 7.3. There Sugisaki and I considered a view in which there is a single parameter for prepositional questions, and two principal options: pied-piping ("*About what* is he talking") or stranding ("*What* is he talking *about?*"). Our conclusion from the acquisitional evidence was that neither of these options is provided to the child as a default: children acquiring English or Spanish wait until they identify the correct option for their target language (stranding for English, piping for Spanish) before they ever attempt a prepositional question.

In the case of prepositional questions we have two main approaches available to us. One approach is to retain the idea of a binary parameter, where neither value leads to a proper superset of sentence-types, and to account for children's grammatical conservatism in some other way. A second approach is to question the idea that there is a single, binary parameter at work here.

In this particular case the second approach receives some empirical support, as noted (in personal communication) by Mark Baker and by Teresa Guasti. For example, the Bantu language Chichewa may be a language in which neither stranding nor piping is available for *wh*-movement of a prepositional object (examples provided by Mark Baker, personal communication):

(10) Atsikana a-ku-nena   za   mfumu.
      girls   AGR-pres-talk about chief
      "The girls are talking about the chief."

(11) *Iyi ndi mfumu zi-mene   atiskana a-ku-nena
      this be chief   about-which girls   AGR-pres-talking
      "This is the chief about whom the girls are talking."
      (*pied-piping)

(12) *Iyi ndi mfumu imene atiskana a-ku-nena   za.
      This be chief   which girls   AGR-pres-talking about
      "This is the chief whom the girls are talking about." (*P-stranding).

Moreover, as noted by Teresa Guasti (personal communication), certain colloquial Romance varieties are similar to Chichewa in allowing neither piping nor stranding. Instead these varieties insert a resumptive pronoun as the object of the preposition.

The existence of languages like Chichewa is unexpected if there is a single parameter, with just two options, that determines how the object of a preposition is to be extracted. On the other hand, if there exist a number of parameters, each of which can make available a particular type of extraction (piping, or stranding, or some other form), then the existence of languages like Chichewa, which disallow both piping and stranding, is unproblematic.

If this idea is on the right track, we should also find languages that provide more than one option for *wh*-extraction of prepositional objects. Certain varieties of English might actually qualify as an example, to the extent that there are speakers for whom both stranding and piping are permissible options. On the other hand, the differences of register associated with piping versus stranding may be an indication that there are really two grammars at work, and that these speakers are "bilingual", in a certain sense. Hence, I will leave the question open.

In sum, certain parameters might indeed have a subset–superset character. In these cases the child can achieve grammatical conservatism by starting out with the "subset" option, and moving to the superset option when she encounters clear evidence that this option is the correct one. Of course, the existence of a "global trigger" for the superset option is far from obvious. Gibson and Wexler (1994) have shown that there exist no global triggers in a parameter space composed of just three parameters: head/complement order, specifier/X′ order, and [+/–Verb Second]. Nonetheless, Gibson and Wexler specifically restricted their attention to parameters that do not have a subset–superset character. The findings might well be different for a parameter space composed entirely of subset–superset parameters, although this remains to be demonstrated.

In any case, however, let us assume that certain parameters will be needed that do not have a subset–superset character. How can such parameters be reconciled with children's grammatical conservatism? One possibility is that such parameters are initially labeled as "unset", and remain so until the child receives clear evidence for one of the settings. To achieve grammatical conservatism, the child will need to refrain from producing any utterance that would rely, for its grammaticality, on a specific setting of an as-yet unset parameter.

For example, suppose that the Head Parameter takes its usual form and offers the child a choice of two actual settings: head-complement and complement-head. The initial state of the parameter, however, would be neither of these settings, but rather a value of "unset". Now, to combine a head with a complement the child would need to make a commitment to one setting or the other. As long as the parameter is unset, the child will have to refrain from utterances that contain both a head and its complement. If there is another parameter determining specifier/X′ order, and this parameter is also unset, the result might be that no multi-word utterances are possible. The child would remain in a holophrastic stage until at least one of the basic word-order parameters received an actual setting.

This scenario is logically possible, although it entails that the language faculty can still function when some of its parameters are in an unset state. Moreover, this scenario requires the child to be able to determine, for a candidate utterance, whether it can be constructed without the use of an actual setting for any of the as-yet unset parameters. The first requirement is a non-trivial constraint on the architecture of the human language faculty, and the second requirement could impose considerable demands on the child's computational resources. Nonetheless, alongside the previous suggestion of strict reliance on subset–superset parameters, allowing unset parameters is a second logical approach to explaining grammatical conservatism.

Does the picture change if we move from switchbox parameters to the constraint rankings of Optimality Theory? Not for the better, as far as I can see. In Chapter 3 I mentioned Tesar and Smolensky's (2000) observation that ranking a set of n constraints is formally equivalent to setting an array of $n(n-1)/2$ "dominance" parameters. Each such parameter determines whether a given constraint X dominates, or is dominated by, a given constraint Y. Moreover, as I discussed in Chapter 3, the use of constraint ranking can make it impossible for these parameters to be set independently of one another. For example, if constraints X, Y, and Z are currently unranked with respect to one another, then moving X below Y necessarily entails that X is also ranked below Z. The ranking of X and Z can be changed later, but temporarily the dominance relation between X and Z assumes a value for which there was no real motivation in the input. Therefore, the use of a constraint ranking simply compounds the difficulty of explaining how children manage to be grammatically conservative. (For further details and discussion, see Chapter 3, Section 3.3.)

A similar conclusion follows for Yang's (2002) Variational Model of language acquisition. In that model, all the possible UG-compatible grammars are available to the child at the outset, and language acquisition takes the form of an evolutionary struggle among these grammars. In testing his model, Yang focuses on areas of grammar where an error takes the form of omitting material that would be required in the adult language. He succeeds in modeling the frequency of English-learning children's null subjects and null objects in terms of grammatical options available in adult Spanish and adult Mandarin.

The problem with the Variational Model is that it predicts rampant errors of comission in other areas of grammar. As discussed by Sugisaki and Snyder (2006), the example of prepositional questions is one such area. If all the possible types of prepositional questions are grammatically available to the child at the outset, then it becomes extremely difficult to explain why a child would ever go through a period of avoiding prepositional questions, as was demonstrated in Chapter 7, Section 7.3. Under the Variational Model, the child might converge rapidly on the correct grammatical option, and thereby avoid errors of comission. Yet, if the child has not yet identified the correct option, then the Variational Model strongly predicts errors of comission, rather than avoidance of prepositional questions, and this prediction is false. In sum, the Variational Model not only fails to help in accounting for children's grammatical conservatism, but actually makes the problem worse.

Thus, we have so far two candidate approaches to explaining grammatical conservatism, namely subset–superset parameters and unset parameters. Neither the constraint rankings of Optimality Theory nor the simultaneous grammars of the Variational Model offered anything else. I do not pretend to have exhausted the possibilities, but will leave it to future research to explore the options fully.

To what extent do the parameters that have been discussed in this book have a subset–superset character, compatible with the first approach? As noted in Chapter 3, Section 3.3, most of the parameters proposed in the literature on Government Phonology have a subset–superset character. One exception, noted there, is Charette's (1991) parameter for the directionality of interconstituent government. Yet, each of the following are subset–superset parameters: the Empty Onset Parameter, the Branching Rhyme Parameter, and the Magic Empty Licensing Parameter (all of which were discussed in Chapter 7, Section 7.1), as well as the parameter for word-final empty licensing (discussed in Chapter 3, Section 3.2).

In the case of syntactic parameters, however, the picture is more mixed. The Compounding Parameter of Snyder (2001), which was discussed in Chapter 5, Section 5.3, is a well-behaved subset–superset parameter. The positive setting simply adds new grammatical options, such as creative root compounding and the possibility of some additional argument structures (e.g. the resultative construction and the verb–particle construction), without removing any option that existed under the negative setting.

Bošković's (2004) DP Parameter, discussed in Section 2.2.5 of Chapter 2, might also be construed as a subset–superset parameter. The child could begin by assuming that her language requires a DP layer above every NP. If in fact she is acquiring a language without such a layer, there will never be any phonetically overt determiner for the child to include in her DP layer, but an overt determiner might not be required in languages that take the DP option. As long as she retains the DP layer, she will be restricted to a proper subset of the word orders permitted in the adult language (i.e. the unscrambled orders). If she encounters clear evidence of scrambling, this will (perhaps) tell her that the DP layer should be eliminated. Note that the child is grammatically conservative, in this scenario, to the extent that she will not produce errors of comission (such as scrambled sentences in a language without scrambling). Yet, from the perspective of the abstract structures that she employs for her utterances, the presence of a DP layer would be a kind of comission error if her target language has none.

More clear-cut are the Referentiality Parameter of Longobardi (2001) and the Split IP Parameter of Bobaljik and Thráinsson (1998). Neither qualifies as a subset–superset parameter. For example, the negative setting (so to speak) of the Referentiality Parameter in English yields the word order facts in (13), while the positive setting in Italian yields the word order possibilities in (14). (These examples are repeated from Chapter 2, Section 2.3.3.)

(13a)   Only Mary telephoned me.

(13b) $^{(*)}$Mary only telephoned me. [*on reading of "no one except Mary"]

(14a)   *Sola Maria mi ha telefonato.
      only Maria me has telephoned
      "Only Maria telephoned me."

(14b)   Maria sola mi ha telefonato.
      Maria only me has telephoned

(14c)   L-a   sola Maria mi ha telefonato.
      the-FEM.SG only Maria me has telephoned

(14d)   *L-a   Maria sola mi ha telefonato.
      the-FEM.SG Maria only me has telephoned
      [*on the relevant reading]

Clearly neither setting yields a proper superset of the sentence-types permitted by the other setting.

The same is true of the Split IP Parameter, as illustrated by the word-order facts in (15) and (16). (These examples are repeated from Chapter 2, Section 2.3.4.)

(15)   ... at   han *ikke* **købte** bogen.   *Danish*
      that he   not bought book.the
      "... that he did not buy the book."

(16)   ...að hann **keypti** *ekki* bókina.   *Icelandic*
         that he   bought not book.the
         "... that he did not buy the book."

The example in (15) comes from Danish, which takes the negative
setting of the parameter and leaves the verb to the right of negation,
while the example in (16) comes from Icelandic, which takes the positive
setting and moves the verb to the left of negation. These word orders are
the only possibilities in (15) and (16), and therefore neither parameter
setting results in a proper superset of possible sentence-types. In sum,
if these latter two proposals from Longobardi and from Bobaljik and
Thráinsson are on the right track, then it will be difficult to account
for the child's success at grammatical conservatism simply by means of
the subset–superset approach to parameters. The idea of initially unset
parameters, however, will still be available.

At this point I would like to introduce another idea: Janet Fodor's
(1998) proposal to identify parameter settings with the distinctive bits
of (surface) syntactic structure to which they give rise. Fodor terms
these bits of structure "treelets", and proposes an ingenious learning
procedure that we might call "learning by parsing". The main idea is
that the child's parser initially has all the UG-compatible treelets at
its disposal, and uses them to identify at least one possible parse for
each sentence in the input. The parser does not produce all the possible
parses, but does note whether there was any point of ambiguity during
the parse that it provides. In case the parse was unambiguous, the parser
identifies the treelets that it used as necessarily correct. The parameter
settings required for those treelets to be available are then identified as
correct choices.

Fodor's approach has a number of properties that could be valuable in accounting for children's grammatical conservatism. First, as
noted earlier, we need a split between production and comprehension.
In spontaneous production the child limits herself to the grammatical options for which she has strong evidence, but in comprehension
she clearly must have access to a much broader range of grammatical options, because otherwise she could not derive new grammatical
information from her input. Fodor's approach permits us to say that
when parsing the input, the child uses all the treelets that have not been
definitively excluded, but in producing utterances of her own, she uses
only those treelets that have been identified as correct.

Note that a treelet can be identified as ungrammatical, in Fodor's system, if UG stipulates that two treelets are mutually exclusive, and the other member of the pair has been identified as correct for the target language. This has interesting consequences for the approaches to grammatical conservatism that were identified above. First, the idea of a subset–superset parameter has a direct expression in terms of the absence or presence of a given treelet in the target language.

Moreover, the idea of an unset parameter finds expression in a very similar way. Even when UG provides a binary parameter, and neither setting leads to a subset language, the initial state of the learner will be that the treelets associated with each setting of the parameter are both available for parsing in the input, yet neither type of treelet is available for use in the child's own utterances. The child will have to wait for unambiguous evidence for one option or the other before she begins to use it in her own speech.

If UG stipulates that two options are mutually incompatible, then the child will remove the treelet or treelets associated with one option when she encounters unambiguous evidence for the competing option. Similarly, UG can set up an implicational relationship between two treelets: if one is available, the other is necessarily also available. In this way Fodor's system allows for the possibility of highly abstract parameters, with proliferating consequences in many distinct areas of grammar. Even if an individual treelet has highly circumscribed consequences, the parameter setting that is required for that treelet to be available might simultaneously make other types of treelets available as well.

In sum, I believe that Fodor's ideas are extremely promising as an approach to explaining children's grammatical conservatism. Her system has three especially valuable characteristics. First, the child's grammar can function even when some (or indeed many) of the parametric decisions have not yet been made. Second, the effect of an unset parameter is that none of the combinatorial possibilities associated with its settings are available for use in production. Third, the child adds a new combinatorial possibility to her production grammar only when she encounters unambiguous evidence for it in her input. Finally, note that Fodor's approach can be extended fairly readily from syntax to phonology, at least if one adopts a parametric approach such as Government Phonology.

8.6 Concluding remarks

In this book I have argued for a parametric approach to child language. The approach focuses on the grammatical information that the child must acquire, and draws heavily on linguistic research concerning the nature of the adult state. A point of emphasis is that the child acquires information of an abstract nature, much more general than the specific examples that she encounters in her input. The information might be represented in the form of switchbox-style parameters, or rankings of grammatical constraints, or perhaps some other format altogether, but by hypothesis the information is more abstract than the particular sentence-types to which it gives rise.

A major claim of the book has been that child language acquisition is an extremely valuable testing ground for hypotheses about grammatical variation. Such hypotheses make strong, eminently testable predictions about the time course of child language acquisition. I have shown the reader, in considerable detail, how to derive these predictions from proposals in the contemporary literature on syntax and phonology, and how to test the predictions with evidence from children's spontaneous speech, elicited production, or comprehension.

In the course of writing this book I have also amassed a fair amount of evidence for what I have termed "grammatical conservatism": in the child's spontaneous speech one finds astonishingly few of the logically possible errors of comission. Instead, the vast majority of children's mistakes are errors of omission. The details vary somewhat for syntax, morphology, and phonology, but some version of the generalization appears to hold true throughout. In this final chapter I have dedicated a considerable amount of attention to what children's grammatical conservatism tells us about the nature of the human language faculty.

Indeed, I believe that this finding has major implications for the explanatory adequacy of linguistic theories. To achieve explanatory adequacy, a theory of grammar must now be able to solve a stronger version of the Logical Problem of Language Acquisition: How, in principle, could a *grammatically conservative* learner identify the correct grammar from among the permitted options, given only the types of information that are in fact required by children?

As a consequence, certain approaches to language learnability are no longer sufficient. For example, consider the Trigger Learning Algorithm of Gibson and Wexler (1994). This algorithm requires the child to take a "random walk" through the parameter space of UG. At each point when the child changes her grammar, the change is motivated by a newfound ability to account for the grammaticality of a single sentence in the input. Yet, in many cases the change will be incorrect, and may very well lead the child to make new errors of comission in other sentence-types. Learnability using the Trigger Learning Algorithm is therefore inadequate for purposes of explanatory adequacy, if actual children are grammatically conservative.

I concluded the last section with a discussion of Fodor's (1998) idea of linking parameter settings to "treelets" of surface grammar, and of having the child use her sentence parser to identify the treelets that are actually available in her target language. To the extent that this idea can be made to work, and in particular, to the extent that treelets can accommodate the types of grammatical variation that are in fact attested, I would suggest it as a promising framework in which to investigate grammatically conservative language acquisition.

References

ABELS, KLAUS. (2003). '*[P clitic]!—Why?', in Peter Kosta, Joanna Blaszczak, Jens Frasek, Ljudmila Geist, and Marzena Zygis (eds.), *Investigations into Formal Slavic Linguistics: Contributions of the Fourth European Conference on Formal Description of Slavic Languages—FDSL IV, Held at Potsdam University, November 28–30, 2001 (Linguistik International 10), Part 2.* Frankfurt am Main: Peter Lang, pp. 443–60.

ADGER, DAVID. (2003). *Core Syntax: A Minimalist Approach.* Oxford: Oxford University Press.

ANDERSON, STEPHEN R. (1982). 'Where's morphology?', *Linguistic Inquiry* 13: 571–612.

AYANO, SEIKI. (2001). *The Layered Internal Structure and the External Syntax of PP.* Doctoral dissertation, University of Durham.

BAKER, MARK. (1996). *The Polysynthesis Parameter.* New York: Oxford University Press.

BALTIN, MARK, and POSTAL, PAUL M. (1996). 'More on reanalysis hypotheses', *Linguistic Inquiry* 27: 127–45.

BARBIERS, SJEF. (1991). 'Telwoorden, adjectieven en lege NP's'. Paper presented at the 1991 Meeting of the Dutch General Association of Linguistics, Utrecht.

BAR-SHALOM, EVA and SNYDER, WILLIAM. (1997). 'Optional infinitives in child Russian and their implications for the pro-drop debate', in Martina Lindseth and Steven Franks (eds), *Formal Approaches to Slavic Linguistics: The Indiana Meeting 1996.* Ann Arbor: Michigan Slavic Publications, pp. 38–47.

_____ _____ (1998). 'Root infinitives in child Russian: A comparison with Italian and Polish', in Antonella Sorace, Caroline Heycock, and Richard Shillcock (eds), *Language Acquisition: Knowledge Representation and Processing. Proceedings of GALA '97.* Edinburgh, UK: The University of Edinburgh, pp. 22–7.

BECK, SIGRID and SNYDER, WILLIAM. (2001a). 'Complex predicates and goal PPs: Evidence for a semantic parameter', in Anna H.-J. Do, Laura Domínguez, and Aimee Johansen (eds), *BUCLD 25: Proceedings of the 25th Annual Boston University Conference on Language Development.* Somerville, MA: Cascadilla Press, pp. 114–22.

_____ _____ (2001b). 'The Resultative Parameter and restitutive *again*', in Caroline Féry and Wolfgang Sternefeld (eds), *Audiatur Vox Sapientiae: A Festschrift for Arnim von Stechow.* Berlin: Akademie Verlag, pp. 48–69.

BERNSTEIN, JUDY. (1993a). *Topics in the Syntax of Nominal Structure across Romance.* Doctoral dissertation, City University of New York.

BERNSTEIN, JUDY. (1993*b*) 'The syntactic role of word markers in null nominal constructions', *Probus* 5: 5–38.

BLEY-VROMAN, ROBERT. (1990). 'The logical problem of foreign language learning', *Linguistic Analysis* 20: 3–49.

BLOOM, LOIS. (1970). *Language Development: Form and Function in Emerging Grammars*. Cambridge, MA: MIT Press.

——(1973). *One Word at a Time: The Use of Single Word Utterances before Syntax*. The Hague: Mouton de Gruyter.

——LIGHTBOWN, PATSY, and HOOD, LOIS. (1975). *Structure and Variation in Child Language*. Monographs of the Society for Research in Child Development, 40 (Serial No. 160).

BLOOM, PAUL. (1990). 'Subjectless sentences in child language', *Linguistic Inquiry* 21: 491–504.

——(1993). 'Grammatical continuity in language development: The case of subjectless sentences', *Linguistic Inquiry* 24: 721–34.

——BARSS, ANDREW, NICOL, JANET, and CONWAY, LAURA. (1994). 'Children's knowledge of binding and coreference: Evidence from spontaneous speech', *Language* 70: 53–71.

BOBALJIK, JONATHAN D. (1995). *Morphosyntax: The Syntax of Verbal Inflection*. Doctoral dissertation, MIT.

——and THRÁINSSON, HÖSKULDUR. (1998). 'Two heads aren't always better than one', *Syntax* 1: 37–71.

BORER, HAGIT. (1984). *Parametric Syntax: Case Studies in Semitic and Romance Languages*. Dordrecht: Foris.

BOŠKOVIĆ, ŽELJKO. (2004). 'Topicalization, focalization, lexical insertion, and scrambling', *Linguistic Inquiry* 35: 613–38.

——and TAKAHASHI, DAIKO (1998).'Scrambling and last resort', *Linguistic Inquiry* 29: 347–66

BROWN, ROGER. (1973). *A First Language: The Early Stages*. Cambridge, MA: Harvard University Press.

——and HANLON, CAMILLE. (1970). 'Derivational complexity and order of acquisition in child speech', in John R. Hayes (ed.), *Cognition and the Development of Language*. New York: Wiley, pp. 155–207.

CHARETTE, MONIK. (1991). *Conditions on Phonological Government*. Cambridge: Cambridge University Press.

CHEN, DEBORAH, YAMANE, MAKI, and SNYDER, WILLIAM. (1998). 'Children's left-branch violations: Evidence for a non-parametric account', in Annabel Greenhill et al. *BUCLD 22: Proceedings of the 22nd Annual Boston University Conference on Language Development*. Somerville, MA: Cascadilla Press, pp. 91–6.

CHIEN, YU-CHIN and WEXLER, KENNETH. (1990). 'Children's knowledge of locality conditions in binding as evidence for the modularity of syntax and pragmatics', *Language Acquisition* 1: 225–95.

CHOMSKY, NOAM. (1964). *Current Issues in Linguistic Theory*. The Hague: Mouton.

_____ (1981). *Lectures on Government and Binding*. Dordrecht: Foris.

_____ (1986a). *Barriers*. Cambridge, MA: MIT Press.

_____ (1986b). *Knowledge of Language: Its Nature, Origin, and Use*. New York: Praeger.

_____ (1993). 'A minimalist program for linguistic theory', in Kenneth Hale and Samuel Jay Keyser (eds), *The View from Building 20: Essays in Linguistics in Honor of Sylvain Bromberger*. Cambridge, MA: MIT Press, pp. 1–52.

_____ (1995). *The Minimalist Program*. Cambridge, MA: MIT Press.

_____ (2001a). 'Beyond explanatory adequacy'. *MIT Occasional Papers in Linguistics* 20.

_____ (2001b). 'Derivation by phase', in Michael Kenstowicz (ed.), *Ken Hale: A Life in Language*. Cambridge, MA: MIT Press, pp. 1–52.

CLARK, EVE. (1978). 'Strategies for communicating', *Child Development* 49: 953–9.

CLARK, ROBIN. (1992). 'The selection of syntactic knowledge', *Language Acquisition* 2: 83–149.

COLE, PETER. (1987). 'The structure of internally headed relative clauses', *Natural Language & Linguistic Theory* 5: 277–302.

CONRADIE, SIMONE. (2006). 'Investigating the acquisition of the Split-IP parameter and the V2 parameter in second language Afrikaans', *Second Language Research* 22: 64–94.

CRAIN, STEPHEN and McKEE, CECILE. (1985). 'Acquisition of structural restrictions on anaphora', in Stephen Berman, Jae-Woong Choe, and Joyce McDonough (eds), *Proceedings of NELS* 16. Amherst, MA: GLSA, 94–110.

_____ and THORNTON, ROSALIND. (1998). *Investigations in Universal Grammar: A Guide to Experiments in the Acquisition of Syntax and Semantics*. Cambridge, MA: MIT Press.

CRAWFORD, JAMES M. (1973). 'Yuchi phonology', *International Journal of American Linguistics* 39: 173–9.

DAVIS, STUART. (1990). 'Italian onset structure and the distribution of *il* and *lo*', *Linguistics* 28: 43–55.

DEJIMA, MAYUMI. (1999). *A Study on Remnant-scrambled sentences in Japanese and their LF Representations*. MA thesis, Nanzan University, Japan.

DEVILLIERS, JILL, ROEPER, THOMAS, and VAINIKKA, ANNE. (1990). 'The acquisition of long-distance rules', in Lyn Frazier and Jill DeVilliers (eds), *Language Processing and Language Acquisition*. Dordrecht: Kluwer, 257–97.

FIKKERT, PAULA. (1994). *On the Acquisition of Prosodic Structure*. The Hague: Holland Academic Graphics.

FODOR, JANET DEAN. (1998). 'Unambiguous triggers', *Linguistic Inquiry* 29: 1–36.

GAVRUSEVA, LENA. (1998). 'Left-branch violations in Child L2 English', in Annabel Greenhill et al. *BUCLD 22: Proceedings of the 22nd Annual Boston University Conference on Language Development*. Somerville, MA: Cascadilla Press, pp. 25–245.

GERKEN, LouANN and SHADY, MICHELE E. (1996). 'The picture selection task', in Dana McDaniel et al. *Methods for Assessing Children's Syntax*. Cambridge, MA: MIT Press, pp. 125–45.

GIBSON, EDWARD and WEXLER, KENNETH. (1994). 'Triggers', *Linguistic Inquiry* 25: 355–407.

GORDON, PETER (1996). 'The truth-value judgment task', in Dana McDaniel et al. (eds), *Methods for Assessing Children's Syntax*. Cambridge, MA: MIT Press, pp. 211–31.

GREENHILL, ANNABEL, HUGHES, MARY, LITTLEFIELD, HEATHER, and WALSH, HUGH (eds). (1998). *BUCLD 22: Proceedings of the 22nd Annual Boston University Conference on Language Development*. Somerville, MA: Cascadilla Press.

——— LITTLEFIELD, HEATHER, and TANO, CHERYL (eds). (1999). *BUCLD 23: Proceedings of the 23rd Annual Boston University Conference on Language Development*. Somerville, MA: Cascadilla Press.

GRIMSHAW, JANE and SAMEK-LODOVICI, VIERI. (1998). 'Optimal subjects and subject universals', in Pilar Barbosa, Danny Fox, Paul Hagstrom, Martha McGinnis, and David Pesetsky (eds), *Is the Best Good Enough? Optimality and Competition in Syntax*. Cambridge, MA: MIT Press, pp. 193–219.

GRODZINSKY, YOSEF, and REINHART, TANYA. (1993). 'The innateness of binding and coreference', *Linguistic Inquiry* 24: 69–102.

GUASTI, MARIA TERESA. (1994). 'Verb syntax in Italian child grammar: Finite and non-finite verbs', *Language Acquisition* 3: 1–40.

HALLE, MORRIS and MARANTZ, ALEC. (1993). 'Distributed morphology and the pieces of inflection, in Kenneth Hale and Samuel Jay Keyser (eds), *The View from Building 20: Essays in Linguistics in Honor of Sylvain Bromberger*. Cambridge, MA: MIT Press, pp. 111–76.

HARRIS, JOHN. (1994). *English Sound Structure*. Oxford: Blackwell.

——— and GUSSMANN, EDMUND. (1998). 'Final codas: Why the west was wrong', in Eugeniusz Cyran (ed.), *Structure and Interpretation: Studies in Phonology*. Lublin: Folium, pp. 139–62.

——— ——— (2002). 'Word-final onsets', in Ad Neelemann and Reiko Vermeulen (eds) *University College London Working Papers in Linguistics* 14: 1–42.

HAWKINS, ROGER and CHAN, CECILIA YUET-HUANG. (1997). 'The partial accessibility of Universal Grammar in second language acquisition: The failed formal features hypothesis', *Second Language Research* 13: 187–226.

——— and HATTORI, HAJIME. (2006). 'Interpretation of English multiple *wh*-questions by Japanese speakers: A missing uninterpretable feature account', *Second Language Research* 22: 269–301.

HENDRIKS, PETRA, and HOOP, HELEN DE. (2000). 'Optimality theoretic semantics', *Linguistics and Philosophy* 24: 1–32.

HEWSON, JOHN. (1972). *Article and Noun in English*. The Hague: Mouton.

HIGGINSON, ROY. (1985). *Fixing: A Demonstration of the Child's Active Role in Language Acquisition*. Doctoral dissertation, Washington State University.

HODGE, CARLETON T. (1946). 'Phonemes of Serbo-Croatian', *Language* 22: 112–20.

HORNSTEIN, NORBERT and WEINBERG, AMY. (1981). 'Case theory and preposition stranding', *Linguistic Inquiry* 12: 55–91.

HYAMS, NINA. (1986). *Language Acquisition and the Theory of Parameters*. Dordrecht: Reidel.

——— (1987). 'The setting of the Null Subject Parameter'. Paper presented at the 12th Annual Boston University Conference on Language Development, Boston, MA.

——— and WEXLER, KENNETH. (1993). 'On the grammatical basis of null subjects in child language', *Linguistic Inquiry* 24: 421–59.

——— SCHAEFFER, JEANNETTE, and JOHNSON, KYLE. (1993). 'The acquisition of the verb particle construction'. Paper presented at Generative Approaches to Language Acquisition. (GALA), University of Durham, September.

ISOBE, MIWA. (2005). *Language Variation and Child Language Acquisition: Laying Ground for Evaluating Parametric Proposals*. Doctoral dissertation, Keio University, Tokyo.

——— and SUGISAKI, KOJI. (2002). 'The acquisition of pied-piping in French and its theoretical implications'. Paper presented at Going Romance 2002, Groningen University.

JAEGER, JERI J. and VAN VALIN, ROBERT D. (1982). 'Initial consonant clusters in Yateé Zapotec', *International Journal of American Linguistics* 48: 125–38.

JAEGGLI, OSVALDO AND SAFIR, KENNETH J. (1989). 'The Null Subject Parameter and parametric theory', in Osvaldo Jaeggli and Kenneth J. Safir (eds), *The Null Subject Parameter*. Dordrecht: Kluwer.

JAKOBSON, ROMAN. (1962). *Selected Writings 1: Phonological Studies*. The Hague: Mouton.

KANG, BOSOOK. (2005). *Acquisition of Language Particular Properties under Impoverished Input*. Doctoral dissertation, University of Connecticut, Storrs.

KAYE, JONATHAN D. (1989). *Phonology: A Cognitive View*. Hillsdale, NJ: Lawrence Erlbaum.

——— (1990). 'Coda licensing', *Phonology* 7: 301–30.

——— (1992). 'Do you believe in magic? The story of s+C sequences', in *SOAS Working Papers in Linguistics and Phonetics* 2: 293–313. Reprinted in Henryk Kardela and Bogdan Szymanek (eds.), *A Festschrift for Edmund Gussmann*. Lublin: Lublin University Press, pp. 155–76.

KAYE, JONATHAN D. (1995). 'Derivations and interfaces', in Jacques Durand and Francis Katamba (eds), *Frontiers of Phonology: Atoms, Structure, Derivation*. London: Longman, pp. 289–332.

—— LOWENSTAMM, JEAN, and VERGNAUD, JEAN-ROGER. (1985). 'The internal structure of phonological representations: A theory of charm and government', *Phonology Yearbook* 2: 305–28.

—— —— —— (1990). 'Constituent structure and government in phonology', *Phonology* 7: 193–231.

KAYNE, RICHARD. (1981). 'On certain differences between French and English', *Linguistic Inquiry* 12: 349–71.

KESTER, ELLEN-PETRA. (1994). 'Adjectival inflection and the licensing of *pro*', in Jairo Nunes, Ellen Thompson, and Spyridoula Varlokosta (eds), *University of Maryland Working Papers in Linguistics* 2: 91–109.

—— (1995). 'Adjectival inflection and conditions on null nouns', in Antonietta Bisetti, Laura Brugè, João Costa, Rob Goedemans, Nicola Munaro, and Ruben van de Vijver (eds), *Console III Proceedings*. Leiden: Student Organization of Linguistics in Europe, pp. 155–72.

—— (1996). *The Nature of Adjectival Inflection*. Doctoral dissertation, University of Utrecht.

KLIMA, EDWARD S. and BELLUGI, URSULA. (1966). 'Syntactic regularities in children's speech', in John Lyons and Roger J. Wales (eds), *Psycholinguistics Papers: The Proceedings of the 1966 Edinburgh Conference*. Edinburgh: Edinburgh University Press, pp. 183–208.

KUCZAJ, STAN. (1976). *-ing, -s, and -ed: A study of the Acquisition of Certain Verb Inflections*. Doctoral dissertation, University of Minnesota.

LASNIK, HOWARD and URIAGEREKA, JUAN. (2005). *A Course in Minimalist Syntax: Foundations and Prospects*. Oxford: Blackwell.

LAW, PAUL. (1998). 'A unified analysis of P-stranding in Romance and Germanic', in Pius N. Tamanji and Kiyomi Kusumoto (eds), *Proceedings of the North East Linguistic Society (NELS) 28*. Amherst, MA: GLSA (Graduate Linguistic Student Association), pp. 219–34.

LEROUX, CECILE. (1988). *On the interface of morphology and syntax. Stellenbosch Papers in Linguistics #18*. South Africa: University of Stellenbosch.

LEVELT, CLARA. (1994). *On the Acquisition of Place*. The Hague: Holland Academic Graphics.

LILLO-MARTIN, DIANE C. (1991). *Universal Grammar and American Sign Language: Setting the Null Argument Parameters*. Dordrecht: Kluwer.

LONGOBARDI, GIUSEPPE. (1994). 'Reference and proper names', *Linguistic Inquiry* 25: 609–65.

—— (2001). 'The structure of DP: Some principles, parameters, and problems', in Chris Collins and Mark Baltin (eds), *The Handbook of Contemporary Syntactic Theory*. Oxford: Blackwell, pp. 562–603.

López-Ornat, Susana. (1997). 'What lies in between a pre-grammatical and a grammatical representation? Evidence on nominal and verbal form–function mappings in Spanish from 1;7 to 2;1', in Ana Teresa Pérez-Leroux and William R. Glass (eds), *Contemporary Perspectives on the Acquisition of Spanish, Volume 1: Developing Grammars*. Somerville, MA: Cascadilla.

——— Fernández, Almudena, Gallo, Pilar, and Mariscal, Sonia. (1994) *La Adquisición de la Lengua Española*. Madrid: Siglo XXI.

MacKay, Carolyn J. (1994). 'A sketch of Misantla Totonac phonology', *International Journal of American Linguistics* 60: 369–419.

MacWhinney, Brian. (2000). *The CHILDES Project (3rd Edition). Volume I: Tools for Analyzing Talk: Transcription Format and Programs*. Mahwah, NJ: Lawrence Erlbaum.

Marantz, Alec. (2001) 'Explorations in post-lexicalist morphology: Recovering locality'. Lecture series delivered at the 2001 LOT Summer School, University of Utrecht, The Netherlands.

Marcus, Gary F., Pinker, Steven, Ullman, Michael, Hollander, Michelle, Rosen, T. John, and Xu, Fei. (1992). 'Overregularization in language acquisition. With commentary by Harald Clahsen', *Monographs of the Society for Research in Child Development* 57.

Marlett, Stephen A. (1988). 'The syllable structure of Seri', *International Journal of American Linguistics* 54: 245–78.

——— and Pickett, Velma B. (1987). 'The syllable structure and aspect morphology of Isthmus Zapotec', *International Journal of American Linguistics* 53: 398–422.

McCarthy, John and Prince, Alan. (1993). 'Prosodic morphology I: Constraint interaction and satisfaction'. MS, University of Massachusetts, Amherst, and Rutgers University, New Brunswick, NJ.

McCloskey, James and Hale, Kenneth. (1984). 'The syntax of person-number inflection in Modern Irish', *Natural Language & Linguistic Theory* 1: 487–533.

McDaniel, Dana and Cairns, Helen Smith. (1996). 'Judgements of grammaticality and reference', in Dana McDaniel et al. *Methods for Assessing Children's Syntax*. Cambridge, MA: MIT Press.

——— Chiu, Bonnie, and Maxfield, Thomas L. (1995). 'Parameters for *wh*-movement types: Evidence from child English', *Natural Language & Linguistic Theory* 13: 709–53.

——— McKee, Cecile, and Cairns, Helen Smith. (1996). *Methods for Assessing Children's Syntax*. Cambridge, MA: MIT Press.

——— ——— and Bernstein, Judy B. (1998). 'How children's relatives solve a problem for Minimalism', *Language* 74: 308–34.

McKee, Cecile. (1992). 'A comparison of pronouns and anaphors in Italian and English acquisition', *Language Acquisition* 2: 21–54.

MILLER, WICK R. (1965). *Acoma grammar and texts.* Berkeley, CA: University of California Press.

MIYOSHI, NOBUHIRO. (1999). 'Compounds and complex predicates: Japanese evidence for a "global" parameter', in Annabel Greenhill et al. *BUCLD 23: Proceedings of the 23rd Annual Boston University Conference on Language Development.* Somerville, MA: Cascadilla Press, pp. 453–61.

MONTES, ROSA GRACIELA. (1987). 'Secuencias de clarificación en conversaciones con niños', *Morphé: Ciencias del Lenguaje 3–4.*

—— (1992). *Achieving Understanding: Repair Mechanisms in Mother–Child Conversations.* Doctoral dissertation, Georgetown University.

MUYSKEN, PIETER. (1983). 'Parasitic trees', in Peter Sells and Charles Jones (eds), *Proceedings of the North East Linguistic Society (NELS) 13.* Amherst, MA: GLSA (Graduate Linguistic Student Association), pp. 199–210.

NEELEMAN, AD. (1994). *Complex predicates.* Utrecht: Onderzoekinstituut voor Taal en Sprak (OTS).

—— and WEERMAN, FRED. (1993). 'The balance between syntax and morphology: Dutch particles and resultatives', *Natural Language & Linguistic Theory* 12: 433–75.

O'BRIEN, KAREN, GROLLA, ELAINE, AND LILLO-MARTIN, DIANE. (2006). 'Long passives are understood by young children', in David Bamman, Tatiana Magnitskaia, and Colleen Zaller (eds), *BUCLD 30: Proceedings of the 30th Annual Boston University Conference on Language Development.* Somerville, MA: Cascadilla Press, pp. 441–51.

PAN, NING and SNYDER, WILLIAM. (2004). 'Acquisition of /s/-initial Clusters: A parametric approach', in Alejna Brugos, Linnea Micciulla, and Christine E. Smith, (eds), *BUCLD 28: Proceedings of the 28th Annual Boston University Conference on Language Development.* Somerville, MA: Cascadilla Press, pp. 436–46.

—— —— (2005a). 'Acquisition of phonological empty categories', in Anna Maria di Sciullo (ed.) *UG and External Systems.* Amsterdam: John Benjamins, pp. 213–22.

—— —— (2005b). 'A parametric account of syllable acquisition and syllable typology', MS, University of Louisiana and University of Connecticut.

PIERCE, AMY. (1992). *Language Acquisition and Syntactic Theory: A Comparative Analysis of French and English Child Grammars.* Dordrecht: Kluwer.

PLATZACK, CHRISTER. (1986). 'COMP, INFL, and Germanic Word Order', in Lars Hellan and Kirsti Koch Christensen (eds), *Topics in Scandinavian Syntax.* Dordrecht: Reidel, pp. 185–234.

POEPPEL, DAVID and WEXLER, KENNETH. (1993). 'The full competence hypothesis of clause structure in early German', *Language* 69: 1–33.

PRINCE, ALAN and SMOLENSKY, PAUL. (1993). 'Optimality Theory: Constraint interaction in generative grammar', MS, Rutgers University, New Brunswick, NJ, and University of Colorado, Boulder.

_____ _____ (2004). *Optimality Theory: Constraint Interaction in Generative Grammar*. Malden, MA: Blackwell. (Slightly revised version of Prince and Smolensky 1993.)

REINHART, TANYA. (2004). 'The processing cost of reference set computation: Acquisition of stress shift and focus', *Language Acquisition* 12: 109–55.

RIEMSDIJK, HENK VAN. (1978). *A Case Study in Syntactic Markedness: The Binding Nature of Prepositional Phrases*. Dordrecht: Foris.

RIZZI, LUIGI. (1986). 'Null objects in Italian and the theory of *pro*', *Linguistic Inquiry* 17: 501–57.

ROOD, DAVID S. (1975). 'The implications of Wichita phonology', *Language* 51: 315–37.

ROSS, JOHN ROBERT. (1986). *Infinite Syntax!* Norwood, NJ: ABLEX Publishing.

SACHS, JACQUELINE. (1983). 'Talking about the there and then: The emergence of displaced reference in parent–child discourse', in Keith E. Nelson (ed.), *Children's language, Vol. 4*. Hillsdale, NJ: Lawrence Erlbaum Associates, pp. 1–28.

SAITO, MAMORU (2006) 'Scrambling and cyclic interpretation'. Lecture delivered at the University of Connecticut, 24 March 2006.

SALLES, HELOISA MARIA MOREIRA-LIMA. (1997). *Prepositions and the Syntax of Complementation*. Doctoral dissertation, University of Wales, Bangor.

SAPIR, EDWARD. (1921). *Language: An Introduction to the Study of Speech*. New York: Harcourt, Brace.

SCHWARTZ, BONNIE D. and SPROUSE, REX A. (1996). 'L2 cognitive states and the Full Transfer/Full Access model', *Second Language Research* 12: 40–72.

SELKIRK, ELISABETH. (1984). 'On the major class features and syllable theory', in Mark Aronoff and Richard Oehrle (eds), *Language Sound Structure: Studies in Phonology Presented to Morris Halle by his Teacher and Students*. Cambridge, MA: MIT Press, pp. 107–36.

SIGURJÓNSDÓTTIR, SIGRÍÐUR. (1999). 'Root infinitives and null subjects in early Icelandic', in Annabel Greenhill et al. *BUCLD 23: Proceedings of the 23rd Annual Boston University Conference on Language Development*. Somerville, MA: Cascadilla Press, pp. 630–41.

SLABAKOVA, ROUMYANA. (2006). 'A semantic parameter with a syntactic trigger in the L2 acquisition of Italian', in Roumyana Slabakova, Silvina A. Montrul, and Philippe Prévost (eds), *Inquiries in Linguistic Development: In Honor of Lydia White*. Amsterdam: John Benjamins, pp. 69–87.

SLEEMAN, PETRA. (1993). 'Noun ellipsis in French', *Probus* 5: 271–95.

_____ (1996). *Licensing Empty Nouns in French*. Doctoral dissertation, University of Amsterdam (Holland Institute of Generative Linguistics).

SLOAT, MELISSA and SNYDER, WILLIAM. (2006). 'The Compounding Parameter: New acquisitional evidence', MS, University of Connecticut, Storrs.

SNYDER, WILLIAM. (1995). *Language Acquisition and Language Variation: The Role of Morphology*. Doctoral dissertation, MIT. Distributed by MIT Working Papers in Linguistics, Cambridge, MA.

―― (2001). 'On the nature of syntactic variation: Evidence from complex predicates and complex word-formation', *Language* 77: 324–42.

―― (2002). 'Parameters: The view from child language', in Yukio Otsu (ed.), *Proceedings of the Third Tokyo Conference on Psycholinguistics*. Tokyo: Hituzi Syobo, pp. 27–44.

―― (2005). 'Motion predicates and the compounding parameter: A new approach'. Paper presented in the Linguistics Colloquium Series, University of Maryland, College Park, 15 April 2005. (Available at http://web.uconn.edu/snyder/papers/Maryland05.pdf)

―― and STROMSWOLD, KARIN. (1997). 'The structure and acquisition of English dative constructions', *Linguistic Inquiry* 28: 281–317.

―― CHEN, DEBORAH, YAMANE, MAKI, CONWAY, LAURA, and HIRAMATSU, KAZUKO. (1999). 'On the nature of children's left-branch violations', in Bart Hollebrandse (ed.), *New Perspectives on Language Acquisition. University of Massachusetts Occasional Papers in Linguistics, Volume 22*. Amherst, MA: GLSA, pp. 177–85.

―― FELBER, SARAH, KANG, BOSOOK, and LILLO-MARTIN, DIANE. (2001). 'Path phrases and compounds in the acquisition of English'. Paper presented at the 26th Boston University Conference on Language Development, Boston, 2 November 2001. (Available at http://web.uconn.edu/snyder/papers/BUCLD26.pdf)

―― SENGHAS, ANN, and INMAS, KELLY. (2001).'Agreement morphology and the acquisition of noun-drop in Spanish', *Language Acquisition* 9: 157–73.

STOWELL, TIMOTHY. (1981). *Origins of Phrase Structure*. Doctoral dissertation, MIT.

STROMSWOLD, KARIN J. (1990). *Learnability and the Acquisition of Auxiliaries*. Doctoral dissertation, MIT.

―― (1996). 'Analyzing children's spontaneous speech', in Dana McDaniel et al. *Methods for Assessing Children's Syntax*. Cambridge, MA: MIT Press, pp. 22–53.

SUGISAKI, KOJI. (2003). *Innate Constraints on Language Variation: Evidence from Child Language*. Doctoral dissertation, University of Connecticut, Storrs.

―― and ISOBE, MIWA. (2000). 'Resultatives result from the Compounding Parameter: On the acquisitional correlation between resultatives and N-N compounds in Japanese', in Roger Billerey and Brook Danielle Lillehaugen (eds), *WCCFL 19: Proceedings of the 19th West Coast Conference on Formal Linguistics*. Somerville, MA: Cascadilla Press, pp. 493–506.

―― and SNYDER, WILLIAM. (2002). 'Preposition stranding and the Compounding Parameter: A developmental perspective', in Anna H.-J. Do, Laura

Dominguez, and Aimee Johansen (eds), *BUCLD 26: Proceedings of the 26th Annual Boston University Conference on Language Development*. Somerville, MA: Cascadilla Press, pp. 677–88.

_____ _____ (2003). 'Do parameters have default values? Evidence from the acquisition of English and Spanish', in Yukio Otsu (ed.), *Proceedings of the Fourth Tokyo Conference on Psycholinguistics*. Tokyo: Hituzi Syobo, pp. 215–37.

_____ _____ (2006). 'Evaluating the Variational Model of language acquisition', in Kamil Ud Deen, Jun Nomura, Barbara Schulz, and Bonnie D. Schwartz (eds), *The Proceedings of the Inaugural Conference on Generative Approaches to Language Acquisition—North America, Honolulu, HI, Volume 2. University of Connecticut Occasional Papers in Linguistics* 4: 354–2.

_____ _____ and YAFFEE, DANIEL. (2000). 'Preposition stranding and prepositional complementizers in the acquisition of English', in Yukio Otsu (ed.), *Proceedings of the First Tokyo Conference on Psycholinguistics*. Tokyo: Hituzi Syobo, pp. 154–70.

SUPPES, PATRICK. (1973). 'The semantics of children's language', *American Psychologist* 88: 103–14.

TESAR, BRUCE, and SMOLENSKY, PAUL. (2000). *Learnability in Optimality Theory*. Cambridge, MA: MIT Press.

THORNTON, ROSALIND. (1990). *Adventures in Long-distance Moving: The Acquisition of Complex Wh-questions*. Doctoral dissertation, University of Connecticut, Storrs.

_____ (1996). 'Elicited production', in Dana McDaniel et al. *Methods for Assessing Children's Syntax*. Cambridge, MA: MIT Press, pp. 77–102.

_____ and GAVRUSEVA, LENA. (1996). 'Children's split "whose-questions" and the structure of possessive NPs'. Paper presented at the 21st annual Boston University Conference on Language Development, Boston, MA.

THRÁINSSON, HÖSKULDUR. (1996). 'On the (non-)universality of functional categories', in Werner Abraham, Samuel David Epstein, Höskuldur Thráinsson, and C. Jan-Wouter Zwart (eds), *Minimal Ideas: Syntactic Studies in the Minimalist Program*. Amsterdam: John Benjamins, pp. 253–81.

_____ (2003). 'Syntactic variation, historical development, and Minimalism', in Randall Hendrick (ed.), *Minimalist Syntax*. Oxford: Blackwell, pp. 152–91.

TORRENS, VICENÇ. (1995). 'The acquisition of inflection in Spanish and Catalan', *MIT Working Papers in Linguistics* 26: 451–72.

TROMMELEN, MIEKE. (1984). *The Syllable in Dutch: With Special Reference to Diminutive Formation*. Dordrecht: Foris.

VALIAN, VIRGINIA. (1991). 'Syntactic subjects in the early speech of American and Italian children', *Cognition* 40: 21–81.

WEVERINK, MEIKE. (1989). *The Subject in Relation to Inflection in Child Language*. MA Thesis, University of Utrecht.

WEXLER, KENNETH. (1998). 'Very early parameter setting and the unique checking constraint: A new explanation of the optional infinitive stage', *Lingua* 106: 23–79.

——and MANZINI, RITA. (1987). 'Parameters and learnability in Binding Theory', in Thomas Roeper and Edwin Williams (eds), *Parameter Setting*. Dordrecht: Reidel, pp. 41–76.

WHITE, LYDIA. (2003). *Second Language Acquisition and Universal Grammar*. Cambridge: Cambridge University Press.

WOLFF, HANS. (1948). 'Yuchi phonemes and morphemes, with special reference to person markers', *International Journal of American Linguistics* 14: 240–3.

YAMANE, MAKI, PICHLER, DEBORAH CHEN, and SNYDER, WILLIAM. (1999). 'Subject–object asymmetries and children's left-branch violations', in Annabel Greenhill et al. *BUCLD 23: Proceedings of the 23rd Annual Boston University Conference on Language Development*. Somerville, MA: Cascadilla Press, pp. 732–40.

YANG, CHARLES D. (2002). *Knowledge and Learning in Natural Language*. Oxford: Oxford University Press.

Language Index

Afrikaans 23, 84, 86
Arabic
    Egyptian 88
    Moroccan 44–45, 47

Basque 88

Chichewa 183

Danish 18
Dutch 18, 54, 72, 83, 119, 122–23, 127, 132,
    172, 187

English 55–58, 83, 86, 98, 127, 132, 147–56,
    165, 174, 177
Estonian 88

French 105

German 18, 131, 132, 170

Hebrew 87, 130

Icelandic 18, 118, 188
Irish 131
Isthmus Zapotec 128
Italian 4–8, 128, 130, 132, 147, 171

Japanese 24, 27, 87, 88, 194–95, 115,
    174–75, 177
Javanese 88

Khmer 87
Korean 115–17

Luo 46

Mandarin 87
Misantha Totonac 128

Norwegian 18–21

Polish 171

Romani 147–48
Russian 86, 87, 98, 167

Seri 128
Serbo-Croatian 88, 128
Spanish 82, 83, 86, 122, 132–46, 147–56,
    165
Swedish 132
Sanskrit 178

Telugu 46
Thai 87

Wichita 128

Yatee Zapotec 128
Yucatec Maya 46
Yuchi 129

General Index

acquisitional testing 7, 9, 17, 173; *see also*
    hypothesis testing
  concurrent acquisition 9, 74, 109, 178
  ordered acquisition 9, 80, 113
  weaknesses 176–77, 178
Adger 9, 25, 27
Agr, *see* minimalism
Argument Identification
    Requirement 26
attributive adjectives 105; *see also*
    resultative constructions

Baker 7, 183
Barbiers 129, 133
Bar-Shalom and Snyder 170, 171
Basic CV Syllable Structure Theory, *see*
    Optimality Theory
Beck and Snyder 85
Bernstein 132, 133
bilingual 183
Binding Theory 105, 107, 168
Binominal Test, *see* hypothesis testing
Bley-Vroman 179
Bloom, Barss, Nicol, and Conway 107
  Bloom, Lightbown and Hood 147
Bobaljik 161–62
Bobaljik and Thráinnson 17, 25, 160,
    187–88
Borer 130
bundling, *see* features
Bošković 23–26, 118, 160–61, 186
Branching Rhyme
    Parameter—BRP 121–23, 173, 186
Brown and Hanlon 70–71

candidate parses, *see* Optimality Theory
case marking 25, 27, 116
Charette 42, 44, 48, 186
Charm Theory, *see* Government
    Phonology

Checking, *see* Minimalism
Chien and Wexler 108
  Chien, Yamane, and Snyder 99, 167
Chomsky 4, 86, 130, 146, 152
Clark 146
Cole 175
commission, *see* error type
computational component—C_{HL} 12, 25,
    161
Conradie 23
constraint ranking, *see* Optimality
    Theory
copy, *see* Minimalism
corpus-based research 52, 76, 133
  CHILDES 52–55, 58–61, 90, 101–103,
    124, 136–43, 153, 166, 169
  CLAN 55, 60–61, 65, 79, 90–91, 124
  data analysis 63–67
  Fikkert-Levelt corpora 54, 122
  hypothesis testing, *see* statistics
  routines, imitations, and
    repetitions 55
Crain and Thornton 104, 106
Crain and McKee 104
cross-linguistic variation 34, 44–46, 84,
    88, 129, 131, 160, 163

data analysis, *see* corpus-based research,
    statistics
DP Parameter 23, 160, 161, 186
Dejima 24
DeVilliers, Roeper, and Vainikka 147
diary studies 52
Distributed Morphology, *see*
    morphology
double object constructions 155–56, 177

Empty Category Principle, *see*
    Government Phonology
Empty Onset Parameter 47, 186

error type 8, 55–58, 62–63, 67, 70, 149,
          159, 165, 171, 176
    commission 49, 73, 170
    epenthesis 172
    omission 55, 63, 70, 72–73
    optional infinitives 170–71
    over-regularization 170
experimental methods:
    elicited production 97, 103–104, 108,
          110
    naturalistic observation 8, 52–53,
          89, 108, 168–70, 176
    Truth Value Judgement Task 104, 106,
          110, 112, 168
explanatory adequacy 6, 154

features 10
    bundle 27, 161
    interpretable/uninterpretable 10, 27
    selectional/non-selectional 10, 28
    strong/weak 11, 29
Fikkert 172; see also corpus-based
          research
First of Repeated Uses—FRU 77–78, 88,
          91, 95, 154
Fodor 181, 188–99

Gavruseva 103
Gerken and Shady 115
Gibson and Wexler 181, 184, 190
Government (Phonology) 40, 119, 121–22,
          186
    Charm Theory 42
    Empty Category Principle 44–45, 47
    licensing 46–48, 119–21, 133
    locality 43
grammatical conservatism 8, 25, 41, 47,
          72–73, 77, 108, 159, 169, 171, 176,
          180–91
grammatical constraints 107
Grimshaw and Samek-Lodovici 30
Grodzinsky and Reinhart 108
Guasti 171, 183

Hale and Marantz 162
Harris 46, 121, 127
    Harris and Gussman 46

Hawkins and Hattori 179
    Hawkins and Chan 179
head internal relative clause—HIRC
          174
Head Parameter 5–6, 13, 181, 184
Hendriks and Hoop 30
Hewson 133
Hierarchy of Projections, see Minimalism
Higginbotham 4
historical linguistics 178
Hornstein and Weinberg 150
Hyams 130, 146, 149
    Hyams, Schaeffer, and Johnson
    Hyams and Wexler 132
hypothesis testing, see statistics

Independence Principle 180
inversion, Subject-Auxiliary
Isobe 174–75
    Isobe and Sugasaki 152

Jaeggli and Safir 130
Jakobson's syllable typology 34, 47

Kang 26–27, 115
Kaye 41, 44, 48, 119–21, 129
    Kaye, Lowenstamm, and Vernaud 41
Kayne 151
Kester 129, 132, 133, 144
Klima and Bellugi 166
Kuczaj 107, 169

Lasnik and Uriagareka 13
Last Resort, see Minimalism
Law 152
learnability 36
learning by parsing:
    treelet 188–91
Lectures on Government and
          Binding—LGB 4–6, 14
Left Branch Constraint and
          left-branch extraction 98, 100,
          101, 103, 167
LeRoux 84, 86
lexical variation 13, 160
lexicon, see Minimalism

licensing/identification, *see* morphology
Lillo-Martin 130, 144
linearization 12, 31
locality, *see* Government Phonology
Logical Problem of Language
    Acquisition—LPLA 154
longitudinal recordings 52, 89, 144; *see
    also* corpus-based research
Longobardi 14–18, 160, 187–88

Magic Empty Nucleus Parameter—MEN
    121–25, 173, 186
Marantz 161
Maratsos 170
Marcus, Pinker, Ullman, Hollander,
    Rosen, and Xu 169
McCloskey and Hale 131
McDaniel and Cairns 145
    McDaniel, Chiu, and Maxfield 147–49
    McDaniel, McKee, and Bernstein 155
    McDaniel, McKee, and Cairns 96
McKee 107–108, 168
MacWhinney 52
Mean Length of Utterance—MLU 79, 81,
    93
Minimalism/ Minimalist Program 10,
    27–31, 85, 151–52, 160, 163
    Agr 11, 18, 30
    checking relation 29
    copy 29
    features, *see* features
    Hierarchy of Projections 18, 24–25,
        29
    Last Resort 15, 173
    lexicon/lexical items 9–11, 13, 27–31,
        82, 160–61
    Merge 11, 28
    Move 11
    Numeration 27, 31, 162
    Spell-Out 14
Miyoshi 87
morphology:
    Distributed Morphology 161–63
    licensing/identification 144
    morphological agreement 133
    rich morphology 129
Muysken 129, 132, 133

Neeleman 83–84
    Neeleman and Weerman 83–84, 86
Noun drop 119, 129, 133–46
null subject 129, 131
numeration *see* Minimalism

O'Brien, Grolla, and Lillo-Martin 97
omission *see* error type
Optimality Theory 30–41, 47–50, 163,
    185
    candidate parses 30, 163
    constraint ranking 31, 32, 35, 163, 185
    evaluation procedure 33
    dominance parameters 38, 163
    mark 33, 35
    phonology 20
        Basic CV Syllable Structure
            Theory 30, 32, 35, 40, 163
        Error Driven Constraint
            Demotion—EDCD 30, 35–40
    semantics 30
    syntax 30, 163
    winner/loser/tie 33, 34
optional infinitive, *see* error type
over-regularization, *see* error type

parameter 4, 180
    default setting 146, 148, 156, 184
    macro-parameter 7
    parametric predictions 153, 173–74,
        176; *see also* DP Parameter,
        Empty Category Parameter,
        Empty Onset Parameter, Head
        Parameter, Magic Empty Nucleus
        Parameter, P-Stranding
        Parameter, Referentiality
        Parameter, Resultative Parameter,
        The Compounding Parameter,
        Split IP Parameter
Pan and Snyder 46, 121, 122, 127
particle constructions 8, 56, 72, 82, 88,
    91; *see also* hypothesis testing
passive 97
phonological data, *see* Fikkert–Levelt *in*
    corpus-based research
phonological theory 30, 163, 176; *see also*
    Government Phonology and
    Optimality Theory

pied-piping 98, 146, 152
    P-stranding Parameter 149, 151, 152,
        154
    preposition stranding 229, 248, 165
Platzack 19
plausible dissent 106
Poeppel and Wexler 170
pragmatic felicity 106
Prince and Smolensky 30, 34, 36, 163
Principles and Parameters—P&P 5, 9,
        160, 162; *see also* acquisitional
        testing
Proper Binding Condition 24

reanalysis 150
Referentiality Parameter 13–15, 187
Reinhart 108
resultative constructions 104–106, 186;
        see also attributive adjectives
Resultative Parameter 85
Riemsdijk, van 180
Rizzi 144
Ross 98
root compounding 82, 86
routines, imitations, and repetitions, *see*
        corpus-based research

Saito 24
Sapir 26
Schwartz and Sprouse 179
scrambling 25, 28, 115–17, 118, 160
second language acquisition—SLA 24,
        178, 179–80
Selkirk 120
Sigurjónsdóttir 170
Sonority Sequencing Generalization 121
Snyder 73, 85, 105, 176
    Snyder, Senghas, and Inman 119,
        135–44; *see also* Empty Category
        Parameter, Resultative Parameter,
        The Compounding Parameter
Spell-Out, *see* Minimalism
Split IP Parameter—SIP 17–24, 160, 187
spontaneous speech *see* experimental
        methods
statistics:
    Analysis of Variance 75
    Binominal Test 75, 88, 90

Binominal Theorem 113
Bonferroni correction 76
correlation 76, 92, 110
Fisher Exact Test 110–11, 114
hypothesis testing 71, 86, 109
t-test 92, 127
Stromswold 71, 166–67
Subset Condition 47–48, 180, 186
Sugisaki and Snyder 119, 146, 182, 185
    Sugisaki and Isobe 104
    Sugisaki, Snyder, and Yaffee 151
syllable 31, 119
syntactic variation 15, 162

tense:
    double tensing 167
Tesar and Smolensky 33, 38, 163, 185
The Compounding Parameter—TCP 85,
        186
Thornton 97, 147
    Thornton and Gavruseva 98, 101, 167
Torrens 171
transitive expletive
        construction—TEC 20
treelet, *see* learning by parsing
trigger 180
    Trigger Learning Algorithm 190
Truth Value Judgement Task, *see*
        experimental methods

Valian 147
Variational Model of Language
        Acquisition 185–88

Weverink 170
Wexler 148
    Wexler and Manzini 47, 180
wh-movement/extraction 119, 146,
        177; *see also* preposition
        stranding
White 179
word order 56, 116, 187; *see also*
        linearization

Yamane, Pichler, and Snyder 99
Yang 185